Guidance and Counselling
(A Manual)

Published by
Saurabh Publishing House

Guidance and Counselling

(A Manual)

Dr. Vinay Rao

Saurabh
Publishing House
4735/22, Prakash Deep Building,
Ansari Road, Daryaganj,
New Delhi - 110002

Published by :
SAURABH PUBLISHING HOUSE

Distributed by:
Lotus Press Publishers & Distributors
Unit No. 220, Second Floor, 4735/22, Prakash Deep Building,
Ansari Road, Darya Ganj, New Delhi-110002
Ph: 23280047, 32903912, 098118-38000
E-mail : loutspress1984@gmail.com
www.lotuspress.co.in

Saurabh Publishing House is an imprint of
Lotus Press Publishers & Distributors

Guidance and Counselling (A Manual)

ISBN : 978-81-89005-88-7 (PB)

Printed at : Lotus Press, New Delhi - 110002

Preface

Guidance is an assistance given to individuals in making intelligent choices and adjustments. It is based on the democratic principles that it is the duty and the right of every individual to choose his own way in life so that it does not interfere with the rights of others. The ability to make intelligent choices is developed through experience and guidance. One of the functions of education is to provide opportunities for development of this ability. Guidance, in this context, makes an integral part of education and aims at fulfiling this function. Guidance helps them make decisions in such a way that gradually they may develop the ability to make decisions independently, without help from others. While in a counselling process the decision-making and learning operate at the emotional level in guidance it is confined to the intellectual level.

Guidance consists of a group of services which assist an individual with the knowledge and the necessary skills to make choices, plans and interpretations for adjustment so that the individual may make an effective member of the group. Guidance services help the individual in understanding his abilities, interests, development and the limitations. On the other hand, guidance services provide information regarding the educational and occupational opportunities and requirements, personality development, effective study habits and other areas which may be of importance to the individual. Guidance services also provide means for determining the placement of the individual in his class, occupation and community. Qualified personnel of the guidance services are able to help the individual understand himself, interpret the environment and make appropriate adjustment to the environment.

This book deals with the topics of—*Introduction to Guidance and Counselling; Education and Counselling; Theoretical Principles of Counselling; Guidance and New Education Policy; Guidance and Curriculum; Vocational Development and Career Planning; Rational Theories and Techniques; Elementary Education to Vocational Guidance; Phenomenon of Transfer of Learning; Tests in Guidance and Counselling; Research and Evaluation in Counselling; Motivated Behaviour;* etc.

I hope that students and those in the education field will find it useful for academic and competitive examinations. I owe a deep sense of gratitude to my publisher for materializing my present endeavour.

Dr. Vinay Rao

Contents

1

Introduction to Guidance and Counselling

Guidance is a commonly used term and familiar to Indian educators. Guidance programmes evolved by the Central and State governments are intimately related to the education of the school and the university students. Such programmes provided information regarding various educational opportunities in the country and outside. No educational planning is possible without information regarding opportunities for technical and vocational education and higher education in general. They also provide information regarding employment situation, different vocations, requirements and qualifications needed for each type, salaries, opportunities of advancement, etc. Provision of all these and related services comes under the purview of guidance. Guidance programmes may also include programmes of orientation of new students. This will involve helping them know the institution they are about to join, its traditions, the facilities made available to the students, the conduct expected of them and their responsibilities as the members of college community. Guidance activities may also involve help with study skills. The difference between the school and the college studies is well known in our country. The student who joins college for the first time needs help with how to study, how he should take notes, where he can find the books and the atmosphere congenial for study. Guidance activities, ideally, should spread over the entire year and aim at helping the student with educational, vocational and personal problems which he may face from time to time. Guidance services should anticipate these problems and render help to the students before the problems really occur.

Administration of tests and interpretation of scores is another guidance activity. Before helping the student with the choice of courses or vocation it is essential that the guidance worker or teacher knows about the interests abilities and the potentialities of the student. For this, the administration of various tests and the interpretation of test scores becomes an essential. Guidance services, therefore, have facilities for test administration and interpretation of test scores. As the description indicates, guidance activities provide the basic information which prevents problems or makes the basis for counselling sessions. Unlike counselling, face-to-face relationship is not an essential condition for guidance activities. Most of the guidance services can be rendered in groups, even when work with individual cases is called for, the counselling interview is not necessary referral to other agencies is a common phenomenon in guidance work.

Guidance is an assistance given to individuals in making intelligent choices and adjustments. It is based on the democratic principle that it is the duty and the right of every individual to choose his own way in life so that it does not interfere with the rights of others. The ability to make intelligent choices is developed through experience and guidance. One of the functions of education is to provide opportunities for development of this ability. Guidance, in this context, makes an integral part of education and aims at fulfilling this function. Guidance helps them make decisions in such a way that gradually they may develop the ability to make decisions independently, without help from others. While in a counselling process the decision-making and learning operate at the emotional level in guidance it is confined to the intellectual level.

Guidance made its beginning as a help with problems related to vocations. It mainly concerned itself with securing jobs for young people. The purpose for this service was to help control juvenile delinquency. Young people with no occupation got involved in delinquent acts and thus added to the problems of indiscipline in the society. However, from the very beginning guidance did not confine itself to just finding jobs. It emphasized making a "wise" choice—the choice which was suited to the abilities and the needs of the individual. Through the years, guidance has acquired a much wider connotation, it now concerns the entire individual in relation with other members of the group.

A very close relationship between education and guidance has been recognized since early in the guidance movement. Through the years this relationship has become closer and more meaningful. Today, the only controversy which exists is between those who consider guidance as a vital part of education and those who consider education as synonymous with guidance. Jones attributes the controversy to two factors: (1) The different meanings attached to the term education, and (2) The failure to distinguish between the part played by the teacher and by the learner in the process of education. He takes the position that guidance is found in that area of educational endeavour which involves assistaoce given by agencies or persons to the individual in making choices and in helping him to choose a line of action, a method or procedure, and a goal. It is not choosing for him or directing his choice; it is helping him to make the choice.

Education concerns itself with the entire development of the individual. From one point of view, education can be interpreted as the conscious effort of the society to develop and modify the individual so that he conforms with the social expectations, takes his place in society, contributes to it and in doing so realizes his own maximum development. Education from this point of view is an interaction between the individual and the society. Guidance is present as long as the two continue to interact but it disappears the moment society starts deciding what the education should consist of, how it should be imparted and stops to seek cooperation of the individual in the choice of things to be learned and how they should be learned.

Guidance consists of a group of services which assist an individual with the knowledge and the necessary skills to make choices, plans and interpretations for adjustment so that the individual may make an effective member of the group. Guidance services help the individual in understanding his abilities, interests, development and the limitations. On the other hand, guidance services provide information regarding the educational and occupational opportunities and requirements, personality development, effective study habits and other areas which may be of importance to the individual. Guidance services also provide means for determining the placement of the individual in his class, occupation and community. Qualified personnel of the guidance services are able to help the individual understand himself, interpret the environment and make appropriate adjustment to the environment.

Need for Guidance and Counselling

The need for guidance and counselling is felt the most during career choice. With our society getting industrialized so, rapidly the young student needs help with information about various jobs available to him and the requirements, responsibilities and the nature of work involved in a particular job or career. The need for counselling is enhanced with larger number of students seeking admissions to colleges. Educational is no more a privilege of the elite; our educational institutions are open to all who may satisfy the minimum standards set for admissions. Under these circumstances the students are coming from a varied social background. A significantly large number of students are the first generation learners. In their family they have no one with experience of college education or the background to guide them in the choice of a career. With a right to the best education available and a wide range of jobs open to him an individual student needs mature help in making his choice. Before he makes this choice the young individual needs to develop a life pattern for himself, an image of what he wants to be. Counselling help can be meaningful in this development.

The individual student brings with him the attitudes, beliefs and the values typical of his own background. In the case of first generation learners and rural population these differ widely from the attitudes, beliefs and values prevalent in the college. Conflicts arise between the two sets of values which require professional help. In order to be able to derive the maximum benefit from the educational facilities, it is necessary for the student to make an adjustment between the values at home and the values prevalent in the college.

The student is required to make a place for himself in the social and co-curricular life of the institution besides maintaining his status in the curricular and academic sphere. This involves the skill to budget his time and energy between the curricular and the co-curricular both of which are equally important to the total development of his personality. A counsellor can help him with this adjustment and budgeting of his time.

Children bring their family to the school in the sense that the tensions, frustrations, and conflicts experienced at home affect their behaviour in school. A counsellor helps children understand and modify emotional attitudes that may have grown out of the home environment. Many other social factors add to the insecurity experienced by the student, competition for positions, fulfilment of ambitions and high goals, unemployment and the economic strain are a few that can be mentioned.

Research evidence to prove the need for guidance is available in the form of an All India study of student needs and problems conducted under the sponsorship of the All India Association of Guidance and Counselling. In this study a total of 1,508 returns were received on a forty item questionnaire sent to various universities situated in different parts of India. An analysis of a representative sample of men and women showed that on an average the boys marked 17 problems while the girls marked 14 serious problems which concerned them. The questionnaire included items on the type of help they were receiving and the help they wanted. They were asked to indicate the sources from which they received "much help", "some help" and "little help".

Students reported that they received most help from their parents and guardians. They received only a small amount of help from the personnel connected with their colleges, with the exception of those who reported receiving help from their professors. Almost 40 per cent of the male students included in this study reported receiving "little help" from their teachers and professors. Female students seemed to have received more help with their problems from this source. One out of five reported much help but one out of four reported" little help". A very small amount of help was reported as received from college guidance personnel. This may be interpreted as indicative of the fact that either the colleges have no organized programmes of guidance or they are not succeeding in their purpose. When asked if they would welcome help if offered by the college or institution, 87.7 per cent indicated a desire to seek help with their problems; 83.3 per cent expressed their need for such help.

Scope of Counselling

The counsellor does not make plans and decisions for the counsellee neither does he solve his problems. He confines himself to help the client gain new perceptions and insights into his problems, change his behaviour patterns so that they are satisfying for him and acceptable to the group he is a member of. This goal the counsellor achieves by providing favourable learning situations to his clients. The learning situations and the process of learning varies with different counsellees according to the emotional stability, native endowments, kind and degree of formal education and the crippling effects which may have been caused by the crises during early life.

Counselling is dedicated to client self-realization and self-direction. It is generally accepted that a vast majority of human beings are capable of solving their problems and achieving adequate degree of self-direction and self-realization without the formal help of a professional counsellor. No counsellor has a right to tell the client what he should do but there are certain things which need to be done for him in order to help him in decision-making. If his decision is blocked because of lack of information, then the counsellor provides him with this information. On the other hand, if his self-realization is blocked due to orthodox religious attachments then emotional attachments need to be modified through relearning or intellectual reasoning.

Counselling aims at attitude change and does not concern itself with action. Actions are the outcome of attitude change. An example will illustrate this distinction. A boy who comes to his counsellor with the problem that he feels shy and cannot participate in debates and other public functions will not be helped with the advice that he should go to the next college debate and force himself to take part in it. Counselling in this case should consist of a study of attitudes related to his emotions and feelings towards other people, his self-image, his ambitions and his future plans. Counselling will help modify these attitudes which in turn may help him to get over his shyness and participate successfully in the social functions.

Counselling is concerned with emotional and not with intellectual attitudes. Often a client thinks that he understands himself and the defences which he is applying but this understanding does not lead to any relief in tension. The reason for this is that this understanding functions at the logical and intellectual rather than the emotional level. The relationship between the two individuals, *i.e.,* the counsellor and the counsellee is the most important factor in the counselling process. This is why the thinking during the counselling process is significantly different from the thinking done individually by the two individuals. The understanding that interpersonal relationship is the most important factor in the counselling process helps the counsellee to improve his relationship with other individuals also. His relationship with persons with whom he reacts in different ways acquires new meaning and so specific changes in his behaviour take place. This completes the counselling process.

In as much as the process of counselling involves problem solving and learning, it can be considered as special teaching which involves both intellectual and emotional aspects of individual's personality. Counselling thus becomes a legitimate and integral part of education. In counselling which requires the student to make his own decisions and discover his own solutions to his problems, much of the procedure consists of listening to what the student has to say about his problem. Having heard him, the counsellor puts his problem in other words and enquires if the student agrees with this version and interpretation of his problem. If the counsellee does not agree with this interpretation then he is left to think over the two interpretations with the awareness that there are alternative ways of understanding his problem. In this way the counsellor plays an active role in helping the student find his solution but he does not prescribe a solution as he himself does not know which is going to be the suitable solution for his counsellee.

Individuals differ in their ability to learn, some learn fast while the others take time in achieving the same level of learning. It may be ideal to provide unlimited facilities and time to learn but the limitations of finances, time and resources may prevent the achievement of this goal. Some controls need to be exercised and they usually consist in the counsellor giving a guided direction to the counselling process. The process of learning and the nature of learning situations primarily depends upon the training and the experience of the counsellor and very little on the experimental data and evidence. The counsellor deals with the problems of human adjustment and no variable in adjustment carries the same weight for all individuals or the same individual at different times. The patterns of behaviour are so complex, variable and changing that a well controlled experimental approach, in the scientific sense, for each client is impossible and unpractical.

A counsellor must have sound working experience with a wide range of psychological tools and techniques in order that he may vary the pattern of their use according to the clients he serves. Insight and skill in the related disciplines also helps his understanding of the problems. The quality of his work depends on the breadth of his specialization. Counselling being a structured learning situation, a counsellor with control on the use of various tools and techniques and understanding of the related fields of knowledge is in a position to structure the learning situation suited to the individual counsellee. It is an accepted principle that the changes in behaviour come about through learning in the counselling situation because the situation is so structured by the counsellor that it facilitates maximum learning and the best kind of learning.

Counselling is centred around the problems and the needs of the counsellee. Basically all counselling is client-oriented. Improvement and protection of society and its standards may be the background but primarily the aim of counselling is to help the individual operate more effectively in his own social set-up. The counsellor does this not through forcing his own views, feelings, thoughts and beliefs on the counsellee but by listening to him, identifying with his problems and by focusing on his feelings, beliefs and perceptions.

Research in individual psychology has proved that individuals show significant differences in personality development, the kinds of problems they face and their ability to deal with these problems. Therefore, the treatment of each case must be individualized and adapted to his needs and problems. The problem of career choice will obviously need a different type of treatment from the one needed by an adolescent boy indulging in petty thefts, and still different from the treatment of a conflict between a businessman and his son who wants to take up painting as his career. The specific symptom against the background of the individual determines the nature of interviews and the specific method and the tools to be used. Practice has shown that a counselling psychologist finds it difficult if not impossible to be dogmatic about his techniques. Eclectic approach in theory, philosophy and techniques seems a common pattern in modern. The specific details are dictated by the needs and the problems counselling.

Good counselling results from client-made decisions. During the counselling process the counsellee acquires insight into his problems and their causes and he experiences a desire to change behaviour in desirable directions. The counsellor can provide situations conducive to these learnings but he cannot actually do these things for the client. The counsellor and the counsellee together can explore the path to decision but the actual decision must be made by the counsellee himself. Once it is made, the counsellor can again get together with the counsellee and mark out the route, the steps and milestones. During this process it is the responsibility of the counsellor to provide his counsellee with facts and information, possible alternatives to the situation, barriers and the hazards he would face in achieving his goals. The decisions, however, must be those of the counsellee.

Counselling is dependent on the accuracy of counsellor prediction. There is very little literature concerning the reliability and validity of counselling results of one counsellor or another. The counselling results can be judged from the predictions which a counsellor makes during the process of counselling. The first prediction he makes when he decides whether he should take the case or not. If he accepts the case he predicts improvements which can be tested through improved study habits, improved social relations, greater comprehension, etc., depending upon the initial problem.

The prediction made by the counsellor, however, does not affect the freedom of choice of the counsellee. Counsellor predictions are both short and long-term forecasts based upon his perception of consequences of whatever plan of action a client may choose out of the alternative plans considered. According to Super "So-called... prediction is therefore not, in reality, a prognostic act, but rather a counselling process in which counselling means to plan, and to act accordingly." One may thus conclude that without prediction there can be no evaluation of counselling results, without evaluation there can be no proof of professional and social usefulness, and without this proof there can be no defence for counselling as a profession.

Last, though not the least in importance, all counselling should be voluntary for the counsellee. He should not be compelled to seek counselling, he should feel the need for help with his difficulties and must seek this help. The willingness on the part of the counsellee contributes to the counselling process because it ensures the cooperation of the client. As pointed out earlier, counselling is a leraning situation. Experiments in learning have proved that it is impossible to force someone to learn. Counselling can be successful only if the counsellee cooperates with the counsellor. We may succeed in sending someone to see the counselor but the counsellor is helpless in his work if the counselee is unwilling or not interested.

●●●

2

Education and Counselling

Counselling, as defined in the previous chapter, is a help offered to an individual in solving his day-to-day difficulties and problems. The Counsellor does not solve his problems for him but he helps him to find a suitable solution of his present problem and any future ones which he may encounter. In other words, it is a help given to the counsellee to develop into an independent and self reliant individual able to meet his own problems and make his own decisions. A review of the aims of education stated earlier will point out the similarity between the basic principles of counselling and education.

One of the assumptions underlying counselling is that the counsellee is a 'more or less' normal individual who is getting on well with his daily life. He has certain difficulties and problems which affect or may affect his academic output. The problems cause tension to the individual which disturbs his studies and results in a drop in the level of his achievement. Often counselling is confused with clinical work—this is especially common with the Indian students and educators. The students have often expressed the fear that if they are seen with the counsellor, people would think something has gone wrong with their minds. We need to underline the fact that counselling is a help offered to normal individuals, with common everyday problems. Everyone has problems and professional help with these problems is meant to check any further complication and strain for the counsellee. Counselling in educational settings avoids unnecessary conflicts and frustrations and in doing so it helps in improving the academic achievement of the student. In recognizing that everyone of us has problems and in offering help with these problems the counsellor is showing his respect for the individual and his personality. This is another common goal that counselling shares with education in a democratic society.

The problems of a counsellee may centre around his courses, career and the job he may be aspiring to occupy or his problems may be purely personal and emotional in nature. The nature of his problems notwithstanding, he needs the help of a professionally qualified individual in resolving certain basic conflicts and making a choice of the best alternative available for his personal growth and welfare of the society he is a member of. The counsellor helps him in the process of making independent decisions and in developing an objective and well balanced image of himself in context with his surroundings. In India, we are familiar with the vital role that the parents play in deciding a career for their children. It is common for them to decide whether their child should become a doctor, engineer or a teacher. Everyone has accepted this role of the parent and we have never felt the need for any professional help in making the vocational choice. When the parent decides what his child should become he is motivated by anyone or all of the following reasons:

1. Parents are known to have urged their children into a particular career for purely monetary reasons. Sometimes the financial gains are possible through malpractices only, but the parents have not cared to stop and analyses these factors.
2. The parent himself wanted to go into a particular line but could not do so due to one reason or another. To make-up for this failure, he often decides that his child would follow the cherished career and make a great success.

3. His love for the child leads the parents to aspire that he should go into a profession which enjoys the highest social prestige.

4. Accidental exploration on the part of a child has often led the parent to decide his future career. Preoccupation with a mechanical toy has made the parent conclude that he is to make an engineer. Playing with the first-aid box or medical instruments may make the parent think that the child is showing an inclination to medicine. These, at their best, are examples of overestimation of the child's ability based on incidental interest shown by the child.

None of these, nor even all of them put together are enough reason for deciding a career for the child. Choosing a career is not a simple process any more. With the industrial and technical expansion, hundreds of new jobs are coming into existence. The optimum development of a society demands that positions be manned by skilled and well matched individuals. From the individual's point of view, working on a job should not be a question of money alone. In order to put his best into the job and to derive the maximum joy out of it, the individual needs to experience job satisfaction. For the developing democracy, that we are, it is imperative that the available man-power is utilized in the best manner possible.

For successful completion every job requires a certain type of person with certain defined qualities and skills; the choice of a job for a particular person, therefore, involves a study of the person, his aptitudes, temperament, interests, skills and his likes and dislikes. On the other hand, it involves a thorough study of the job and its requirements. After this study of the individual and the job, we need to match right individuals with right jobs. The above mentioned process calls for an objective study and handling of the situation rather than a subjective and biased one. It also requires training in testing, interpretation of tests, interviews and other techniques involved in counselling. Thus we may conclude that the parents with a subjective bias for their own child and no professional training, except in the case of a few, are not qualified to decide the career for him. The child needs the help of a counsellor for this great decision of his life. Moreover, by making a decision for him the parents deprive their child of the right to make his own choice and an opportunity to experience independent thinking and decision-making. Decision-making is a skill which is best acquired through practice under guidance of an experienced adult. For the optimum development in this direction the child needs help and guidance and not ready made solutions of his present problems. Ready made decisions make him dependent on adult help and do not equip him with the skill to meet future problem situations.

Emotional Problem

In the case of an emotional or personal problem, the youth is afraid to talk to the parents or anyone else. The very nature of their problems forbids sharing them with others. When the problems are related to a taboo area, the students are afraid of punishment from the parents and a disapproval of others. They need a great deal of assurance and confidence before they can express themselves to even the qualified counsellor. A qualified counsellor knows the techniques of interviewing and helping the counsellee talk of his most intimate problems. He is also trained in the art of helping the counsellee with these problems without trying to pass a judgment on his behaviour.

Counselling thus described is necessary in an educational set-up with the optimum development of the individual as its aim. Counselling does not easily fit into the system which limits itself to providing knowledge and literary skills only; on the other hand, it easily fits into an education that aims at an all round and maximal development of the individual's potentialities. It fits in with the education which aims at helping students put in their best effort without tension and struggle with the problems.

Counselling as understood in the modern context is developing spontaneously in response to the needs of the students communicated to the teachers through a warm and friendly relationship between the two. Democratic education aims at exploring the individual's interests and providing optimum opportunities for the development of every student. To achieve this aim education should consist of a wide variety of subjects and courses out of which the student may choose the ones which he likes to pursue. The youth is rarely bound to the decision of his parents regarding his career. He is expected to make his own choice in determining his life vocation. Therefore, it is necessary that he should have the help of a professionally qualified individual in taking such an important decision of his life. This has been the beginning of educational and vocational counselling in modern education.

In India, though we claim to be a democracy yet our system of education is far removed from democratic practices. We are going through a transition. Not very long ago our education was meant for a few privileged individuals. The aim of education was not to provide for optimum development of the individual but to train a few selected individuals so that they may fill positions in the governmental machinery of those days; it was more of 'schooling' than 'education'. Since independence we are groping for a suitable system of education which should cater to the changed needs of our society, provide for optimum development of the individual and his potentialities. With the uncertain state which our educational system is passing through, counselling may seem out of place and foreign but we can hope to achieve the ultimate aim of education only, if, through professional counselling, we make provisions for the best possible development of the individual and his abilities.

Indian education is still more like the British system which lays down a large number of requirements without much choice in courses. In the light of inflexibility which this system leads to, it is often argued that there is not much point in offering help in career planning. However, a curriculum, no matter how rigid it may be, does offer courses which prepare the individual for more than one career. A selection is called for in deciding the best choice out of the available alternatives, limited though they may be in number. The help with career planning is important so that the student selects his vocation carefully and does not waste his time in making inappropriate choices and the forced shifts from one career to another. The presumption here is that the courses are so grouped that they do prepare an individual for a specific line. Often this is not the case in educational institutions in India. The courses are introduced without any specific line in mind and the students are permitted to take electives which do not combine well in preparing the student for a particular line. This type of curriculum planning, besides leading to a waste of time, causes unnecessary tension and confusion in the mind of the student.

Planning of courses is not only educational problem of Indian students. Study habits, how to budget time, how to read fast and how to make notes on assigned readings are some other difficulties encountered by the students. They need help with these in order to show optimum academic achievement. Many of the educational problems are expressed in general terms by the counsellee 'I can not concentrate'. 'I cannot read properly'. 'I do not understand what is read'. Counselling sessions reveal a variety of causes responsible for these vague and undefined symptoms. Close to the examination time another problem 'how to answer questions' raises its head and the students, proceed to the counsellor for help with this seasonal difficulty.

Most of the above problems can be helped through programmes of group guidance. A few sessions on topics such as how to study, how to take notes and how to answer question papers can be included in the school and college curriculum. Answers to these questions are as important to the academic success of the student as the classroom teaching. Many a time the group guidance sessions do not provide sufficient help to the counsellee; individual counselling is necessary in such cases.

Academic backwardness or underachievement is often caused by personal and emotional factors which the counsellor needs to study and work on. Failure in examinations is known to be due to unhappy family life, emotional insecurity, sibling rivalry and such other psychological factors. Counselling service becomes an essential aspect of education if optimum educational achievement is the aim. The counsellor aims at helping the student to find relief from these factors and put in his best performance. Achievement is significantly high when the emotional stress is reduced.

As far as the personal and emotional problems are concerned the needs of Indian students are identical with those of American students or students anywhere else in the world. They need someone sympathetic, unbiased, understanding and professionally qualified to help them make proper adjustment to the surroundings. Going to school is not an easy job, it means competition, pressure of studies, examinations and the need for meeting the set standards. All this causes a lot of strain on the mind of the student and if not helped with, may cause tension and frustration which, in turn, may affect his performance in the classroom.

For a major part of the school period the student is passing through adolescence; adolescence makes its own demands for adjustments. The individual is going through rapid physical changes which contribute to a change in his self image and often a feeling of insecurity. Parallel to the physical change is the sexual development and the attraction for the opposite sex which is a spontaneous expression of sexual maturity. Our society provides for very little preparation or education to facilitate the adjustment required for this development. The young individual goes through a conflict between his natural urges and the strict taboos prescribed by society on the expression of these urges and desires. Often he faces serious emotional problems which can be helped through counselling to achieve an objective understanding of himself and his surroundings.

This is the age when the youth struggles with social adjustment. He is very self-conscious and as a result clumsy in his behaviour. He feels awkward in the presence of others and nervous in talking and dealing with others. At the same time he starts thinking of the important problems of marriage and home-making. In short, the age is full of conflicts, struggles, tensions, adjustments and the young individual needs help so that he may make a smooth and peaceful transition into adult life.

It is common for Indian educators to emphasize the differences between American and Indian conditions and draw the conclusion that Indian students do not face the problems which are common among the American youth. Extensive counselling work with school and college students however, has brought out the striking similarities between the youth of the two countries, and the counsellor is convinced that the struggles of growing up are the same in every culture. The differences found during counselling are minor in nature and can be attributed to the differential manifestations prescribed by different cultures rather than the differences in basic needs and problems themselves.

Even when there are obvious differences in the problems manifested by Indian and American youth the intensity of their impact on the adjustive behaviour and educational achievement is the same. Examples of specific cases will clarify: Indian students are usually more dependent on their family for some of the important life decisions. Their parents decide the school or college they should join, the subjective they should choose and the career they should prepare for. The parents are rarely equipped with the training to guide in an objective and scientific manner. To draw the parallel with the American scene, the young people there are expected to be independent, make their own decisions with parental and other adult guidance but not under directions from the parents. Some of the life decisions, under these conditions, become momentous for the young adult to take by himself. Wrong decisions in either case can upset the individual his adjustment to life and his achievement in school. Counselling assistance at the right time can save the individual from the strain and frustration which can result from a wrong decision.

Let us now examine the problems related to sex and marriage. It is commonly assumed that the Indian youth does not have any problem related with sex and marriage simply because the sex expression is not permitted to him as it is to the American youth. Marriage is also considered a settled issue and as such an area in which Indian youth does not face conflicts or struggles. Very little research evidence is available on this aspect of students' life yet whatever little research has been conducted has failed to support this belief. Through an all India survey 54 per cent of the students marked their inability to make friends among the opposite sex as one of their troublesome problems and 52 per cent felt that they did not possess sufficient information about matters on sex. The report of this survey mentions an interesting incident which reflects the opinion and attitudes formed by the older generation without reference to scientific evidence: " The principal of one women's college was shocked and indignant that her students were asked whether they were satisfied with the amount of knowledge they had with regard to sex and marriage. The good lady was certain that her students had neither interest nor problems in such matters. However, after she learned the findings of the study with regard to her college student body, she changed her opinion, and to her credit must be added that she immediately arranged for a series of lectures on the very topics which she had assumed were not troublesome to her girls".

The case histories reported from counselling practice have also reflected evidence which clearly contradicts this belief. They have proved without doubt that inter-sex adjustment is a vital problem for college students especially when the college population is drawn from both the urban and the real backgrounds. Differences in the expectations, background and experiences of the two groups cause a great deal of conflict and confusion in their behaviour on the college campus. Lack of education in this area adds confusion and insecurity to the behaviour of the student. Many students have come for counselling help due to their preoccupation with problems of sex and marriage and the consequent effect on their academic performance.

Students, contrary to the estimates of their parents and teachers give free expression to these problems, if and when an appropriate opportunity is provided to them. Once they are assured of an objective hearing, professional help and no judgement or reprimand, they express the conflicts, tensions and the problems regarding sex and marriage which occupy their minds and often interfere with their academic achievement. In our society, because sex has a severe taboo attached to it, it does not mean that the young people do not think about it and do not experience certain difficulties and problems in this area. The strong repression exercised by the individual often gives rise to more frustration and further complications in the already existing problems. The counsellor can help the counsellee develop an objective image of himself which should include sex and sexual maturity as the natural phenomenon of life. He can learn to relax the unnecessarily rigid repressions on its expression.

Indian Education System

Though patterned after the British system of education yet Indian education has somehow failed to show the same recognition and understanding of the needs and problems of the student that the British education has exhibited in more than one way. There is ample evidence that student services and counselling are recognized as an integral part of education in British schools and colleges and that facilities for such services are made available to the students. The spirit of student services prevalent at Oxford and Cambridge has been well expressed by Dongrekery, "... each undergraduate has his own tutor or supervisor, who, fellow of his own college, interviews him from time to time, supervises his work and looks after his welfare generally... and gives him personal guidance and instruction ... "

In all British universities the undergraduate knows his teachers personally and receives personal instruction from them. Personal contact and communication between the teacher and the taught is considered by British opinion as essential to true education. Sport is an important aspect of British education. All forms of sport are entirely managed by the students themselves. "No university would think of assigning any member of its staff to organize or even to encourage the sports of its students".

All universities have a tutorial system in one form or another. The tutorial system, however, is significantly different from the tutorials that we are familiar with in Indian universities. Oxford enjoys the status of a pioneer in this system of instruction. The main objective of tutorial system is the close personal relationship between the teacher and the undergraduate student. The first communication between the tutor and his pupil is established soon after the student joins the college, it continues through the period of his stay at the college and usually continues even after graduation. Most of the tutors do not confine their guidance to finding a suitable career for their pupils but take a continuing interest in their progress through life. "Often the tutor stands in loco parents to his pupil. He is invariably the guide, philosopher and friend, to whom the pupil can turn for advice in his daily conduct as well as in his studies."

Under tutorial system each junior member of the college is placed in the care of a senior member who guides him in his studies, sets him essays, tells him what lectures he should attend and regularly discusses with him his readings and the work of the week. The university makes a large number of lectures available to the students but the attendence at these is not compulsory. The tutor advises his pupil which lectures he should attend and the student makes his choice out of the lectures offered by the college keeping in mind the guidance given by his tutor. In this way, the major part of undergraduate instruction is based on individual guidance given by the tutors.

At Cambridge the system of advising is slightly different from the tutorial system of Oxford and functions under the nomenclature of 'supervision'. The 'tutors' at Cambridge do not teach classes, their main responsibility consists in the welfare of the students. They look after their needs, their problems and are responsible for student conduct and discipline. On admission each student is assigned to a 'Director of Studies' who advises him on his academic problems and makes arrangements for his weekly supervision.

The University of St. Andrews practices student advising through its 'Regent System'. The aim of this system is to maintain contacts between the teachers and the students. The regent is expected to give friendly advice to the students regarding their academic and personal problems. The regent system has been adopted by many civic universities in England with sight modifications to suit their conditions. In these universities all freshmen are assigned to a number of tutors who are mostly junior lecturers expected to "see them, singly or in groups, several times a term; help them to coordinate the various aspects of their work; to organize their time and invite them to discuss their private interests, home circumstances and anything else they like."

The social life is mainly centered in the college which has different societies for the extra-curricular activities located in the student union and organized by the students themselves. In most of the colleges there is a guild of undergraduates or students' representative council. The students select their own officers and they organize the activities which are held in the students' unions.

It is important to note that the student activities are managed and organized entirely by the students. Most of the Indian colleges report student activities, clubs and societies but a close look at the activities reveals the dominating role which the faculty member in charge of these activities plays in their organization. Student activities dominated by the staff are of no use to the students. They do not help them develop leadership or organizational skill which is the aim of student activities. An opportunity to organize their own activities helps students to take independent decisions, understand various protocols develop skills to conduct various academic and social meetings. All of these abilities and skills promote general overall development of the student and makes him a well groomed and capable citizen.

The universities operate student employment services which not only seek to provide work but find employment for their students on completion of their courses. This service is operated under the name 'Appointments Boards' and is building a bridge between the university and the world of work. It is meaningless for a university to confine itself to the award of various degrees and diplomas of doubtful value. If the university aims at producing better citizens capable of handling professional jobs and successfully occupying responsible positions then it is one of the most important duties of the institution to sell its degrees and diplomas to the, public. This can be best done by placement of its graduates in responsible jobs. In fact, the value of its degrees is established only if the public approaches the university for its graduates to fill responsible positions in industry and various administrative positions.

Most of the colleges provide health services to ensure the health of the student body. The first general check-up and a chest X-ray are compulsory for all students. After this, how much advantage they take of the provision depends upon the individual student. Closely connected with the health services, is the compulsory physical education for the students. The colleges also provide for help with other student problems, in form of advisory services. In case of problems connected with welfare each student knows to which staff-member he has to go so that he may confide in him and ask for his counsel and help. There is often a special adviser for foreign students.

Most of the universities have an accommodation officer who has a complete list of the approved lodgings for students. All universities have financial aids, scholarships and awards available to students which are governed through the financial aid office of the university. It is important that the financial aids are centralized and not scattered in various departments of the universities. The latter arrangement can lead to duplication and possible waste of funds while the centralized financial aids help the institution in making the optimum use of the funds available for student aid.

Oxford and Cambridge give evidence of their understanding of the need for student-teacher interaction by making it a requirement that the students and the fellows live together during a part or the entire academic year. This gives a number of opportunities to the undergraduate student to mix with his 'fellows'. All the colleges provide their undergraduates with personal tuition in addition to residence and a corporate life. The opportunity to meet formally and informally with other undergraduate students and the 'fellows' creates a peculiar *esprit de corps* which makes the students take pride in their college and all that it stands for. Indian colleges need to develop this esprit *de corps* so that education may become meaningful.

No regular lectures and no compulsion regarding attendance of these lectures is in itself an evidence that Oxford and Cambridge do not limit themselves to the classroom teaching only. The university and colleges put out a list of lectures arranged on various subjects, during the term. Thereafter the students are left free to choose the lectures they are interested in and ignore the ones that do not interest them. The tutors advise the students as to which lectures they should attend and which ones they could omit.

Even the non-residential colleges consider student teacher contact an important aspect of college life and make tutorial system an integral part of their education. Tutorial system personifies intimate personal contact between the tutor and the undergraduate student. For a good tutor, a pupil becomes his son; he is a guide, philosopher and friend to his pupil. The pupil seeks his advice in his daily conduct as well as in his studies. The tutor emphasizes individual instruction but realizes that over doing tutorial work can be harmful to the student, so he practices it with restraint and does not allow it to lead to spoon-feeding.

Tutorial System

The tutorial system is not a new development in British education, as it has existed in Oxford from the very inception of the university. By Constitution, the students were to be assigned to tutors. In the early days, arrangements for tutors were informal and unofficial. Their functions were mainly to guide students in proper conduct and regulate their personal allowances and the finance. With the larger number of students coming to the university this informal contact between the tutor and the pupil was not possible. A regular tutorial system needed to be devised. Today, the first day a student joins the university, he is introduced to his tutor who assesses his level of achievement and guides him in his studies accordingly.

Indian colleges and universities have borrowed the tutorials from the British universities but, unfortunately, the practice has been reduced to academic help and coaching only. The usual pattern of tutorials followed in Indian institutions consists of the selection of a few topics on which each student writes an essay and presents it to the tutorial group for evaluation. In many institutions tutorials are held equivalent to periodic tests the marks of which are counted towards the internal assessment of the student; this cannotation of tutorials has become so deeprooted in Indian educational thought that a change of terminology sounds imperative. During conferences and educational gatherings, the educators have discussed the aims of tutorials—theoretically the aims of the tutorials include personal help to the pupil also—which are the same as those of student advising. However, in practice the tutorials have amounted to academic coaching only. In effect, the Indian student is deprived of the most important help which the tutorials are supposed to render to him—the help with his personal and emotional difficulties which may, in the long run, affect his academic achievement.

So much for the place and meaning of counselling in Indian higher education. The status of guidance and counselling in high schools is not very much different. Though guidance and counselling is included as an area in the teachers' training programme yet, on appointment, these teachers find very little scope to practice the principles of guidance and counselling in their classrooms. Very few schools have a full time position of a counsellor. Some appoint a teacher with a background in guidance and counselling and expect him/her to look after the educational and vocational planning of the students as well as help them with their personal and emotional problems. This, however, is only a part of the counsellor's responsibility; he/she has a teaching load slightly less than the full time teacher.

Though our school system is patterned after the British system yet the positions of a school psychologist and the vocational psychologist, so well known in England, have become almost unknown in Indian set up. Unlike his counterpart in England, an Indian child has no facility for periodic testing and consultation with the psychologist or the employment officer. Career conferences for school children are a recent development in Indian schools. Supported and encouraged by the Education departments and State Bureaux of educational and vocational guidance the career conferences started as series of talks on various professions and vocations. !n the early years they were more or less a routine during a certain period ill the academic session; through the years, however, they have become more meaningful by becoming a starting point for group discussions and individual consultations.

Under the leadership of National Council of Educational Research and Training and the State Bureaux, a programme of guidance and counselling is being developed for adoption by Indian schools. Certain schools have been taken up in the experiment, children are tested for various abilities interests and aptitudes, their profiles are prepared and predictions made. This has been helpful in interpreting to the principals and the administration, the job and the responsibility of a school councellor. In the meantime, there have not been many training programmes for counsellors and guidance workers, therefore, the difficulty in locating qualified personnel to fill the positions. The National Council of Educational Research and Training and a few other institutions are offering training programmes which turn out a small group of qualified counsellors every year.

With the introduction of multipurpose schools and the availability of choice in curricula the guidance and counselling service for school children has become imperative. In order to make the most effective use of his abilities and potentialities and to make the most suitable choice of a career the student needs professional guidance through evaluation and testing of his abilities, understanding the world of work and its requirements and finally in matching his abilities with the most appropriate vocation.

The area of personal and emotional problems is more ignored in the case of school children than college students. Because of their age the school teacher tends to put his students at the end of the receiving line. With a few exceptions the children are 'talked to' and not 'talked with'; sharing of experiences, ideas and problems is a prerequisite for a counselling situation. The school teacher has to develop a respect for his students which is an absolute necessity for a counselling relationship. By and large, a school teacher in India gives information to his students perhaps a lot of good information—but not the personal assistance which the child requires for optimum development of his potentialities. Though guidance is making inroads into the Indian school system yet, requiring a change of attitudes, it will take a long time before it is accepted as an integral part of High School education.

The British system of education has given evidence of its concern about educational and vocational guidance through regular conferences on the training of the young worker. These conferences have been periodically arranged with the basic theme that the education and vocational training of the young worker, who joins work after school, should continue. The young worker usually comes into the job at the approximate age of fifteen. It becomes necessary that he gets an apprenticeship, acquires skills to live happily and to maintain happy relations with his fellow workers. The conferences recognized the need for education so that the young worker may successfully reach the above goals. If we draw a parallel between this concern and the American system then there is nothing more appropriate than to call it by the name of educational and vocational guidance.

Thus we find that in the British system of education there are adequate provisions for student services especially counselling with educational, vocational and personal problems both at the high school and college level. On the other hand, the Indian education has taken over the academic system leaving behind the student services, individual instruction and the warm and friendly relationship between the teacher and the taught. In doing so our education has become confined to the classroom learning and mastery of academic skills, mainly through rote memory. Outside the class our students are left with plenty of unoccupied time during which they seek activities and methods of spending their unused physical and mental energy.

No guidance is provided for the selection of constructive and useful activities; often the students choose exciting and adventurous preoccupations which are destructive and in disciplined in nature. We tend to presume that discipline and good behaviour are inborn and inherited. Psychological research has provided us with plenty of evidence to prove that this is not true. Discipline and ethics are learnt abilities and can be helped through education and proper guidance. Education when confined to the classroom learning has no place for the development of these abilities but if defined as the help given to an individual to develop his potentialities to the full, education is vitally concerned with the intellectual, social and emotional development of the individual. Discipline and values—esthetic, ethical and others—make a part of this all-round development of the individual.

A well organized set-up of student services can fill this gap and provide opportunities for continuing development and education even outside the classroom. During these hours the teachers could join students in organizing various student activities, meet with their pupils, discuss their academic plans and progress and help them with personal and emotional problems causing concern.

A change of attitude is necessary for the organization of such a set-up. Unless the teachers accept the broader interpretation of "education", the practice of education as a continued process even outside the classroom is not possible. It has become common for teachers to limit their responsibility to the classroom teaching and correctional work only, this is a clear indication of a 'teacher centred' education. Education is defined through what a teacher finds easy and convenient to do; for a really effective and productive education, we need to bring the student to the centre of education. The activities and responsibilities of the teacher and administration need to be defined according to the needs and problems of the students.

On the other hand, the meaning of education for the students and their parents needs to be changed. For most of us, going to the college has unfortunately become a prestige symbol and a mode to spend the student's unoccupied time. The students fail to demand quality education as their right. A strike is not interpreted as a waste of their own time and money; the education is so dull for them even a strike at their own cost is interesting and exciting. If student activities were made interesting and exciting and yet educational the students would not seek destructive and meaningless avenues for release of unspent physical and mental energy.

●●●

3

Theoretical Principles of Counselling

Counsellors and educators need to follow a specific psychological theory to explain human nature, but that does not mean that every-one of them sets himself the task of evolving individual theories. The usual practice is to adopt a general theory that seems reasonable and stick to it. Usually, theories are not accompanied by a great deal of empiricill data because it is not possible for the a laboratory scientists to experiment with all kinds of life situations. The laboratory psycholigist is used to studying behaviour under controlled conditions and there also the emphasis in his study is on the physical activity and not on the study of symbolic behaviour like language, feelings and attitudes. Therefore, the counsellor whose emphasis is on the study of symbolic behaviour, is led to try the theory of his choice in explaining and modifying behaviour of his clients. In doing so he collects evidence in favour or against this particular theory. As his experience accumulates he is in a position to modify this particular theory or to borrow concepts from alternative theories and integrate them with his choice theory.

Theory has been aptly defined as a meaningful organization of all the knowledge available on a particular subject. Knowledge about human behaviour has numerous facets; different theories have thrown light on one or the other of these facets. It is quite common, therefore, that a theory may be able to explain the behaviour of "A" individual and not that of "B". On the other hand, an alternative theory may work in the reverse, it may adequately explain the behaviour pattern of "B" and not that of "A". For practical purposes a counsellor needs to develop an overall view of human behaviour and in doing so he uses different varieties of theoretical concepts organized in a peculiar way to make his own individual theory of human behaviour, which is a life long project.

Having discussed how the individual counsellor develops his theory of human behaviour to apply to his counselling practice we will now discuss some of the theories and their sources. As mentioned earlier, every theory of human behaviour throws light on only one aspect of it; this, it does according to the source it is derived from. A theory derived from research in physiology is bound to emphasize the physiological aspect of human behaviour. Physiological phenomenon of homeostasis, for example, has given rise to the concept of "general adaptation syndrome". As homeostasis means maintenance of a constant inner state in spite of drastic changes in the external environment of the individual, so, on the psychological front it is believed that the "general adaptation syndrome" indicates the individual's reaction to stress of any kind, in an attempt to equalize mental tensions and disturbance. In accepting this concept we are thinking in terms of complicated dynamic behaviour patterns which maintain themselves by constant delicately balanced changes.

Psychological research has added significantly to the counselling approach and practice. If counselling is defined as a learning process then learning research is of particular interest to the counsellor. Through successful counselling the client learns to form better relationships between himself and the world he lives in. Counselling is a situation designed to help the client to learn more effectively and efficiently than is possible in most life situations. Assuming that counselling is a learning process it is natural for us to expect that learning theories would apply to the counselling problems.

Learning Theories

Learning theories can be classified into two types (1) Stimulus-response theories, and (2) Cognitive theories. The stimulus-response psychologists emphasize the end product that is the behaviour of the individual under varying conditions and situations. Attitudes, emotions, feelings and social behaviour are classified as behaviour under this system. When we come to the questions how habits are formed and tendencies to respond in a particular way are strengthened or weakened then the stimulus-response theory uses the concepts of reinforcement, extinction and generalization of responses to new situations. Reinforcement if positive would strengthen a habit or tendency to respond in a particular way, if negative it will result in extinction. When positive reinforcement is applied to similar or near similar situations the set habit or tendency is carried to the new situation also.

Interpreted in this way, the stimulus-response theorist emphasizes one-to-one relationship between stimulus and response, there is very little reference to inter-relationships or organization between experiences. The cognitive learning theories, on the other hand, recognize the internal relationships between experiences. Cognitive theorists believe that the changes in behaviour as the learning proceeds are determined by the way a person, consciously or unconsciously sees things. The most striking example of this, one finds in problem solving situations when the person suddenly sees the way to the solution. The concept of insight can be explained through the internal relationships and intergration of experiences only.

The sophisticated researches in learning concent-rate on isolating factors and studying the process of learning under the most controlled situations. In doing so they become atomistic and concentrate on small bits of the problems encountered in counselling. They have little application beyond the simplest behaviour while the behaviour pattern, which the counsellee presents is complex and involves the entire personality. Learning theories apply to the "process of learning" while counselling is mainly concerned with the "person who learns"; the two points of view are vastly different. Counselling deals with problems requiring personality reorganization, which may call for learning concepts but of much broader connotation than the ones defined in learning theories developed under the controlled conditions of a laboratory.

A parallel can be drawn between the application of learning theory to education and its application to counselling. Learning theory, so far, has failed to produce any significant movement in education, as a matter of fact, in some instances the learning theory has produced negative effects. The example is that of emphasis on drill and rote memory in our classrooms, which is a straight application of Ebbinghaus' experiments of three generations ago. As education shifts its emphasis from subject matter to children and from processes to people, the learning theory will be gradually replaced by personality theory. In counselling we have already stated our purpose to serve persons who have problems and are keen to learn to make new adjustments to their environment, it is a problem of people rather than processes. Therefore, like education, counselling needs to look more to theories of personality than learning.

The Counsellor needs a dynamic personality theory, which would help him in understanding human behaviour outside the laboratory, in free situations where few, if any, variables are likely to be in the control of the observer. Some psychologists feel apprehensive about the research performed on uncontrolled variables; such work is considered less "scientific" than the controlled research. For psychological practice this is unfortunate, it equates science with minuteness rather than understanding. Minute theories have proved inadequate in providing a guide to classroom learning; they are equally inadequate in providing an explanation of what happens during the counselling process. Though these theories have successfully explained certain isolated aspects of what seems to happen to clients, they have generally failed to explain the changes, which a counsellor observes almost daily in the course of his practice. Neither are they able to provide a guide in improving practices or to understanding behaviour problems encountered in counselling practice.

Perceptual Field Theory

Research on perception is closer to the cognitive theories of learning and seems to offer a more adequate explanation of human behaviour than the stimulus response theory of learning. Perception implies the process of inner organization. Experimental work on many specific areas of perception such as illusions, colour constancy and size, has proved how pervasive and universal this organizing process is. Recent research has brought out the relationships between motivation and what is perceived in ambiguous situations and between personality traits and general perceptual characteristics. This has further emphasized the fact that each person's world is to some extent an individual creation. Therefore, a counsellor cannot analyse a client's relationship to his family and assume that he sees it as the counsellor does.

Field theory of personality organization is based on the growing understanding about the nature and functions of perception and the concept of self. Perceptual theory does not claim to answer all questions or solve all problems related to counselling but it has proved satisfactory, logical and helpful in explaining behaviour under various conditions. It is also useful as a personal guide to behaviour.

According to this theory, all behaviour is a function of the individual's field of perceptions at the time that behaviour takes place. In other words, people behave according to how things seem to them. For example, when a person believes that icecream causes stomach upset he will avoid eating it himself and would advise others against it. Each individual behaves differently because he perceives himself and his surroundings differently. Perceptions are 'real' to the individual who perceives; beliefs, stereotypes and prejudices are nothing else but the perceptions of individuals. This frame of reference is being accepted by an increasing number of counselling psychologists. It is consistent with client centred therapy and to a great extent with psycho-analysis. It applies well to educational and vocational development and guidance. If we accept the above statement, that is, behaviour is a function of perception, then the goal of counselling must be to help the counsellee to change perceptions. Effective, efficient and satisfying behaviour, both from the point of view of the counsellee and society, requires maximum freedom of perception. Rogers describes the adjusted person as follows:

> "It would appear that when all of the ways in which the individual perceives himself all perceptions of the qualities, abilities, impulses and attitudes of the person and all perceptions of himself III relation to others are accepted into the organized conscious concept of self, then his achievement is accompanied by feelings of comfort and freedom from tension which are experienced as psychological adjustment."

In terms of field theory of perception, the aim of counselling becomes one of assisting the counsellee to acquire a rich, varied, accurate and undistorted perception. If the case involves self-perception then counselling must help the client with more accurate, precise and clearer picture of self and its relationship with the world in which he lives. While accepting change of perception as the aim of counselling, due recognition must be given to the fact that the perceptual field of the counsellee is a personal and internal organization, not directly open to manipulation. No counsellor can change his client's perception; he can only help the latter to review and if possible change his perception. Counselling is not a situation in which something is done to the counsellee, it is rather a situation in which he is assisted to change: his own mode of seeing things according to his own free will.

If it is true that behaviour is a function of perception then it becomes necessary for the counsellor to understand factors, which influence perception. Though a great deal remains to be investigated in the field of perception yet a good amount of relevant research evidence is available which can be usefully applied to the process of counselling. Some of the factors are:

1. Perception is a function of the physical condition of the perceiver. Perception affects and is affected by the physical organism which works as the vehicle for perceiving.
2. Perception is a function of time. Effective perception requires sufficient exposure to the outside world.
3. Perception cannot occur if the opportunity for experience has been denied to the individual.

Besides these three factors, which have been amply experimented with, there are some more which have not yet accumulated so much of research evidence, but are gaining importance in practical application of perceptual principles. These are:

1. Perception is a function of individual's values and goals. The values and goals of the individual make his perception selective in nature. Other things being equal, an individual perceives more clearly and effectively if the perceived matter fits in with or violates his value system.

2. Perception is significantly affected by the self-concept of the individual. A person who considers, himself unintelligent fails to perform at the average level of intelligence. The psychologists have just started realizing the importance of self-concept upon every aspect of human behaviour. Perception of self seems to be the nucleous around which all perceptions of reality are formed.

3. Perception is seriously affected by the experience of threat.

The effects of threat are of two types:

1. When a person feels threatened his field of perceptions gets limited to the object of threat only. This phenomenon is known as the "effect of tunnel vision".

2. When threatened, the individual seeks to defend his existing self-organization and in doing so, he often goes to the other extreme of having grandiose perceptions of self.

Understanding of these factors has a direct bearing upon the process of counselling and they can serve as useful guides to the counsellor in his practical work with counsellees.

Psychoanalysis

Psychoanalysis has given a rich theoretical background to counselling. It may not be possible for all counsellors to accept psychoanalytic theory in totality yet some of the principles of this theory can simply not be denied in actual counselling practice. An apt example is the concept of unconscious. Many of us may not like the unconscious as a part of personality but during our counselling experience we do come across behaviour, which the counsellee is totally unaware of Repeated occurence of such evidence has led to the acceptance of unconscious as a concept in counselling.

Psychoanalytic belief that personality is a dynamic process in which wish and aspiration play a vital role has deeply penetrated the thinking of counselling psychologists. The significance of personality development during the first few years of life and early childhood experiences has been well realized by counsellors. Ample evidence has been found to support the theory that the root of later personality problems can always be traced to the early childhood experiences of the individual.

Jung, Adler and other neo-Freudians have made their own contributions to counselling theory and practice. Some of the examples are creative constructive unconscious emphasized by Jung and Adler and the social emphasis of Adler and other neo-Freudians. The assumption that man is basically a social creature and that his socialization process progresses with nature has influenced counselling theory a great deal. Rank's emphasis on the will and his belief that the individual has a right and need for free choice is well reflected in the current counselling thought.

Individual Differences

The theory of individual differences is the sole support of counselling. If individuals were not different from one another there was no need for indivıdual study and guidance or counselling. Because individuals are so different in their interests, attitudes, beliefs, likes and dislikes, intelligence, needs and problems, the counsellor's services are required to study and help them understand themselves and find solutions to their problems relevant to their own mental and environmental set-up.

The study of developmental patterns has come to two significant conclusions (1) All human beings share a likeness in developmental patterns (2) In spite of general similarity, individuals are different from each other. As far as the basic structure is concerned all human beings are alike; they are alike in physical as well as in psychological structure. They have the same senses in that they all can see, hear, smell and experience the outside world. People of a particular group are alike in their behaviour or responses to certain stimuli, therefore, it is possible for us to predict their behaviour. Language is interpreted by members of a particular group in the same fashion expression of emotions is the same and patterns of social behaviour have the same interpretation for all the members of a group.

The similarity, however, is limited to general characteristics of behaviour only; refined observation and controlled research indicates the vastness of differences in individual behaviour and makes one realize that the differences are as important, if not more, as the similarity in behaviour. One person is more intelligent than the other while a third one has facility with numbers better than both of these. These examples can rightly lead us to the conclusion that the differences between individuals are quantitative rather than qualitative. All persons have intelligence but some are more intelligent than others; all persons are capable of working with numbers but some are better than others.

Nature of Individual Differences

Abilities differ quantitatively and not qualitatively. Often abilities are viewed as an all or none phenomenon; either people are intelligent or not, they are sane or insane. All or none conception of abilities is deter-mental to counselling practice. What is basic to the philosophy of counselling is that all persons are capable of reacting intelligently, only some do it more intelligently than the others. Similarly, all of us have characteristics and behaviour patterns, which if carried to the extreme, enter the realm of neurosis or psychotic disorders. No one can be labelled absolutely normal or sane. Counselling has a case only if we accept that everyone at times, can require help with some of the problems which are an outgrowth of peculiarities and idiosyncracies of individuals; and that there is no stigma attached if the individual seeks such help. On the contrary, seeking help with problems should be an indication of the individual's awareness of his needs and sensitivity to human problems. Individual differences of degree in various abilities play an important role in the adjustment, which an individual makes with his environment; understanding of this role is of vital importance to the counsellor and the counselling psychologist. A great deal has been written about the factors responsible for individual differences, which in brief, boil down to heredity and environment. Research in this area has come to the conclusion that heredity and environment are so related to each other that it is difficult to seperate factors entirely hereditary in nature from the ones, which can be labelled purely environmental. The research evidence in this field has double application. The results can be interpreted so as to suit the two schools equally well. In fact the effects of heredity and environment are so interwoven that it is difficult to distinguish between the two.

The areas and the aspects of individual's life in which we should expect differences are difficult to define; individual differences can be expected in every aspect of the individual's life. However, the student of counselling psychology will be more interested in the areas closely related with learning and attitude change. In a school situation, the first and the foremost difference is that of age. There are attempts at controlling the age but this control can be exercised in a limited way only. Within the year students can be as far removed as eleven months. Physically it may not seem to make much difference but mentally this age difference is known to have created problems for individual counsellees. Age determines the learning tasks. A child of eight for example, is not expected to do the intellectual tasks, which we expect of a twenty-five year old individual.

Physique and physical development is another factor determining Individual differences. Physical disabilities contribute to the self-image of the individual and the accompanying emotions and feelings. Emotional stability and development, temperament, interests and attitudes are some of the other areas in which we should look for individual differences. These differences affect the personality of the individual and so the counselling practice.

One important lesson, which a counsellor can learn from the study of factors responsible for individual differences is that it is wrong to assume that heredity cannot be acted upon. Often it is reflected that nothing can be done with an individual who has inferior intelligence. Environment can play an important role in improving or impairing the intellectual potential of individuals. Studies of twins brought up under different environment have amply proved this fact.

General intelligence is one more major area of individual differences, which influences human behaviour significantly. On Binet's distribution based on intelligence quotient, individuals who fall in the subnormal category do not come for regular schooling, they are cases for custodial care and should be admitted to residential institutions. In India, there are very few institutions of this type and most of these function at substandard level; as such the situation is rather grave. The educational set-up, usually, works with the "above subnormal" group within which also three levels can be distinguished: (1) the lowest most at which the individual is expected to learn very little except in the simplest learning situations; (2) at a little higher level individuals experience difficulties in learning but with special remedial help, they can learn to some extent; (3) the level at which regular school learning is possible. At school, learning skills require a minimum I.Q. of 75. In the group going to regular schools there is a significantly large number of children who fall in the dull and borderline category; they have difficulty in learning materials meant for normal children. These are the guidance cases for remedial help and special education; with special help also they are capable of mastering only the simple materials. Many children with an I.Q. of 90 aspire to master more complicated materials. They have persistence and inspiration, which is limited by restricted intelligence. A normal school is geared to individuals in the I.Q. range of 95 to 105; children aspiring to go into higher education should have significantly higher intellectual level. The guidance counsellor shoulders the responsibility of guiding these children to the most suitable institutions.

Some of the research findings, which may prove equally helpful to the teacher and the guidance worker are:

1. The slow learner reaches his limit of educability sooner than the average and the superior child. Favourable environment or learning conditions do not affect the educability level.
2. If favourable conditions are provided the average child may show better progress in basic learning and mastery of special skills.
3. Favourable conditions help the mentally superior child in learning as far as his interests and educational facilities make it possible for him to learn.
4. Unfavourable conditions interfere with the learning of superior, average as well as dull children.

For better educational results children need to be grouped accordmg to their intellectual status, which can be assessed only if adequate intelligence testing programmes are provided in schools. Testing also helps in diagnosing the extent to which a particular child's anti-social behaviour is related to the level of his mental ability.

Individual differences in special abilities are also relevant to counselling. During early life of the child special abilities escape notice because the child is engaged in mastering the basic tools and techniques of learning. However, a little later when he comes to the middle and higher secondary level, aptitude testing and discovery of special abilities, which the child may possess becomes an important guideline for his education. Though intelligence has been proved a major factor in all learning yet it has also been established that intelligence plays a more important role in academic learning than in motor skills, music, art and physical education.

Children also differ in educational achievement. In any particular class, children show a vast range in the level of materials, which they can learn. Sometimes this range becomes so big that the teacher finds it difficult to adapt his subject matter to all the levels. Wide differences have been found in the ability of children to learn specific subjects. Some may achieve better in history while others may show better results in science subjects. These differences may be due to differences in intelligence and special abilities but more often they can be traced back to aptitudes and interests. With the help of aptitude and interest study there is great possibility of improvement in learning efficiency. A more important aim of education is to help the child acquire skills of learning and acquiring knowledge rather than the knowledge itself. Unfortunately, our education has emphasized information giving so much that it has become loaded with memory rather than reasoning. Higher secondary and college programmes should have courses on reading or study habits because underdeveloped reading and study habits have become a frequent problem during higher education.

Attitude towards education and school is an important area of individual differences and contributes to the individual's adjustment to school and studies. Aims of education are different for different people especially in case of boys and girls. In our society, for a boy the aim of education is to secure a job and earn a living for the family.

On the other hand, for a girl it is a period of general education and often a means of improving matrimonial prospects. It is a major responsibility of the school and the guidance programme to help students develop positive attitudes towards School. Differences in attitudes towards various occupations, social customs, traditions and the problems related to school and society influence the child's adjustment to school and his achievement. Diagnosing individual differences and providing adequate facilities for people to develop within these differences is one important function of guidance and counselling programmes in educational institutions.

Research in other Social Disciplines

As has been brought out in the previous section testing and measurement have been accepted in counselling and made use of as the most important method of classifying people and diagnosing their problems. The whole science of testing and measurement is based on the concept of personality traits. It has been proved that each personality trait can be drawn out and measured. The concept of quantitative differences, has been influential in this development. Concepts from testing and measurement have been liberally borrowed and used in counselling practice.

Thinking on personality done in cultural anthropology has given another dimension to personality theory. This type of thinking is different from the laboratory theorization because it is based on objective observations of people in natural settings. A person is not only a biological system affected by social environment but he is a system in which the biological and the social aspects are so merged that it is impossible to separate the two. The concept of social role is a contribution made by the anthropological and sociological thinking. Man and woman, mother, teacher and businessman all have a social role to perform. Our behaviour is determined by these social roles. It is approved by others if it conforms with the social roles; if not, it becomes the subject of question, surprise, ridicule or fun.

Philosophy and religion have a major contribution to make to counselling practice. In the Western world the emphasis on the individual soul and its significance has already come to be recognized in the counselling world. Its reflections are obvious in the emphasis that psychologists lay on the self in personality, individual choice, freedom and responsibility. Counselling in India has a far richer philosophical and religious bases to work on. Learning from whatever experience we have in counselling the young people in India, we will need to reinforce the importance of individual choice, freedom and responsibility.

Indian youth is, usually, inexperienced and hesitant to exercise free choice and to make independent decisions. The reason for this may be the lack of practice in exercising free choice. In our homes children are rarely given the opportunity of making their own choice and decisions. They are usually helped by the elders—parents and others—to make what they think is the best choice. In due course they get so used to others doing their thinking and making decisions for them that the cases are common when, in a counselling situation, the young adult asks the counsellor for a decision and instructions about what should be done.

The counsellor, under Indian conditions, also has the temptation to give advice right away. He is so used to doing this that he finds it easier to "tell" the student what to do rather than to help him to think for himself and find his own solutions to his problems. We need to remember that the main aim of counselling is to help the individual discover himself, realize his individual freedom and the responsibility, which he must take on himself for his own decisions and actions. Having attempted this brief survey of the theoretical concepts applicable to counselling, we are in a position to sum up into an individual counselling theory.

Our general framework, which can combine the various theories disscussed above is that of development. Development is a continuous process-taking place in every individual through his life span. At every moment the individual is changing and is a little different than what he was. This change, however, is accompanied by a pattern in the development.

Tyler has developed this synthesis of the theoretical concepts in great detail. She stresses that the development is a continuous and a one-way process. Once a developing structure has been made it can never be eradicated. Life can be visualized as a series of stages of development. At each stage the individual faces special tasks and challenges which, in the psychological literature, are called developmental tasks. Different periods in the life span can be definitely marked by these specific developmental tasks. The general framework of development provides for complex, multiple causation of whatever happens in a human life and is comprehensive enough to provide a place for the various theories. A counsellor who adopts this framework finds himself working with nature in each individual case. The ability to grasp the complex pattern of each developing life and the nature of the changes that are occurring or can occur becomes basic to his practice; sensitivity is the most valuable asset for him to possess. Acceptance also emerges as important because nothing can be done with the developmental patterns which have already set in, determined as these are by factors in the unrecoverable past.

4

Guidance and New Education Policy

It is now widely accepted that government is inefficient in producing economic goods and services. We have therefore abolished the licence-permit raj in the economy. The economic liberalization has increased competition and consumer choice. Instead of the government determining what and how much of goods and services should be produced, under market principles of choice and competition, we now allow businesses and consumers to make those decisions. In the economy, government sovereignty has been abolished and consumer sovereignty has been established.

Many however, feel that in the area of education, the government must play a dominant role. Education is very different from economic goods and services. Market principles of choice and competition and of consumer sovereignty cannot be applied to education. Education is a "public good" a "social good," a part of "social infrastructure." Education is so important to our economy and society, the argument goes, that it cannot be left to the choices of poor, illiterate peasants and the vagaries of the market. The government must take the primary responsibility for education; it must expand its role and involvement to improve basic literacy and to produce trained labour force that can compete in the global economy. But is education that different from other economic services to make it antithetical or immune to market principles? In answering that question, let's first begin with the proposition that we all agree with—Compared to the market, the government is inefficient in producing economic goods and services. Why is the government seen as being inferior in the economic arena? The answer exists in various forms. One is what I call the "Dialectics of Three is"—Interest, Incentives, and Information. The (self interest of government employees, like everyone else's, is to take care of themselves. Individuals do not suddenly become altruistic (other regarding), just because they work in a government factory as opposed to a private one. The conflict between the public interest and the interest of government needs no further proof than a reminder of the recent pay raises for government employees.

Incentives for increasing efficiency are also weak. Government employees have little incentive to minimize costs, to find and correct mistakes, to innovate, and to acquire necessary information about resource availability and consumer demand. The collapse of the Soviet Union, where everything was managed by the government, showed that the stories of nails weighing a kilogram and ice cream with only vanilla flavours were no exaggeration. Soviet employees were just concerned with fulfiling their prescribed quota of producing certain kilograms of nails and ice cream. They did not worry about who would use their products and how their products would be used, or whether the products were in line with consumer preferences. Information on which, government decisions are based, is as reliable as statistics of literacy rate or balance of payments. In addition to poor quality, information is generally manipulated of political and public-relation purposes. Economic data and forecasts during the annual budget are always rosier than the reality. The "Dialectics of Three is" is what explains the general agreement on the proposition of government inefficiency in comparison to the market.

It is not that the people who work in the government are inferior to those in the private sector. It is the institutional structure-incentives and information—within which their self interest plays out. that institutional structure determines whether the pursuit of their interest would generally lead to increased social welfare. Unfortunately, their is no visible hand to guide government employees. In the competitive private sector, the pursuit of self-interest by business—maximization of profits-compels them to obey the desires and preferences of customers. If government is inefficient in producing food—cultivating land—then how could it become efficient in producing education—cultivating the mind? Tilling land is certainly a far simpler task than training the young. The reasons that make the government incompetent in the economic arena also make it inept in the area of education. India's poor performance in education is the result of government monopoly and excessive intervention. After sixty years of managing our education system, the government can show only fifty per cent literacy rate. Even that number, many analysts believe, is overly exaggerated. The dropout rate in elementary and secondary schools has been rising, so is the failure rate in colleges, and the quality of education at all levels has been falling. If government monopoly and controls play havoc in the production of economic goods and services, they could not be expected to offer opposite results in the production of education.

Education and other economic goods and services are alike; they all perform poorly when left to government management. The economy is being liberated from government control and is increasingly operating under market principles of competition and consumer sovereignty. It is time to do the same with education. Education is too important to be left solely in the hands of the government. It should be opened up to encourage experimentation and competition—to unleash the marvel of private initiative, imagination, and effort.

As in the economy, where the government provides financial support (subsidies) to the needy, the government may choose to subsidize education. But subsidizing education is not the same thing as producing education. I however think that if the quality of education were high and if it were tailored to the needs of individual parents and children, even the poor would pay for it. As recent studies have shown, today with the government-quality education, households with less than Rs. 3000 in annual per capita income spend 10 to 36 per cent of their income on their children's elementary education (NCAER 1994). Even if the government was to undertake financing of education, effectiveness of that expenditure depends heavily on where and how the money is spent. A detailed study of two states—Kerala and West Bengal—illustrates the significance of the distribution of the forms that government expenditure on education. Where and how the government spends the money is critical in determining the degree of education and therefore the efficiency of the education system.

A Tale of Two States

Kerala and West Bengal are chosen for the analysis in order to remove any doubt about the stale government's ideological commitment to the improvement of people's education. Both states for long have had popularly elected Marxist governments. The conclusions of the comparative analysis are however generally valid.

The crucial differences in the educational structure and the nature of government spending on education in the two states. The effect of those differences on the performance of the education system in terms of literacy rate and the proportion of children never enrolled in school. (All data are from the NSSO 1991, 1993; NCAER 1994; see also Tilak 1996. The data are for the years 1986-87 or 1991-92.) Kerala is one of the few states in the country where elementary education has not been made compulsory by law. Both governments spend about an equal fraction of the total budget on education (about 25 per cent). In West Bengal, 84 per cent of rural children do not pay, any fees for primary education but that number is only 48 per cent in Kerala. Sixty per cent of rural primary school children get free textbooks and supplies in West Bengal, only two per cent in Kerala. Households with less than Rs. 3000 in annual per capita income spend 25 per cent of the income on elementary education in West Bengal, but in Kerala it is 36 per cent. The poor in Kerala spend the highest fraction of their income on their children's basic education compared to the poor in any other state in the country.

Given these facts—more children get free education and supplies in West Bengal and the poor are asked to spend more of their own money in Kerala—one would expect that West Bengal would have a much higher literacy rate than Kerala. The facts speak otherwise. Kerala has 91 per cent literacy rate, while West Bengal only 57 per cent. Moreover, in West Bengal 46 per cent of children (age 6-14) have never enrolled in school, only two per cent in Kerala suffer from that fate. What explains this vast difference in performance? Kerala undoubtedly has had a head-start: There have been strong education movements in the state since the pre-independence days and the government has consistently spent a much larger proportion of its budget on education since independence. It then seems unfair to compare the two states in terms of their educational performance. It is legitimate to argue that cross-section comparisons at a single point in time do not control for variations over time. Kerala's current spending on education is almost the same as West Bengal, but since Kerala had a head-start, current literacy rates and the reach of education are likely to be different.

But leaving that comparison aside, it is instructive to examine the distribution of their education spending. Kerala and West Bengal have chosen to spend their education money rather differently. Though the data are for one year (1986-87 or 1991-92), it would be difficult to maintain that the pattern of education expenditure that year is rather different from that in other years. There would be variations from year to year in any given category of expenditure, the basic pattern could reasonably be expected to have altered little.

It is surprising that in a thoroughly Marxist state like Kerala 60 per cent of the rural primary schools are private, as compared to only 11 per cent in West Bengal: The proportion of private primary schools m Kerala is the highest in the country; the second highest is Meghalaya at 21 per cent and the national average is only 5 per cent. The government of Kerala also pays expenses of almost half of the students enrolled in private primary school. The number for West Bengal is 15 per cent which is the third highest in the country (Tamil Nadu is at 20 per cent); the national average is again about 5 per cent.

Kerala has the highest proportion of private primary schools and it also subsidizes the highest proportion of students in private schools. Both of these facts give the citizens of Kerala wider effective choice in selecting primary schools for their children. Many pf these private schools are run by various religious groups in the state and they are generally more likely to be successful in exerting pressure on parents to send their children to school. Since religious education, formal or informal, is part of schoolwork, parents are also more likely to have their children go to school Religious education at that age is one of the most effective ways to teach values, to impart ability to discern right from wrong, and to foster good behaviour. The private primary schools provide what many parents desire. The choices available to parents must increase attendance as well as retention rate in the state. The efficiency and effectiveness of the education system is determined not just by how much a state spends, but by how the money is spent.

Moreover, Kerala uses its public funds to encourage competition among schools. Surveys indicate that transportation costs are the biggest expense incurred by households in educating children. Most parents therefore choose to send their children to the nearest school. The resulting "geographical clustering" of schools and their customers lessens competition among schools. Each school has a captured customer base. By subsidizing transportation costs, Kerala helps parents send their children to the school they consider the best, irrespective of the distance. This in turn increases competition among schools. Provision of direct scholarships to students in Kerala also leads to the same result. With the scholarship money, students can go to any school of their choice. Among all the states in the country, the highest proportion of children in Kerala receives transportation subsidy and direct scholarships.

The focus on how the two governments spend their education rupees indicates that Kerala by offering more choices to parents and increasing competition among schools actually practises market principles. Given the ideological bent, one must assume that this is an unintended consequence of the nature of educational spending in Kerala. Nonetheless, Kerala's citizens have received far better educational service than those of almost any other state in the union have. The Kerala model of education—of choice and competition—is unique in the country and so is Kerala's educational performance. It is not just how much a state spends on education but how it spends that determines efficiency and effectiveness of the education system.

Criteria for Good Education Policy

A good education policy must foster choice of and competition among schools, make schools student-centred and not teacher-centred, and increase accountability of schools by linking their revenues with performance.

Increase Choice and Competition

It is more readily accepted that increased choice and competition are good for higher education. The central government had introduced a bill which would have allowed establishment of private universities. Private colleges already exist in professional fields such as medicine and engineering. But there is no full-fledged private university in the country. The bill would have helped increase choice in higher education. It would also have lessened the financial burden on central and state governments of subsidizing higher education. As students who could afford to pay the tuition go to private universities, less subsidy would be necessary, or more resources would be available to now smaller number of students in government universities. Choice and competition is the most effective means to improve the quality and financial viability of higher education.

Choice and competition to improve the quality and financial viability of primary and secondary education is actually more urgent. Though that, proposition is not as readily accepted. It is argued that market principles may be good in higher education but they are inoperative, irrelevant, or even harmful in basic education. People are so poor and often lack understanding of the significance of literacy that if the government did not take the full financial responsibility and did not make elementary education compulsory, our literacy rates would never improve. Many maintain that in achieving basic education in a poor country like ours, the government must run and fund schools.

In reality, the poor, especially the rural poor, have been spending a substantial portion of their income on their children's basic education, and their lack of interest in education, as revealed in various surveys, is actually reflective of the poor quality of education in our public schools than their poor understanding of education's importance. The NCAER (1994) and NSSO (1991, 1993) studies suggest that in a given year people spend anywhere from Rs. 100 to more than Rs. 4000 per child on primary education. For the year 1986-87, the total household expenditure on primary education was Rs. 7388.5 million. And primary education is supposed to be free in the country. This private spending on primary education is not just by the rich and the middle class in urban areas. Out of the Rs. 7388.5 million, Rs. 4202.5 million were spent by rural areas, more than half of the total private expenditure. In that year, the total government expenditure on primary education was Rs. 17,000 million. So the private expenditure is by no means an insignificant amount; it was more than 40 per cent of what the government spent on primary education.

Surveys suggest that 40 per cent of children do not enroll in school are due to economic factors, one per cent because of domestic chores, and 25 per cent because they are not interested in education. These results are used to conclude that economic necessity compels parents to use children to earn a living instead of sending them to school and that people do not really understand the importance of education. The poor and the illiterate then cannot be relied upon to educate their children. The government must intervene to safeguard the interests of children as well as of the society.

When the same surveys inquire about the actual activities of non-enrolled children, they find that less than 10 per cent are economically active. Economic necessities are less of a reason for non-enrollment than the first impression may suggest (40 per cent). Field researchers widely believe that supply and not the demand factors make people less interested in education. The quality of infrastructure (buildings, furniture, and supplies), teaching, and the concern for learning is so poor as to make the whole Idea of education worthless, a waste of time. Whenever these drawbacks have been rectified, generally due to the initiative of some individual teacher, or principal, or bureaucrat, enrollments improve dramatically.

(In the Total Literacy Programme, a few districts performed exceptionally well because of particular individuals.) People do not lack understanding of education's importance; they simply cannot be fooled into spending their time and money for a mediocre education.

The reflexively deployed argument that poverty and illiteracy of our people necessitates the government to run and fund education has little basis in facts. Despite the government's claim of providing free primary education, the poor have been spending a significant part of their income to acquire it. Their spending on education is a prima facie evidence of their desire for education: is the Kerala experience demonstrates, the poor are willing to spend more—up to 36 per cent of income—if they are offered a better quality education, the kind of education that they desire.

Basic literacy is crucial for a globalizing economy and growing democracy. Relying solely on the government to educate such a vast and diverse population of India is not only foolish, but also gravely disastrous. To serve our diverse student population, we need diverse types of schools. In general there is more choice in urban areas, but that needs to be extended to rural areas where the majority of school age population resides. Once direct and indirect entry barriers are removed, government schools, nonprofit schools run by community, religious, fraternal, and other voluntary organizations, and for-profit schools can coexist. Flowering of such varied institutional arrangements has been thwarted by the licence-permit raj that exists in the field of education.

To establish a new school requires a licence from education authorities. In theory a school can operate without a licence as an "unrecognized school", but the students of that school will not be able to appear for any of the board examinations. This discourages most serious and genuine interests. The licence-permit raj must end in education as it did in the economy. It has the same effect in education as it had on the economy. The government limits competition and arrogates the power to decide what type of schools can serve educational needs of the people. It creates artificial scarcity of schools and allows existing schools to exploit their customers. To curb such exploitation, the government puts further restrictions on the amount of fees that can be charged for tuition, laboratory, transportation, and on the amount and purpose for which donations can be asked from parents. The restrictions are impossible to enforce because the artificially created scarcity compels parents to pay up; they have no other choice. This morass of controls is what the "potato chip theory of regulation" predicts. One restriction creates situation that demands further restrictions which in turn require more restrictions. Once a bag of potato chips is opened, it's hard to stop at one or a few chips.

In addition to the licensing requirement, regulations governing the use of land are a major hurdle, especially in urban areas. Often, the government is the sole legal owner and it must allocate land for school use. Difficulties or costs of getting such allotments so not require description. There is also the problem of finance. Nationalized banks offer preferential interest rates to industrial houses because they work in the areas which are recognized as "industry" by the government. No such consideration is given to entrepreneurs in the vital field of education. I am reluctant to advocate grant of cheaper loans for education because it would open another bag of potato chips. The government would then specify the type, size and location of schools that can qualify for subsidy; credit controls would replace explicit licensing. All that the government needs to do is to abolish the licence-permit raj in education and free the entrepreneurs from the non-profit and for-profit sectors to serve the cause of education.

A good education policy must satisfy three criteria: there must be increased choice and competition, schools must be student and not teacher-centred and revenues must be linked with performance.

Even if the government chooses to finance elementary education, it should be done in a way so as to foster more competition. Financing can take the form of scholarships or education vouchers. These means of financing would allow the government to help only those who need it and let those who can pay for their children's education do so. The increased choice and competition can only improve the quality of our basic education as well as its financial viability. Choice and competition are as crucial in elementary as in higher education.

Make Schools Student and not Teacher-Centred

The education system of today is designed for the convenience of teachers and not students. Teachers are going to be at the school from 8 to 2 or 10 to 5, so students must get educated at the designated place and time. What if one has to help on the farm during 8 to 2 or attend to younger siblings? That is seen as a clear indication that the person is not really serious about education. Why should all schools run on the same schedule? Why can't the convenience of students be the factor in determining school timings?

But school schedules are fixed all over the world. India by no means is unique. They certainly are. That is because almost everywhere education is government's business. All government businesses work for the benefit of those who are employed there and not for the welfare and convenience of customers. Consider the telephone or electricity service provided by the government in India. Not only do we have to beg and bribe to get connections we get extremely unreliable and poor quality of service and we have to also spend a working day just to pay for the services we purchase. The *sarkari babus* cannot be even bothered to take our money promptly and courteously. They don't care for the money;

nothing in their life depends on it. They actually are doing us a favour by taking our money. They certainly act that way.

On the other hand, private businesses go out of their way to earn our money. They provide a good value for our money; not because they are nice people, but they know that we can always take our business somewhere else. They are polite solicitous, and always trying to find easier ways for us to pay for the purchase of their goods and services. They invent credit cards, debit cards, and smart cards. Incentives do matter. Businesses that face competition are more responsive to customers' needs Government businesses hardly ever face competition and therefore their self-interest and incentives do not generally align with the needs of customers. It is then hard to expect government teachers to work at the convenience of students. A dramatic change in the institutional structure of our education system is required. Competition must be introduced into our education system. Some teachers and schools would then find it in their interest to accommodate students who cannot attend classes at the designated time and place. The education system must be made student-centred; consumer sovereignty must be established in the market for education. The student-centred education system will bring back many of the 25 per cent of "not interested" students. As pointed out earlier, 40 per cent claim to not enroll because of economic compulsion, but only 10 per cent are actually economically active. The student-centred system would also bring back many of the 30 per cent of the children "missing" on economic grounds. And even those who need to work would be accommodated by schools facing a higher degree of competition.

Link School Revenues with School Performance

Currently government grants to schools are automatic based simply on the number of students and physical infrastructure of the past with an eye on the growth in the head count and the need for maintenance and expansion of facilities. A school's budget does not depend on its performance. Linking government grants with performance would help realign self- interest and incentives of the school with the needs of it customers. The school's task is to educate; it should receive its revenues depending on whether the school has met its responsibility.

There are multitudes of ways to measure performance of schools and the issue needs a deeper analysis. But a simple way to gauge performance is to consider the number of students who pass the standardized board examinations. A school's revenues could be linked with that number. Success in passing board examinations is probably not the best way to judge the quality of education; we should think of better and yet easier ways to assess the quality. The basic objective nonetheless is to make schools earn their revenues by fulfiling their responsibilities.

A Proposal to Improve Literacy: Open Schools

State, or preferably local, governments should offer anyone who educates a child up to the third standard a specified sum of money if the child passes a standardized examination. That basically is the scheme. The proposed scheme meets the three criteria which is described earlier. It increases choice and competition in primary education. Anyone could become the "open school" and educate children. Choices for parents would be unlimited and competition really stiff. It would help make education up to the third standard truly student-centred. The open schools are very likely to run at a place and time convenient to students. Individual teachers not only have interest and incentives, but also ability to accommodate different learning styles and schedules of students. The scheme links revenues of open schools (teachers) directly to their performance. All the three criteria are then met.

The open schools will unleash millions of educated unemployed in India to attack the debilitating problem of illiteracy, while providing them a meaningful and accountable employment. It is a practical way to implement a little flippant proposal of the former Prime Minister I.K. Gujral: Each one teach five. Under the open school scheme, each one will likely teach twenty-five.

Golden Rules for Guidance

- Guidance should be viewed as a continuous process spanning the entire education system, and should be directed towards aiding all to make conscious and positive educational and occupational choices. It should ensure that individuals are provided with the prerequisites:
  - to become aware of their interests, abilities and special talents, and to help them frame a plan for life;
  - to pursue courses of education and training designed to realise their potential and fulfil their life plans;
  - to acquire flexibility in decision-making concerning their occupations, in the initial and later stages, for developing a satisfying career;
  - to facilitate transitions back and forth as needed, between education, training and the world of work.
- Guidance should take into account the needs of industry, the individual and the family while preparing students and adults for the real possibility of frequent career changes, which could include periods of unemployment and employment in the informal sector, to be achieved through:

  - close liasion and coordination between lifelong learning, training, the workplace and placement services;
  - ensuring that those engaged in work have access to information concerning continuing education and training as well as other work opportunities;
  - ensuring that all necessary information concerning the world of work and career opportunities is available, and actively disseminated using all available forms of communication.

- While emphasizing the needs of individuals, guidance should be accompanied by information that gives them a realistic view of the opportunities available, including trends in the labour market and employment structures, the environmental impact of various occupations, and what may be expected in terms of remuneration, career advancement and occupational mobility.
- Particular attention should be given to guidance for girls and women to ensure that:
  - guidance is gender-inclusive and covers the whole range of education, training and employment opportunities;
  - girls and women are encouraged to pursue subjects such as mathematics and science, which are prerequisites for vocational education and training programmes;
  - girls and women are encouraged and motivated to take advantage of the opportunities available.
- Guidance in the formal schooling context should promote technical and vocational education as a

viable and attractive choice for young people. It should:

- cover a broad range of occupations, include supplementary visits to workplaces, and make the student aware of the eventual necessity of choosing an occupation and the importance of ensuring that this choice is made as rationally as possible;
- assist students and their parents/guardian in making a positive choice concerning educational streams, and encourage learners to keep open a wide range of options so as to increase their learning and occupational flexibility.

- Guidance in technical and vocational education as preparation for an occupational field should:
  - inform students of the various possibilities open in the particular field of interest, the educational background required, and the subsequent possibilities for continuing education and further training;
  - encourage students to choose educational programmes that will not limit their later employment options;
  - follow the students' progress through their educational programmes;
  - supplement the programmes by short periods of work experience and study of real work situations.
- For individuals engaged in continuing technical and vocational education as a part of their lifelong learning, guidance should:

– help to choose the programme best suited to their needs;

– enable them to make effective choices regarding their entry into suitable levels of specialization.

- Guidance should take into account:

  – educational achievements and/or work experience;

  – economic, social, technological, cultural and family factors influencing the learners' attitudes, expectations and choice of career;

  – opportunities and prospects in the occupational sector of interest;

  – individual preferences and special needs, including medical conditions, physical limitations and disabilities.

- Guidance systems need to be accountable to the beneficiaries and sponsors of the service. Quality assurance and long-term results should be continually monitored at national and institutional levels through:

  – a system of evaluation both of staff performance and of the methods used to determine the long-term effects of guidance and the degree of self-reliance of beneficiaries;

  – accurate records of clients, needs addressed, programmes and interventions used and resultant employment including self-employment.

The Learning Process

- The challenges facing technical and vocational education in the 21st century demand learner-centred innovative and flexible approaches including a reoriented curriculum to take account of new subjects and issues such as technology, the environment, foreign languages and cultures, entrepreneurship and the requirements of rapidly growing service industries.

- Full use should be made of contemporary educational technology, particularly the Internet, interactive multimedia materials, audiovisual aids and mass media, to enhance the reach, cost-effectiveness, quality and richness of programmes, especially in the promotion of self-learning.

- Theory and practice should form an integrated whole and be presented in a manner that motivates the learners. Experience in the laboratory, workshop and or enterprises should be linked to mathematical and scientific foundations, and conversely, technical theory, as well as the mathematics and science underlying it, should be illustrated through their practical applications.

- The methods and materials used in technical and vocational education should be carefully adapted to the learners' needs. In this respect:
  - where the language of instruction differs from the native language, teaching materials should make maximum use of numerical and graphical representation, written material being kept to a minimum;
  - where materials developed in one country are adapted for use in another, this adaptation should be carefully made with due regard to local factors;
  - considering, however, the increasing mobility

of labour, the acquisition of foreign language skills should be considered a vital aspect of the curriculum.

- Machines and equipment used in workshops in educational institutions should be geared to the needs of the workplace, and should simulate it as closely as possible. Learners should be capable of operating and maintaining the equipment.
- Evaluation/assessment should be an integral part of the teaching and learning process, and its major function should be to ensure the availability of appropriate programmes for the development of learners in accordance with their interests and capacities, and competence in the world of work.
- The learners' performance should be evaluated/ assessed on an overall basis that considers class participation, interests and attitude, aptitude for acquiring practical skills and competencies, and relative progress, allowance being made for aptitudes and examinations and other tests.
- Learners should participate in the evaluation/ assessment of their own progress, and this system should have an in-built feedback mechanism to identify and correct learning problems.

Staff

- The emoluments and conditions of service which are offered should compare favourably with those enjoyed by persons with similar qualifications and experience in other occupational sectors. In particular, promotions, salaries and pension scales for technical and vocational education staff should take into account any relevant experience acquired in employment outside the educational sector.

- To ensure the high quality of technical and vocational education, priority should be given to the recruitment and initial preparation of adequate numbers of well-qualified teachers, instructors/trainers, administrators and guidance staff, and to the provision of continuous professional upgrading throughout their career, and other facilities to enable them to function effectively.

Teaching Staff

- All teachers in technical and vocational education, including instructors/trainers who teach practical skills, should be considered an integral part of the teaching profession, and should be recognized as having the same status as their colleagues in general education. In this regard:
  - the recommendation concerning the Status of Teachers adopted by the Special Intergovernmental Conference on the Status of Teachers on 5 October 1966 is applicable to them especially as regards the provisions concerning preparation for a profession, continuing education, employment and career, the rights and responsibilities of teachers, conditions for effective teaching and learning, teachers' salaries, and social security;
  - arbitrary distinctions between teachers in specialised technical and vocational institutions and those in general education institutions should be eliminated.
- Technical and vocational education teachers, on a full-time or part-time basis, should possess the appropriate personal, ethical, professional and teaching qualities, and a strong initial preparation

that will enable them to operate in and adapt to an ever-changing scientific, technological and social environment.

- Teachers of technical and vocational subjects in general education should:
  - develop the ability to relate these to each other as well as to the larger social, economic, environmental, historical and cultural context;
  - be familiar with a broad range of specialities;
  - where these subjects serve primarily an occupation or educational orientation function, be able to give guidance.
- Teachers of technical and vocational education for occupational fields should have relevant qualifications so that:
  - if the occupational field requires primarily practical skills, they should have significant experience in the exercise of these skills; if learners are to be prepared for technician or middle-management positions, teachers should have a thorough knowledge, preferably acquired through appropriate practical experience, of the special requirements of this type of position;
  - if the occupational field requires research and theoretical analysis, *e.g.* an engineering field, teachers should have a background in research methods.
- Skilled professionals working outside education should be invited to teach in schools, universities or other educational institutions in order to link the world of work more closely to the classroom.

- Teachers in technical and vocational education as continuing education should, in addition to the special preparation for teaching adults, have an adequate knowledge of the working environment of the learners, and be able to provide distance and individually paced education and training.

- Teachers of general subjects in technical and vocational education institutions, in addition to qualifications in their own field, should have an appreciation of the nature of the learners' specialized technical and vocational education programme.

- Preparation for technical and vocational teaching should preferably be offered as a tertiary programme, requiring completion of secondary education or its equivalent for entrance. All programmes should be designed with the following objectives in mind:

  - to maintain standards of education and professional preparation in effect for the teaching profession as a whole and to contribute to raising these overall standards;

  - to develop in future teachers the responsibility for keeping up to date with trends in their field, as well as with the related work opportunities;

  - to develop in future teachers the ability to teach both the theoretical and the practical aspects of their field, with special emphasis on the need to use, whenever possible, the information and communication technologies;

  - to ensure that future teachers are equipped, by means of supplementary training, to teach other subjects related to their primary subject;

  - to develop in future teachers the ability to guide learners with special needs.

- When local conditions prevent future teachers from receiving practical work experience in their training, the teacher-training institution should attempt to simulate workplace conditions as part of the curriculum.

- Flexible training and retraining programmes, combining instruction on the campus and in the workplace, must be adapted to suit the concerned subjects and the needs of the learners and the workplace by developing new and appropriate instruments of assessment, accreditation and articulation, and certification standards.

- The professional preparation of all technical and vocational teachers should include the following elements in pre-service training and in-service upgrading programmes:

  - classroom management, special teaching methods appropriate to the subjects/fields of the future teachers and methods of evaluating/assessing the students' work;

  - educational psychology and sociology relevant to the subjects/fields to be taught by the future teachers;

  - educational theory in general and particularly as it applies to technical and vocational education;

  - training in how to create and produce appropriate teaching materials, including modular and computer-aided instructional materials, whenever such materials are in short supply;

- training in the choice and use of contemporary teaching techniques and aids, including information/communication technologies;
- a period of supervised practice teaching before appointment to a post;
- planning the instructional environment of practical classes and laboratories and managing! maintaining these facilities;
- an introduction to educational and occupational guidance methods as well as to educational administration;
- a sound training in safety, with emphasis on teaching safe working practice and setting a good working example.

- Staff responsible for the preparation of technical and vocational teachers should have obtained advanced qualifications in their field:
  - teacher-educators responsible for special technical and vocational fields should have qualifications in their field equivalent to those of special subjects staff in other higher education institutions and programmes, including advanced degrees and employment experience in related occupational fields;
  - teacher-educators responsible for the pedagogical aspect of teacher preparation should themselves be experienced teachers in technical and vocational education, and should possess advanced qualifications in education.
- Staff responsible for the preparation of technical and vocational teachers should be actively engaged in technical research and analyses of work opportunities

in their field. Provision should be made for this in terms of a reasonable teaching load, and access to appropriate facilities.

- Teaching staff should be encouraged to continue their education and training, whatever their specialized field, and should have the necessary means to do so. Lifelong learning should be made available in a wide range of facilities, and should include:
  - continuous review and updating of knowledge, competencies and skills;
  - continuous updating of specialised professional skills and knowledge;
  - periodic work experience in the relevant occupational sector.
- When questions of promotion, seniority and status are considered, teachers' achievements in continuing education and training as well as relevant work experience should be taken into account.

Administrative and Guidance Staff

- Administrators of technical and vocational education programmes should be equipped with the following qualifications:
  - teaching experience in a field of technical and vocational education;
  - a broad vision of technical and vocational education as a vital element in personal, social and economic development;
  - some work experience in one of the fields taught in the programme;

- knowledge of administrative techniques and procedures.

- The heads of technical and vocational education establishments should devote a significant portion of their time to the educational and scientific aspects of their work. Sufficient staff should be available to provide the following services:
  - the preparation, supervision and coordination of all practical work and experiments;
  - the maintenance of instruments, apparatus and tools in workshops and laboratories;
  - counselling and guidance for candidates and students;
  - academic support services such as libraries, information and communication technology centres and information resource centres.

- Administrators should keep up to date with new administrative techniques and trends, especially through relevant lifelong learning programmes. They should receive special training in the methods and problems associated with the specific features of technical and vocational education programmes such as flexible entry and re-entry patterns continuous training in the workplace, and relevance to the needs of the world of work. This preparation should include:
  - financial planning methods that facilitate the allocation of available resources, given the objectives and priorities of the various programmes, and ensure their efficient utilisation;

- management methods appropriate to educational administration, including techniques that utilize information and communication technologies;
- contemporary human resources management and development methods.

- Guidance staff should receive special preparation for their tasks. They should be equipped to make objective assessments of aptitude, interest and motivation, and have up-to-date information concerning education and work opportunities. They should acquire a direct knowledge of the economy and the world of work through systematically organized visits to enterprises and training periods in enterprises. Guidance staff should be provided with facilities—including the opportunity for practical experience—to keep up with new information and methods of guidance.

***

5

Guidance and Curriculum

A curriculum is made by a teacher and his students as they work together. Teacher and students receive continuous assistance directly and indirectly from many persons and from many sources. The superintendent, principal, supervisors, subject-matter specialists, school psychologists, lay groups and social agencies, advisory commissions all contribute, usually through the teachers' guides and through the curriculum-improvement programme which developed the guides. The development of a specific curriculum is, then, a cooperative activity in which many persons participate. The amount of help or guidance a given teacher may receive from several sources will vary with amount of training, professional skill, and professional attitudes possessed. Teachers of less training and with mediocre professional insights, attitudes, and skills will of necessity receive far more guidance, even direction, than alert, dynamic teachers. One aim of in-service programmes of growth through curriculum improvement is to raise the levels of teacher initiative and responsibility.

Educational workers in order to participate well in curriculum developments will either possess or will develop in the course of the activity.

1. A critically appraised philosophy of education.
2. Detailed knowledge of the growth and development of children.

3. Skill in locating and developing pupil needs.
4. A clear conception of how the reorganization of experience or the inter-grating process proceeds.
5. Knowledge of how and when to help children in selecting and using educational materials and experiences; how to guide without dominating.
6. Skill in developing the various specialized types of learning outcomes concepts or understandings, attitudes, appreciations, generalised abilities, skills, functional knowledge.

The writing of a course of study or teachers guide, or of source units is a specialized task requiring certain specialized skills, sufficient time, facilities, and money. Committees or groups are given responsibility for developing a bulletin or series of bulletins known as the course. The work is that of selecting, organizing, editing, and unifying materials from many sources into such form that the teacher may use it easily in the synthesis which is the specific curriculum. The modern course, as has been indicated, should grow out of a curriculum improvement programme, or develop simultaneously with it. This chapter will therefore open with a discussion of curriculum improvement programmes. Three types of improvement programme are recognized by Saylor:

1. Programmes designed solely for the preparation of courses of study.
2. Programmes planned in terms of course of study preparation, but organized so as to promote acceptance of the completed course by teachers through participation of representative teachers in its preparation.
3. Programmes planned on a broad basis for the improvement of instruction with course of study

preparation only one, though an important aspect of the programme.

The above types illustrate the development of thought from the traditional preparation of formal, static courses, to processes used in the modern development of dynamic curriculums.

An improvement programme includes study of all the major elements which affect the individual teacher's curriculum and which enter into production of documents. A reputable curriculum programme necessitates for flung study by all staff members and by groups, based upon defined local needs. The political, economic, and social structure and aim of the surrounding society, its hopes and aspirations, its tensions and shortcoming need to be understood.

The aim and philosophy of current educational practice need to be studied and understood. The nature of learners, their growth and development, their characteristics at various levels of growth all need to be examined and used. The abilities, needs, purposes, and individual differences among learners must be studied. The origin and nature of subject-matter, the development of present curriculums, all need to be scrutinised. The nature of the educative process and the effect upon it by persons and material facilities must be analysed.

A programme of curriculum improvement will go further than developing curriculums in given classrooms, further than writing course-of-study aids. A programme of curriculum improvement to be successful must bring about many important changes within persons and within the elements constituting the setting for learning. Charges within persons will be in their attitudes and understandings, in appreciations and skills. Participants in a curriculum programme will develop knowledge and conviction concerning the aim and philosophy of education in a democracy. They will develop facile knowledge of the nature of experience as the essence of the educative process. They will have a wider grasp of subject-matter and better understanding of its uses. They will learn better how to evaluate the complex and subtle outcomes of modern education. The discussion to follow draws heavily upon other summaries given tarlier and hence is abbreviated and cross-referenced to avoid tedious repetition.

1. A dynamic leadership will accept from all sources suggestions leading toward initiation and development of curriculum programmes. Leadership will assume that change is the order of the day, will provide for it. This prevents crystallization and tends to prevent periods of violent disturbance from time to time. The programme will originate ideally in some out-going activity, interest, argument, criticism, dissatisfaction, suggestion the improvement, proposed new departure, individual experimental work underway. Any item may be capitalised upon by the group under leadership. In some instances it will be necessary and desirable to set the stage to suggest, or in some indirect way to motivate the programme. To the degree that a suggested programme meets the needs of the group and the actualities of the situation, it will be accepted. The normal motivations of all human beings may be utilized readily. A programme may start in and of a score of specific ways and be based upon any aspect of the total educational programme. A wide survey of programmes now operating in the country reveals a number of procedures.

The more dynamic procedures seem to be as follows:

(a) Focus at first may be upon the improvement of whatever teachers and other staff members are now doing.

All earnest teachers are interested in improving their knowledge and technique. They will ask questions and bring problems to a group discussion when democratic leadership prevails. A programme of improvement should not be imposed, but assistance offered upon problems as met by teachers. Modern and traditional teachers will be interested in improving different things and will not always agree on what constitutes improvement. Discussion develops which leads naturally to study and eventually to more organized attack. Discussions growing out of disagreements upon techniques and upon immediate practical problems understood by all teachers lead naturally into discussions of objectives, remote aims, philosophic principles scientific evidence. Study of the background is thus approached functionally rather than through formal courses, lectures, or discussion of purely theoretical problems. This heterogeneity of attack produces also a great variation of suggestions. Creativity and originality of response seem to be strongly stimulated.

(b) Utilize the results of the evaluation programme.

(c) Seize upon any discussion of a suggested new departure, new research finding, and so forth.

(d) Ask for pupils' statements of needs, strengths, and weaknesses in present curriculum.

(e) Encourage any teachers who are carrying on experimental work or who wish to do so; utilize any creative contribution. This is another equally dynamic and functional approach which will develop similarly to the second one.

(f) Utilize comments, inquiries, criticisms from parents and lay groups.

(g) Provide, when possible, for discussion by students who have had experience under both traditional and modern curriculums.

A good but less immediately functional method is to:

(h) Initiate a community survey to determine needs, facilities, and possibilities.

A community survey is also often used within a curriculum programme as an important means.

A reputable but still less dynamic method is to:

(i) Eengage in the study of a set of fundamental questions concerning the nature of education, its relation to the individual and to the social order; the nature of the learner and his learning activities.

The survey of the field revealed a number of other procedures said to be used to initiate a programme; these procedures are more properly means aged within a programme. Writers citing these as initiatory methods are overlooking some more basic item lying behind these means. The following then are not actually methods of starting a programme, though often listed as such:

(a) Call a series of conferences either within the professional staff or on conjunction with lay groups.

(b) Organize intervisitation within the system, visitation to other systems, organize exhibits and visit other exhibits.

(c) Equip and open a local workshop or encourage attendance at summer workshops.

(d) Organize a series of study groups either within the staff be with ticipation.

(e) Examine a collection of courses of study.

(*f*) Set-up a curriculum bureau or planning council within the system.

(*g*) Organize formal courses at nearby teachers colleges or universities which the staff may attend.

(*h*) Organize committees of teachers to study or to produce materials, or to tryout suggested organizations.

2. An adequate process for achieving desired changes must be developed. The desired changes are not merely in materials and methods of instruction but in the beliefs, values, attitudes, and practice of the persons concerned. A successful process must therefore provide for *(a)* growth of the personnel, *(b)* observable results within the instructional materials and methods. These in turn produce a third characteristic of good process, *(c)* a desirable type of security within the staff, the pupils, and the community. The process must also provide for *(d)* continuity of effort. A few persons are irritated at discussions of process. They focus on the goal and drive toward it regardless of methods used. A number of evils result, not the least of which is that the chosen goal may not be reached at all. Others regard process as a collection of clever techniques, "tricks of the trade," a list of "how to's." This gives rise to distrust and itself process; it is merely manipulation and becomes an end in itself Process should never be regarded as a set of techniques, should never be permitted to become an end; it must be designed for solving stated problems within a given setting. We may disregard those who regard attention to process and its control as futile. The result is *laisser faire* and drift. Progress is not possible without attention to and effort to direct a desirable process. The process which seems to carry the best guarantee of success is that of participatory group study, group decision and try-out, and continuing study.

All the facts are not in dogmatic statements are not

warranted in social problems. The best available evidence, however, now points to the cooperative democratic process as desirable. This calls for wide use of the techniques of group discussion and action, division of labour, careful record keeping of discussion, decision, and try-out, continued critical analysis of records and observed results.

3. A functional organization and machinery will be developed. An organization of some sort is necessary carry forward any complex undertaking. An error of the past has been to assume that the form of this organization was the important thing, instead of functional relation to. problems and needs under consideration.

Caution concerning the uncritical acceptance of organizational forms. Far too many curriculum programmes have accepted a formal organization developed logically, or developed in some other situation, and imposed it upon the local programme. Trillingham examined the organization of curriculum programmes in several large cities and found a general pattern operating.

1. In direct charge is a curriculum director, assisted by a curriculum specialist or consultant who is "to aid and stimulate teacher groups" and "critically evaluate the progress of the curriculum programme."

2. The superintendent of schools initiates the curriculum programme and is ultimately responsible for the curriculum.

3. A curriculum councilor cabinet is chosen by the superintendent to determine the philosophy of the school and general guiding principles, "to set-up general objectives of the programme," to serve as a clearing house and, finally, to approve work submitted by various committees.

4. A production committee for each subject and each division that becomes active determines subject aims, subject content, student activities, materials, and so on.
5. An aims committee has the job of formulating the aims of education and determining the programme of studies to be offered.
6. A course installation committee sees to it that the course is properly installed after study by the principals and teachers who are to use it.
7. A continuous course improvement committee keeps bringing the course up to date.
8. A course appraisal committee for each new course of study oversees the try-outs of new materials.

The programme was then recommended for general adoption anywhere. It violates the first principle of good administration, namely, that organization should develop functionally. The recommendation rests upon several naive but serious errors in thinking.

1. Programmes are system-wide prdcedures, instead of being initiated, based upon, individual classrooms or buildings with coordinating mechanisms developing as needed.
2. Programmes are to be launched from the top down, the administration taking all responsibility for initiating, organizing and carrying on. This reverses the desirable order.
3. Programmes start with statements of philosophy or viewpoint developed by a few "leading" thinkers and handed down to the whole group. The philosophy and aims are then broken down

mechanically into smaller area aims; materials and teaching organizations are developed in order. This reverses the psychological order.

4. The learners and the lay public are ignored in this suggested organization.

5. Programmes of curriculum development are clearly confused with programmes of course of study writing. The two are not alike.

Doubtless Trillingham would not today adhere to his recommendation of eleven years ago. The number, size and kind of committees cannot be stated in advance nor inter-relationships indicated. Any and all kinds of study groups, production committees, experimental groups, editing committees may appear. A succession of leaders may arise to serve different pin poses. Consultants and specialists will be called on as needed.

The situation here is similar to that of developing functional organization for administering a school system. The functional organization, may appear to be very similar outwardly to the formal. So, it is with organization for curriculum improvement. The differences, however, are more fundamental than the likenesses. The functional organization grows up from the problems and is fashioned to meet needs. The formal organization grows down from the central authority and is fashioned to meet abstract logical principles. The difference in general structure, in number and names of committees, in provisions for intercommunication may be slight; but they are the key to the basic principles.

The following summary emphasizes points presented many times in preceding pages. The curriculum organization devised in any given situation:

1. Should be close enough to the actual problems and be flexible enough to ensure free-flowing

interpersonal exchanges, to ensure the utilization of the contributions of many types of persons within typical heterogeneous groups including students and lay groups.

2. Should provide for the necessary coordination between groups and units within the system as the programme develops from its simple beginnings.
3. Should grow out of the problems found there.
4. Should provide for continuity of effort.
5. Should be subservient to its purpose and not become the important feature of the situation.
6. Should keep records, publish summaries, and eventually produce materials of use in improving instruction.
7. Should develop all committees functionally as needed to serve temporarily or with membership rotated.
8. Should develop all standing committees to deal with major persistent factors.
9. Should develop a general policy under which the group operates.

The best situations use cooperative group study of local problems in committees, in area or regional conferences, in local workshops, or those in nearby institutions. Extension courses and summer-school work are also widely used. The amount of cooperation differs widely within and among local units since this depends upon local leadership and enthusiasm. The state and city administrations will encourage, stimulate, and aid, but will never impose or coerce the local programmes.

A democratic functional organization for a curriculum programme is desirable first because it is the most efficient method in the long run. Second, it provides full opportunity for individuals and minority groups who often have important contributions to make. Third, it is likely to encourage and to utilize social invention. Fourth, it ensures, as far as anything can ensure, group solidarity, growth for individuals and groups, and accomplishment, all of which give that security necessary to mental hygiene. Accomplishment of desirable results is more likely to ensue.

In USA, a range in teacher participation from 1,500 to 30,000 has been shown between two well-known state programmes. The Kansas programme indicates participation as follows:

"The large number of teachers who participated in study groups indicates that Kansas teachers are seriously desirous of improving their teaching. There were organized in the state during the year approximately 17 large study centres and work of some type was carried on in 101 counties and in 55 first and second-class cities. Approximately 100 parent-teacher-association groups gave special study to the lay bulletin."

The Virginia programme which was probably the most widely particpatory of all programmes so far noted the following methods participation.

1. The preparation of curriculum materials.
2. Try-out and experimentation illustrative curriculum materials.
3. The group study programme.
4. Conferences of all kinds.
5. Service on various committees on many aspects the programme.
6. Utilizing consultative and advisory services provided by the state department.

The two preceding principles indicate the fundamental importance of wide participation by the personnel. How can this be stimulated? What are the obstacles? An excellent study of this factor in the Virginia state programme was made by Saylor. His general conclusions have been corroborated by other fragmentary studies of various programmes. He lists the chief facilitating factors as:

1. Economic ability sufficient to finance a good programme. The two factors are interlocked. Good leadership is undeniably attracted by better rewards and by better support of the programme High economic ability is, however, no guarantee of competent leadership. Many wealth systems employ mediocre leaders and teachers. Good leadership is sometimes found in systems of low economic ability, exercised usually by young men and women on their way to better positions. The economic factor does clearly affect items which facilitate cooperation:

(a) Provision of competent and sufficient supervision.

(b) Provision of better salaries and conditions for teachers.

(c) Provision of more generous supplies of books, instructional aids, and other material factors.

Saylor notes a further factor which becomes of great importance in rural states, or rural areas within states:

2. Physical and cultural isolation. The general challenge in curriculum programmes is to provide in so far as humanly possible, the factors which facilitate cooperation and to prevent or alleviate the effects of weakness in those factors.

Saylor believes that leadership is the critical factor, going so far as to say. In fact, a dynamic superintendent of schools can if he so desires, probably overcome almost any handicap to participation by his school system in a state cooperative curriculum programme of the stimulative type organized in Virginia.

Isolation as a factor presents one of the most direct challenges in any programme. Urban situations and non-isolated rural areas are likely to possess good economic ability, first-class leadership, reasonably well trained and paid teachers, ability and willingness to carry on a competent programme. Cooperation is not too difficult to secure if the leadership is good. Isolated communities, on the other hand, are not handicapped merely by distance and transportation difficulties which make supervision, inter-visitation, and various cultural contacts difficult. Isolated communities develop a feeling of segregation and neglect. They become sensitive about backwardness, feel hopeless about improvement and develop-unconcern if not antagonism, toward developments in more favoured areas.

Saylor believes that the Virginia programme did not always succeed in securing active participation in the more remote rural and isolated areas, low in economic ability and lacking leadership. The programme was one of the earliest state programmes and doubtless progress has been made.

The developing programme in Maine has the problem of isolation in serious proportions. Distances are great and Maine contains a large area of "unorganized territory" The challenge is being met squarely by the state department. Maine has the only state officer "in charge of unorganized territory" in the United States. The general consultant has visited a number of the most isolated one-room school, to observe conditions, to get the teachers' problems at first hand, thus to participate in developing aid for these teachers. The state supervisors and district superintendents make earnest effort to bring supervision to these isolated schools the 1915 workshop included a rural section. Teachers in this group attacked their own problems with vigor and produced excellent materials which will become a state bulletin for distribution among rural teachers.

Discussions of the functional approach have made clear, first, that the widest possible participation by teachers, principals, and all types of supervisory and administrative officers is vital Second, participation by consultants, both general and special, and by small specialized committees will be provided. Third, the participation of lay groups will be greatly extended over that provided by early programmes. The details concerning the first two groups have been made amply clear throughout this and other volumes.

Lay participation needs a further brief note. Lay groups serve best as sources of public opinion concerning the strength and weakness of current programmes, of opinion on the soundness of proposed improvements. Lay groups render excellent service in helping to develop general policy through discussions with professional leaders. They serve also as sounding boards before which to present explanations or denials of criticism, explanations and research backgrounds for new developments. Convinced of the soundness of technical explanations made by the professional staff, the lay participants then become centers for dissemination of information about and support for the new programme. Proposed improvements, no matter how sound will fail if public misunderstanding arises; are far more likely to succeed it there has been public discussion and review. Lay participation is not to "sell" a programme after its development, but actually to aid in the development of the new programme. Definite provision for study by lay members must be made, not of technical details but of general principles and trends.

3. A balance must be maintained between gradualism and rapidity. Social change is a long, slow, tedious process.

Human beings simply do not change ideas easily and quickly, especially ideas dealing with any aspect of organized social life. Ideas dealing with mechanics, machinery, material things will change far more rapidly but we can make no such assumption about changes in more subtle affairs. Time and study plus demonstration continue over a period of time. A curriculum programme must, therefore, be a gradual progress. At the same time, however, it must be kept ever in mind that "civilization is a race between education and disaster." We must not be misled by those who mouth the old cliche "you must not go too fast." We cannot sit around and wait for progress to take place. The deliberate control of social change is necessary.

4. The programme well be based upon a geographic and administrative unit small enough to permit face to face contact, with provisions for necessary coordinations among small units. A city or state-wide attack upon improvement of instruction is likely to become a course writing programme because of sheer size the situation. Participation by personnel is of necessity limited to representatives, thus curtailing opportunities for growth by the whole group. Courses are written with varying degrees of participation and presented to the total group for approval and acceptance. Extensive try-outs are sometimes used to reduce the gap between the materials and the total group.

The individual school is increasingly used as she unit in modern programmes. Small districts may be used in small towns or in semi-urban areas. The Maine programme began with the individual classrooms and is developing appropriate co-ordinations. The advantages of the individual al school as unit are first that the school staff and local community have in most instances come to know each other. The resources of the community are known. The patrons have some understanding of the aims and methods of the school. Second, the ideal situation for curriculum development exists and is under some control, a known group of learners within a given setting. Third, face to face contacts between persons engaged in a common task are usually far more satisfactory than exchanges over a distance. Fourth, participation by all is more easily arranged The principal, the teachers, the pupils, the parents and others interested may each have responsible and important parts In the programme Fifth, the large group of indifferent and drawn in by their own neighbours and because the problems can be brought home sharply.

The heterogeneity of attack through small local units stimulates originality and individuality in meeting problems. The chances for social invention, for the development of new departures for genuinely creative contributions are multiplied. The advantages of this "broken front" attack must not be lost, however, through pure scattering of effort, or through attention to diverse fragments, Balance must be secured through coordinations of various types. Certain needs are common to many units. Agreements on certain specified instructional-policies and practices are necessary for the development of rounded programmes.

Coordinations within the school itself may be secured first by constituting the faculty a committee of the whole. In larger schools a representative committee or council may be used. Needs common to several areas within the school, and the common agreements referred to above may be worked out through these agencies. The student council is also a coordinating device of this type. Coordinations between schools will thus be, second, an extension of an already familiar technique. In large cities, third, there will be more numerous committees and a central council. These will include committees and conferences for interschool effort as well as for wider coordination. An excellent method of securing coordination is fourth, to have all members' of the central stall participate directly in activities on the local firing line. First hand contacts of this type will greatly aid common agreements, understandings between groups, and closer coordination of activities between the centre and the periphery. The interchange among units of any advances made anywhere within the system not only accelerates the programme but is another method of coordination.

5. The necessary financial aid, material facilities, specialists, and adjustments on the loads of local participants must be arranged. This principle is self-explanatory. Its importance was indicated in preceding discussions of factors facilitating participation.

***

6

Vocational Development and Career Planning

Various psychologists have given lists of needs, which a man tries to satisfy by taking an occupation. Cleeton has listed food, physical comfort activity, mating, sharing thoughts and feelings, dominance over people and elements, self-determination, achievement, approbation and ideation as some of the needs, which seek satisfaction through work. Hendrick has postulated a " work principle" according to which work is motivated primarily by the need to make an efficient use of muscular and intellectual energies. It does not exclude the possible satisfaction of other needs such as aggression, sex and self-preservation but the work principle does emphasize that the man seeks and finds primary pleasure in the efficient use of the physical and mental potentialities in order to control and modify his environment. Vernon conducted a study in which he discovered social admiration, pleasure, social conformity, altruism, activity, independence, power, superiority and ease to be significantly influencing the choice of career for the university women. He also came to the conclusion that different drives can operate in different individuals and lead to the choice of same career and that identical or near identical drives operating on different individuals do result in the choice of extremely different careers. An important role is played by personality in determining the type of job a person is likely to choose.

Peerbolte emphasizes that the labour, which is merely self-preservative and seeks satisfaction of the basic physical needs of the individual only, does not give a very high index of job-satisfaction. In order to be really satisfying, the job needs to give some kind of spiritual self-realization to the worker.

While discussing the basic needs of human beings, Maslow warn against direct parallels between the animal and human behaviour. He argues that the individual is a highly integrated and organized whole, distinctly different from any animal, therefore, the understanding and classification of his motives should be human centred and not derived from animal studies. A distinction should be made between the goal objects and the fundamental need 'or goals and any classification of human needs should be based on goals rather' than goal objects. Fundamental goals or needs are often unconscious and express themselves through particular patterns of behaviour. For proper understanding of the individual we must take into account the biological, cultural and social environment of the individual together with the motivation and the basic needs.

Maslow has arranged the basic needs in a hierarchy of prepotency. He claims that the prepotent needs are more urgent and insistent than the others under equal deprivation; the prepotent needs have to be satisfied before the others can emerge as consistent motivators of behaviour. Needs less to say this explanation of behaviour through the hierarchy of basic needs is important in understanding the occupational choice behaviour of the individual. The hierarchy as given by Maslow is:

1. The physiological needs.
2. The safety needs.
3. The need for importance, respect, self-esteem, independence.

4. The need for belongingness and love.
5. The need for beauty.
6. The need for information.
7. The need for understanding.
8. The need for self-actualization.

They have been arranged in order of potency and Maslow claims that a completely unsatisfied individual would start with the search for food. Once he is provided with enough food he would start seeking shelter and safety; it is rarely found that a man with the most basic and potent needs unsatisfied looks for beauty or self-actualizations. Some exceptional persons have shown such an imbalance by suppression and sublimation but then the exceptions prove the rule.

An analysis of our cultural environment would reveal that there is no other single situation, which provides so much of satisfaction for all of these needs as an occupation. Work is the most common and acceptable mode of satisfying physiological needs of hunger, thirst, shelter and safety. Besides the daily bread a job provides the individual with means for long-range safety and security in form of medical and life insurance, old age pension or savings. The occupation also satisfies the need to belong, be a member of a group and be wanted and loved; to work with a congenial group, to be appreciated for the part one plays in a cooperative venture all enterprises and professions, ideally, are cooperative ventures to be respected by colleagues and to feel independent at various levels.

The need for esteem is also satisfied by an occupation; being in a job by itself is esteem. The importance of a job is realized most clearly in the demoralizing effect that being out of job has on the individual. The socio-economic status of the individual depends very much on his occupation and so the respect he enjoys in his particular group. Personal esteem has a direct relationship with the amount of responsibility a particular job entails. The more responsible a position the better it is in the socio-economic ladder and so the regard it holds in the eyes of others. Studies of job satisfaction and ratings of the prestige of occupations have revealed that the amount of responsibility and freedom enjoyed by a worker is a more significant determinant of prestige than the levels of skills involved in a job or the salary drawn by the person.

As discussed the need for information and knowledge is most obviously satisfied in learned and professional occupations. Studies of job satisfaction have established by now that any job is more interesting and satisfying to an individual if he understands the importance of it and knows the relation his particular assignment holds with the entire pattern of the project. Most of the modern employers follow the practice of briefing their personnel and explaining to them the significance of the position they hold and that of their job assignment. The output has shown a definite decline when ad hoc assignments are given to workers without explaining the significance of the positions they hold and the contributions they make to the entire picture Walker and Guest have reached the conclusion that the feeling of anonymity, of becoming depersonalized, is more disturbing than either the boredom or tension that arises from repetitive and mechanically paced work. The degree of satisfaction from a particular job depends on the number of potentialities that it can draw on.

The implications of Maslow's theory for occupational psychology have been well explored by Centers in his study of relationships between certain motivational phenomena and occupational stratification. He set out the hypothesis that "..... men's satisfactions,' desires, aspirations and goals are strongly conditioned or determined by their present roles, statuses and levels of achievement as these are manifested in their placement in diverse occupational strata." His sample consisted of a cross-section of 1,100 white male adults classified into the following occupational groups: Large Business, Professional, Small Business, White Collar, Skilled Manual, Semi-skilled, Unskilled, Farm Owners and Managers, and Farm Tenants and Labourers. For analysis of results he grouped them into rural and urban workers and found that the greatest job satisfaction was experienced by the urban workers which included professional workers, owners and managers and white collar persons, and that the greatest dissatisfaction was experienced by the manual workers. Some of the reasons given for satisfaction experienced by the first group included freedom and independence, interesting varied activity, congenial colleagues, pay security, creativity, responsibility and status, and utilization of the individual's abilities and potentialities. The reason for dissatisfaction was the lack of almost the same factors. It would be interesting to note how the needs mentioned by Maslow have been corroborated through this study.

Centers further discovered from his data that the persons in lower socio-economic levels manifest a safety and security need more frequently than the persons functioning in higher levels. The latter are more concerned about independence, self-expression and interesting experiences. This does not mean that the people in lower strata are not interested in these needs, the only difference is that they give more importance to and show greater concern for the security and other physical needs.

The above discussion of the role of occupation in the life of the individual automatically leads us to the consideration of questions such as how does the individual reach the stage where he starts thinking of taking up a vocation? How and when does he show definite attitudes towards occupation and a vocation? Do these attitudes differ at different age levels? What kind of attitudes should be considered normal for an age and which should be unusual or abnormal? The discussion of these questions would lead us to the consideration of the concept of Vocational Development and Vocational Maturity.

Vocational Development and Vocational Maturity

According to Super work, like social life and intellectual activity, is one specific medium through which the total personality can manifest itself. Like other aspects of development, vocational development may be conceived of as beginning early in life and as proceeding along a curve until late in life. Thus a four year old child who plays the postman or a shopkeeper is in a very early stage of vocational development and the old man of sixty who does not work for money but still participates in intellectual discussions, attends scientific lectures and keeps himself busy with writing books in the field of his specialization is going through the late stages of vocational development.

Vocational development follows the general pattern of development; it can be conceived of as a continuum with definite life stages, which can be defined through their peculiar characteristics. Buehler has classified the vocational life stages as 1. Growth; 2. Exploratory with the sub-stages of fantasy, which may be tentative or realistic with appropriate attitudes towards work and occupation; 3. Establishment beginning with trial and progressing into a stable position as the individual begins to make his place in the world of work; 4. Maintenance stage characterised by stability in the field in which establish-ment has taken place earlier in life; and 5. The decline stage characterised by deceleration during the early part and progressing into one of retirement.

The concept of vocational development brings to mind the question of the level of vocational development at various stages of life and so the question of vocational maturity.

When we ask how suitable an individual is for taking up a vocation, we are talking of vocational maturity. Vocational maturity is in question when we try to evaluate the vocational choice that he has made and the adjustment he is making in that vocation. Vocational maturity is used to denote the level of vocational development of an individual.

Vocational adjustment, which previously was considered to be vocational maturity is the state achieved as the result of the interaction between the individual and his resources on one hand and the reality on the other. The individual makes vocational adjustment when he is confronted with vocational problems and is called upon to solve them. Vocational problems solved by others do not lead to vocational adjustment; only when the individual struggles with the problems himself he experiences the phenomenon of vocational adjustment. Defined in this way, vocational maturity is assessed in terms of the types of behaviour whereas vocational adjustment is defined in terms of the outcome of this behaviour.

Dimensions of Vocational Maturity

From the above definitions vocational development can be visualized as a continuum while the vocational maturity is a point on this continuum. The question now is how do we determine this point, is it a mathematical point so that it has no dimensions or is it a point defined by certain dimensions?

Super *et al.* in a Career Pattern study have developed the rationale for measurement of vocational maturity during adolescent years. The patterns of dimensions, it is assumed, will change with the age of the subject. Therefore, there would be a need for defining the dimensions of vocational maturity at all stages of life. According to the above study the adolescent stage of vocational development is characterised by: 1. increasing orientation to vocational choice; 2. increasing amounts of vocational information and more comprehensive and detailed planning; 3. increasing consistency of vocational preferences; 4. the crystallization of traits relevant to vocational choices; and consequently 5. increasing wisdom of vocational preferences.

Orientation to vocational choice implies concern with the choice. The underlying assumption is that a person who is concerned about the choice is better prepared for making the actual choice than the one with no concern for the vocational choice. This index of vocational maturity may be low during preadolescent years merely because of the lack of opportunity. It may not be there after adolescence because once the choice has been made there is no need for concern over the vocational choice. During old age this may be replaced by a concern for giving up the profession or the vocational choice one made earlier in life.

Vocational information and planning from another dimension of vocational maturity in as much as the individual at the preparation stage is more fit for taking up the vocation if, he has gathered information and done some planning about his vocation. The information may not be complete and the planning may be inadequate but it is there and the amount of it determines the level of maturity. For the later stages of life the information and planning for retirement may form the dimension.

Consistency of vocational preferences is worthy of consideration as a dimension of vocational maturity because greater maturity should help to narrow down the goal and crystallize preferences. Through exploration and trial the individual eliminates many less attractive and inappropriate alternatives and it is presumed that the retained preferences would be higher in consistency, which is indicative of vocational maturity.

Crystallization of traits and aptitudes has been listed as a dimension of vocational maturity because the individual whose abilities and potentialities have been more developed and integrated would be better prepared to cope with the developmental tasks of vocational choice and adjustment. . Since development takes place from general to specific it is assumed that a mature person should be more differential person than the one in whom development to the same degree has not taken place. It is further assumed that these differentiated characteristics would be more stable and crystallized.

Wisdom of vocational preferences is one of the most complex, difficult to manage but the most satisfying dimension of vocational maturity.

Dynamics of Vocational Development

The choice of vocation is a major decision, which causes a great deal of concern to the growing adult. The basic cause for this concern is the urge for economic independence, which the individual adolescent is known to seek early in life. Vocational interests and choices do not appear all of a sudden during adolescence; they appear as a result of a developmental process, which has been traced to the early days of the individual's life. Very often this development can be traced back to the influences exerted before birth. Child Development studies have proved the powerful influence which the thwarted ambitions and frustrations of the parents have on the vocational choice of the individual. Vocation being the implementation of the self-concepts, when the parents have failed to achieve it during their own career choice, they have sought it through the choice of career for their children. In other words, they have forced their own unfulfilled career choice on their children. Some times this has worked but more often it has led to dissatisfaction for the child and often a revolt and a change of vocational choice. This has involved frustration for the growing adult, waste of energy, money and precious time.

The Family

The family is the first social, psychological and economic unit in which the individual lives and the family influences the vocational development of the individual in all three aspects, that is, it exercises social, psychological and economic influences on the vocational development of the individual. The family provides the individual with opportunities to identify with certain adult roles. A male child usually identifies with his father; only in exceptional cases, when the child has developed negative feelings towards the father, this does not hold true. The occupation of the father thus becomes the preferred role for the child. With the opportunities provided by the family he explores this role and finally decides to choose or reject it. The family is also instrumental in helping the individual develop attitudes and values. It has been proved through research that children are not, born with attitudes but that they acquire them gradually through various experiences and influences. The family is the most intimate and important institution, which affects the formation of attitudes and values especially attitudes towards jobs and vocational choice.

The family exerts indirect influences on the vocational development of the individual by providing or depriving him of facilities and equipment necessary for him to experiment with various types of jobs. Thus there is a subtle family pressure on the individual's preferences, training, work, success and satisfaction in a particular job. Children start forming social attitudes and values rather early in life. Family and the peer group are the two main influences on their attitudes and values. 'Since vocational development involves attitudes and values it is significantly influenced by the family, especially the parents, and the peers. The values held by the parents have a subtle influence on the job preferences and so the vocational development of the individual. The jobs that the parents look upto are preferred by the child. Usually the parents respect jobs higher to their own status; therefore, logically the children seek and prepare for jobs superior to the ones held by their parents.

Ability

Adolescents with higher intellectual ability tend to seek and prepare for jobs requiring higher level of intelligence. Intelligence by itself is not a single and independent variable in the sense that research has proved that the individuals with higher intelligence usually come from middle and higher socio-economic families, from better background and with parents who have achieved higher educational level and are capable of providing richer experiences to their children.

Though no systematic and thorough study made on Indian samples is available yet some of the foreign studies have produced results to illustrate the difference in vocational achievement of the intelligent and dull individuals. In one of the studies it was possible to follow-up eight individuals who had been diagnosed as feeble-minded or of borderline intelligence some eighteen years earlier. When their vocational achievement was studied two of them were working as truck drivers; another was a taxi driver; a welder; a office clerk; a motor mechanic; a labourer; and an assembler at an electronic factory. All of these persons were earning meagre money but each one of them was self-supporting and a productive citizen. On the other hand, a group of above average intelligence was followed after a considerably long period. The members were found occupying positions of significant importance. Eighty per cent of those had graduated from college; 75 per cent were employed in professional or semi-professional positions. Many of them were university teachers, physicians, lawyers, architects, authors, engineers and artists. The study was successful in proving that the persons with higher ability' achieve vocations with better social and economical status while the ones with lower mental ability, though self-sufficient, stay in positions of almost no importance.

Personality

Personality of the individual affects his vocational interests just as it does his general interests and their development. A quiet and an introverted personality would be unhappy if placed in the job of a salesman or a publicity officer, he may be quite content and happy as a reference librarian or a research scholar. Similarly, a social and an extroverted rerson, in all probability, would make a successful public relations officer but not a scholar or a librarian.

Every job can be described in terms of the personality characteristics it requires for the person to be happy and satisfied in it. For example, good teachers are usually social, communicative, self-confident, self-sufficient and aggressive. On the other hand, bankers, dentists and musicians are more conservative, self-contained and less aggressive. Good clerks are usually lacking in self-confidence, are less willing to take responsibility and less social. One very important method to measure peoples' personal suitability to a particular job is through the study of their interest patterns. A considerable amount of work he gone into the Strong Vocational Interest Test wherein an individual is required to express his likes and dislikes for some 400 different activities. On the basis of analysis of a large number of responses, the interest blank claims to separate men and women suitable for particular vocations. The test of their suitability has been their satisfaction with the job studied during the follow-up some years after their placement.

Prediction of the most suitable career for an individual is based on the numerous profiles of successful individuals in various jobs. The profile of the individual wanting guidance can be compared with those who have already been successful in that particular field. The similarity and divergence between their personal qualities is a reliable guide for prediction of a career for the individual tested. Studies of reliability of these predictions have proved that young people choosing a particular career have interest profiles markedly similar to those of the successful persons in that particular line. Another study has indicated that persons most stable in their jobs showed interest patterns most suitable to work of their choice. Research has also found a significant difference in the earnings of persons in jobs most suited to their personality characteristics and the one who have been placed in jobs not suited to their interest patterns. Here it is appropriate to mention that these studies give group results, which should, in general, hold good for individuals also but exceptions are possible. Some individuals may not fit into these patterns and they should not be labelled abnormal. However, ample research evidence exists today to warrant prediction of career patterns for the young adults. Besides job satisfaction, suitable personality and interest patterns provide the individual with an opportunity for the development of vocational drive. Certain modern industries and commercial firms have already started emphasizing the importance of personality on the job, good personal adjustment and skills of inter-personal communication.

Various Drives and Influences

The relative importance of various factors in determining the individual's choice of career is difficult to ascertain; the only way to investigate it is through detailed case studies and their analysis. The available research evidence, however, is clear that as a child the individual is influenced by the factors and forces working in his immediate environment only. The family is the major influence at this stage. As the child grows, his experiences expand and spread over a wider area and his contacts reach beyond the immediate environment and the family. At this stage the broader social considerations start influencing him and his vocational choice. Money and security were important factors for men while they did not come very high for the women. Teachers developed a subculture providing much more vocational stimulation than the factory workers. Factory workers, in general, tended to lack stimulation and their planning was least affected by the factors like money, security and status. Male teachers were found to be highly stimulated and more vocationally motivated than the women teachers. Drives like self-expression, status and association with others figured significantly high with teachers and pretty low with the factory workers. One general conclusion of this study was that it is impossible to specify one single drive determining the career choice of the individual; many factors together exercise a complex influence on the career choice of the individual.

Economic Factors

Economics, in general, has confined itself to the social and business problems and has given very little attention to the individual and the vocational adjustment, which he is forced to make. When people need jobs as economic measures, they have to take the job that is available rather than to wait for the one, which they like or possess appropriate qualities for. The phenomena of demand and supply; business cycle; technological change and labour problems are as much individual problems as they are social and business problems. A few studies of occupational distribution and unemployment have contributed to the knowledge that may be called vocational economics and have highlighted the role that economics plays in the vocational choice and development of an individual.

It is one of the basic principles of economics that when labour or a particular skill is rare the wages for it go high but when it is available in plenty it is in no position to bargain so the wages and its prestige goes low. It is but natural therefore, that while planning his career the individual would avoid the vocations with low wages and prestige even though these may be the ones in which he is interested the most.

Business cycle is another economic factor affecting the vocational development of young persons as well as the vocational pattern and adjustment of older adults. It is an established fact that business completes a cycle of success failure and success. The business expands and brings the society to the condition of complete prosperity followed by another period of depression and again enters another period of prosperity. This cycle has definite effects on the vocational development and employment of the individual. A young adult who passes college during depression is faced with the strain of scarcity of employment, which is unfamiliar to another young man who may have passed college during more prosperous times. The two are forced to make very different vocational adjustment. During depression there is a general down grading which results in dissatisfaction among the workers. During prosperous times, on the other hand, there is scarcity of suitable individuals so there is a trend of upgrading. Persons with ordinary qualifications are able to secure good and above expectation jobs. This process can be painful because by putting people in strange situations and ways of life unknown to them it calls for readjustments, which cause considerable amount of strain on the individual.

Industrialization

Technical change and industrialization is another major factor, which influences vocational adjustment of an individual. Industrial development is accompanied by many new jobs and so people have more varied positions to fill. They are usually not familiar with these jobs; they had never aspired for them neither have they had the opportunity to explore their interest and aptitude for these jobs. Publicity is the only source of their knowing about various positions and the training required for them.

Industrialization has a different type of effect on the workers already settled in jobs. For many, it may mean getting uprooted and looking for new jobs; for others it may mean acquiring new skills to fit into the positions requiring skilled labour. A few instances of industrial change leading to a complete displacement of workers in certain occupations are available in World history. The use of water and electricity in place of coal led to mass displacement of coal miners, which caused a major problem of rehabilitation. With the lack of mobility to other geographic regions this would have meant a major disaster but with mobility and versatility the effect of economic forces could be contained and limited. In some states extensive studies of rehabilitation were undertaken and the possibility of retaining the displaced workers in newly created jobs was explored.

Public Policy

Human action in form of public policy has drastic effects on the vocational development of the individual. Legislation forbidding employments of a certain section of the population in the occupation for which they are trained and prepared can cause serious problems of displacement. An example in Indian history is the Gold Control Order, which led to serious problems of employment for the goldsmiths trained in the art of making gold ornaments. When the legislation restricted the use of gold for ornament making there was hardly any business for these craftsmen.

Certain taxes imposed through public policy are another important factor in adjustment and vocational development of the individual. Severe trade restrictions force individuals to change vocations and make vocational adjustments. State patronage to a particular industry acts as a boost while another erstwhile flourishing industry may suffer an obvious set back.

Changes in fashion and style, calamities caused by nature such as earthquakes, floods, etc., and the depletion of natural resources are some other factors, which affect the vocational adjustment and vocational development of the individual.

In conclusion we may say that the family, its economic status and resources, the general and specific abilities of the individual, his personality, motivation, general economic structure of the social group, industrialization, public policy, state patronage, changes in style and acts of nature are some of the factors which determine the vocational development and affect the vocational adjustment of the individual.

Vocational Development and Vocational Counselling

Much before the individual decides the particular occupation he is going to pursue he has formed an image of himself. The choice of occupation is very much determined by this self-image or self-concept. Before choosing a career the individual is bound to think of what he is and what he has aspired to be. The choice of a job is dependent on two considerations: (1) the job should permit the individual to play the role which he has imagined for himself; (2) the role that the job makes him play should be compatible with the self image he has held of himself. When in the job, the individual is testing his self-concept against reality. In adjusting to the job he is testing whether he can really live up to the picture he had built of himself.

If we accept this interpretation of vocational choice then vocational development is very similar to the personal development. Vocational development thus defined is only a specific aspect of the personal development. During the process of vocational guidance, therefore, the guidance counsellor is helping the individual with personal development. In guiding the individual with his vocational choice he is helping him to develop an appropriate, satisfying and realistic self-concept.

Often vocational guidance is considered as a mere information giving service. Vocational counsellor is viewed as a person who has all kinds of vocational information accumulated in his office; when the student comes for guidance the vocational counsellor is to make this information available to him and expect him to make the vocational choice based on this factual information provided to him. The procedure followed consists of interviewing the counsellee and trying to get the complete history of his background, experience, family, likes and dislikes, etc. Often tests are administered to get information of his intellectual level, aptitudes, interests and abilities. Often self-administered questionnaires and inventories have replaced the interviews but the aim is the same that is to get an inventory of the individual's assets, likes and dislikes and any special skills which he may possess.

On the other hand, the vocational counsellor has the lists of jobs, their requirements, the qualities necessary for the job and any other information regarding each job that may be available. With these two profiles the vocational counsellor compares the student's profile with the job information—the process has been known as matching the persons with the jobs. This matching is most empirical when the counsellor compares the two profiles and explains the comparison to the individual. The more practical method is to compare the individual's profile with the profiles of the successful individuals in different vocations and explain the comparisons to the counsellee. Many counsellors would choose to compare the profiles and the job requirements together with the counsellee; the counsellor and the counsellee sit together during the process and read the two sets of information. The last step in the process consists of the counsellor helping the counsellee study a few occupations which he may have liked and considered worth pursuing.

It is implied that the key to good adjustment in a job is the amount of information about the self, the job and the proper matching of the two. This interpretation reduces the process of vocational guidance to facts and information excluding the role that emotional and personal factors play in vocational adjustment. Without minimizing the role played by facts and information in career choice one must remember that the picture is incomplete without consideration of the emotional and personal factors. This brings us to another interpretation of the vocational guidance namely, personal counselling.

Interpretation of vocational guidance as an aspect of personal guidance implies that vocational guidance is not as much a matter of facts as it is of attitudes. By now it has been well established that many vocational problems are due to emotional and personal difficulties and not so much due to the lack of information and fact finding. The psychiatrists and psychotherapists claim that the vocational maladjustments are a matter of attitudes and that the problems of vocational choice and adjustment are personal problems calling for psychotherapeutic help. So in contrast with the traditional view when vocational counselling was considered as a process of fact finding and information giving the modern thinkers consider it a process of help with the emotional problems and personal adjustment. When the student or client come with a vocational problems the counsellor starts his work with how the student feels. If he is undecided about his career, the counsellor helps him to express his feelings and tries to understand how he feels during the state or-undecisiveness. He is helped to feel free in expressing his feelings and frustrations without restraint. The counsellor listens to all that he has to say, encourages him to talk unhesitatingly and helps him to experience a feeling of acceptance. He is helped to feel that his problem is like anyone else's problem and that there is nothing unusual and wrong about it.

Though there is no obvious attempt at exploration and inventory taking yet the individual is permitted to talk as much as he likes to. In doing so he is helped to understand himse!f, his feelings and attitudes and the self-concept he has developed. This expression gives emotional relief to the individual and helps him to plan his future occupation with clarity, confidence and self-assurance. Having acquired an objective estimate of himself, the individual is able to view his aspirations in a more objective manner than he was doing befote. Some of his aspirations may prove too unrealistic now with the revised estimate of himself and understanding of his assets and drawbacks. The counsellor works with the cluster of his counsellee's aspirations; he helps him in discarding the unrealistic ones while the realistic and compatible ones are encouraged and helped to develop.

After the process of vocational counselling has reached this stage, the counsellee may still have some doubts and discrepancies to reconcile with but by now he feels sure enough of himself and his clear understanding of himself and the reality. He considers himself capable of handling these problems and making his own vocational and personal decisions. This is the stage where the student feels that now onwards he could do without the help of the counsellor and he seeks the opportunity to proceed on his own and try his newly acquired emotional independence and self understanding.

The two interpretations of vocational guidance as discussed above are essentially theoretical. In practice, it has been observed that a purely vocational or education problem never comes to the counsellor. They are always interwoven with the personal adjustment. When a person fails to choose his career or finds himself in a wrong job, he experiences certain feelings and reactions from others and starts developing attitudes or emotional reactions to his being unemployed or in the wrong job. Similarly, when a student fails his examination or feels uninterested in studies or in a particular subject, the problem is not failure or lack of understanding or the lack of concentration only, relatives and friends show certain reactions to these incidents, which affect the feelings and the self-image of the individual. This sets in the vicious circle, others' reactions affect his behaviour, which in turn causes new reactions in people around him.

In practice, therefore, it is very difficult to suggest either the pure logical vocational guidance based on facts and information or the personal guidance emphasizing the emotional content of the problem. Usually, the counsellor goes through an eclectic process wherein he gives facts and information whenever necessary but is all the time watching for the emotional content. Whenever expression is given to the emotional aspect, the counsellor helps the student experience free expression with security of acceptance and no judgement on the good or bad of the problem. For a student wanting to take up engineering as a vocation, information regarding various openings, the type of work involved and the branches of engineering is as important as the consideration of his feelings about the profession. No successful and effective counsellor, therefore, should pledge himself to either of the interpretations of vocational guidance. Just as information without feelings and consideration for the client is hollow, the consideration for the client without precise and accurate information is ineffective.

It is accepted now in practice that the three types of problems educational, vocational and personal are so mixed together that it is difficult to group them in distinct and completely independent categories. Statistics of counselling practice and its analysis has revealed very clearly that a particular case can be categorized both as a vocational and a personal problem. Another case can be both educational and personal in nature. As a matter of fact there is hardly ever a case of educational guidance, which is not complicated with personal problems. People have feelings and attitudes towards every aspect of their life. Therefore, personal counselling must enter the vocational choice, vocational adjustment and the vocational problems. People who need to make decisions about the courses they should take, the jobs they should prepare for and the required training are faced with facts. Vocational counselling of the rational type, therefore, also has a place.

The distinction between the vocational and personal counselling is artificial and emphasis on one at the cost of the other is unjustified. When counselling a person with a problem of, vocational choice or vocational adjustment the counsellor does both vocational and personal counselling. A good vocational counsellor uses information and helps the counsellee to make use of information concerning psychological, educational and occupational matters; he also recognizes and helps the client to recognize the emotional factors that are operating. Through the process of vocational choice the individual is exploring his own self concept and reaching a compromise between his ideal self and the real self as he knows and experiences it. Problems of vocational choice are emotional in nature because they involve the self; while choosing an occupation the individual is choosing a means of implementing a self-concept.

If we proceed on the basis of the above discussion then a redefinition of vocational guidance and development is in order. In the process of redefinition, the vocational guidance becomes the process of helping a person to develop and accept an integrated and adequate picture of himself and his role in the world of work, to test his concept against reality and to convert it into reality, with satisfaction to himself and benefit to the society.

Information Service and Career Planning

Educational Information. One of the most important functions of guidance is to provide adequate and usable information regarding the educational opportunities to the counsellee. For proper educational guidance we need to follow the following three steps: (1) understand the individual, find facts about him; (2) know details about the schools and courses he has attended; and (3) guide him in choosing courses by matching individuals with the requirements of different courses. These three steps integrate and make the process of educational guidance. They may be treated separately for discussion purposes but in practice it is difficult to separate them. During educational guidance we are confronted with a real difficulty which is inherent in Indian education. Many facts about courses can be gathered only through experience which can be possible through orientation, tryout and preview courses provided in American set up but completely missing in Indian education. Once he has made his choice, the Indian student is compelled to follow a course throughout his school or college career. If he finds it difficult or uninteresting, there is no way for him to change and take another one in line with his likes and interests.

Information service can help by providing exploratory information on various aspects of education. To be prepared to help the students in educational difficulties the educational information should have facts about the following subjects:

1. Value and rationale of education: why should people study? How does education help the development of an individual?
2. The institutions that offer courses in various lines, for example, the institutions that offer vocational courses after high school, the institutions which offer higher courses in special branches like Indian Institutes of Technology and the national laboratories.
3. The type of education available at every stage of the educational career: after middle school what courses are available? What can be done after higher secondary? And finally, what careers are available for college students?

4. Evaluation of the courses and information regarding general facilities available in schools and colleges.
5. Purposes of these institutions, qualifications and special qualities required for entrance, cost, duration of courses and details about the organization of institutions.

Some of these facts are easily available and can be secured by the teacher or the counsellor, others are more difficult to secure and may take some time for us to compile but the job can be done. But there are some acts which can be acquired through experience only and the student has to wait until the time when he can gain the specific experience.

Information about colleges is important because every year a larger number of young people are passing high school and aspiring to go to college. When they come to the higher secondary stage they need guidance about the various schools, their good points and poor ones.

The Ministry of Education has collected a lot of information and compiled it into a booklet giving various facts about education in general, elementary education, middle and higher secondary schools. This should be a valuable addition to the counsellor's library. This booklet has further value in that it gives a comparative study of education in various states in India and the state-wise status of education at different levels of school.

The counsellor also needs to have facts about the requirements of various schools in different parts of the country so that the counsellee required to move from one place to another may find this information useful. Information on individual states is available with the Education Department of the respective states, what the counsellor needs to do, perhaps, is to put this information together in one unit and have it available for the counsellees. Because guidance and counselling is a new discipline in India, a lot of information which is available has not been integrated in a usable form. The counsellor has to be resourceful and imaginative in gradually collecting these scattered bits of information through the years and compile them in a form appropriate for the guidance of young people. An apt example is that of periodic employment figures. From time to time figures of employment need for persons in certain technical fields and the surplus in certain others is published. If a counselor puts the figures for a few years together he would find out the trend of employment from which he can calculate the demand and supply situation four or five years hence and use this as a reliable index for guiding his students. We need not wait for an extensive study on this subject before we can guide students.

Information regarding various colleges and the courses offered by them is also important. Though fewer students go to colleges than higher secondary schools yet the ones who go are the top of the intelligentia. They are presumably the best of the high school graduates; for full development of our country it is important that we use every individual available and use him in the right place. Therefore, it is essential that when we send our best brains for higher studies they should go to the best and most appropriate institutions and take the most suitable courses. The information on individual colleges is usually made available by them, the counsellor needs to have it available in his library and help the students with interpretation. This is the area in which the schools and colleges in a particular locality can cooperate. Usually the children from schools in a particular community go to particular colleges only; in rare cases do they go to colleges in a different area. By making information about their college available to the schools the administration is preparing their students before they come to college. This can rightly be called pre-college orientation of the students.

Information regarding institutions of higher study in the country should be available with the Student Information

Bureaux set up in almost all universities by the Central Ministry of Education. The purpose of these Bureaux is to collect and disseminate information to students on institutions of advanced study in India and abroad. Unfortunately, these Bureaux are not so well organized and effective as one would wish them to be. Each university is required to put a staff member in charge of this set up but the general indifference to this service is obvious from the lack of adequate information and literature available with the Bureaux. A guidance oriented teacher has scope to render a valuable service by putting this organization in order and making its services adequate and available to the students.

Vocational Information

In the process of assistance to a student in making vocational plans the first important step is to help acquaint him with the information available on various vocations. Personnel workers differ in their opinions on how this information should be given, whether it should be given through special classes or through assignments related with various courses and subjects but there is no disagreement that dissemination of appropriate occupational information is basic to vocational planning. If we accept that the basic philosophy of vocational guidance is to help the counsellee decide on the occupation he would like to follow then the provision of information is a must. In order to make the right decision the counsellee must have all the information available about as many occupations as possible. The individual must know what is available and what steps he needs to take to achieve his goal before we can expect him to make a wise decision.

The type of information which the individual requires to have depends upon the stage he is at. If he is still in school with many years of study ahead of him then he needs information which would give him a general view of the educational and vocational choices available to him. The information may be general but should be extensive. It should give him ample scope to look around and explore. This type of information would help him decide on the general line of studies he should take up namely science, commerce or arts. On the other hand, when he is ready to graduate, that is, after he has chosen the line of study and has taken certain courses then what he needs to know is the specific and detailed information about a few occupations available to him.

The vocational information which we provide to the counsellee needs to be systematic and comprehensive, covering all the possible questions which a counsellee can ask such as:

1. The Nature of Work. The counsellee is keen to know what his duties would be and what kind of work he could be expected to do in a particular job. This is especially true of our society in which people are extremely conscious of manual work or work that would dirty their hands. With a "white collar" mentality it is essential that the vocational counsellor provides information regarding the type of work required in each suggested occupation.

2. Status of the Occupation. Our society being class and caste conscious, people are sensitive about certain jobs which do not enjoy social prestige. Only some occupations like medicine, engineering, civil services etc., enjoy social status; the others either do not provoke any positive or negative response or are definitely looked down upon. When a young adult comes for guidance he and his parents both are interested in the kind of status which the suggested occupation enjoys in their social group.

Besides the social prestige the counsellee as well as his parents are interested in knowing the future prospects in the occupation. How many people does it employ at present?

What is the employment trend for the future? Is it going to take in more or less workers? The counsellee wants to prepare for it only if there are good prospects of his finding a job when he graduates.

3. Preparation Necessary. Certain occupations require long and expensive training which a particular counsellee may not be able to afford. In view of his limitations and circumstances he would need to change his vocational plans so that they fit in with his means. An example is that of a boy who had secured 85 per cent marks in his higher secondary and came for admission to the first year of college. While asking for a form he talked of his plans to join an arts course. This was an unusual behaviour because in general everyone wants to go to science even if the marks secured are not so high. This boy with 85 per cent marks would have had no trouble whatsoever in getting admitted to a science course. An interview with the counsellor revealed that the boy bad lost his father a year ago and was now responsible for looking after an old mother and a young sister with no income except the sale of milk from one cow. With these means and responsibilities the counsellee could not plan a career in science which would have required long and expensive training.

4. Compensation and Working Conditions. The remunerations and the conditions of work are another aspect of an occupation on which the counsellee would require information before he decides to take up one or the other. Not only compensation but the counsellee is also keen to know whether the compensation he receives is commensurate with the length of training and the expenditure he has incurred. Pay may be adequate or high but the counsellee also wants to know the kind of organization with which he would need to work and the kind of working conditions that would be provided.

5. Personal Qualities. Different occupations require different personal qualities for the worker to be successful. A research worker may not need so much of social skills as a lawyer and a salesman would, a surgeon cannot afford to be indifferent to precision and accuracy while a scientist is no good without patience and hard-work. For an appropriate vocational decision the counsellee needs to know the qualities required in a job so that he may assess his own qualities against those required by a job.

6. Advantages and Disadvantages. This is a general heading under which the counsellor can summarize the information given under all the above headings. This is also an opportunity for him to add any other features of the occupation which might have escaped his notice and is helpful in winding up the session for dissemination of occupational information.

Information on the above mentioned aspects of an occupation is useful in individual guidance and it can be beneficially used for group guidance in classes before the children are required to choose their vocation. We have failed to realize the value of vocational information in junior classes. Many of us tend to think that consideration of occupations is too early for the junior classes while others gave preference to other subjects and push occupational information to a lower priority. But occupational information, if given under supervision of a qualified and sympathetic teacher, can lay a sound foundation for wise career choice. The two main aims of occupational information are:

1. To provide the student with better understanding of various occupations and the workers in these occupation.
2. To help the student in making a wiser choice of a career and in preparing him for the chosen occupation.

The first and the most difficult problem for the occupational counsellor is to collect occupational information.

The difficulties are manifold. For one, the occupations do not stay still for long enough time. In the rapidly changing world of ours the scientific and technological development affects the occupations almost every moment. They change their nature, the type of work required and the demands which they make on the individual. The rapid change and development requires that the investigation of occupations be repeated periodically and kept up-to-date from time to time. This obviously means that some persons should be assigned the responsibility of looking after this aspect of the guidance service.

In order to get systematic and reliable information the guidance workers need to investigate certain other aspects such as (1) where to get facts (2) how to distinguish between facts and attitudes, prejudices and fancies (3) methods of research so that if need be they can conduct small-scale local investigation and supplement or verify the information given to them. They also need to develop a uniform outline along which the information should be collected so that it can be more effective in its use. One may argue that every additional information about an occupation should be useful and should make the description more clear and complete but on the other hand, certain facts are more useful than the others. It is the responsibility of the counsellor to sift the useful information and make it available to the counsellee. The following list of the basic facts which the occupational information must include has been drawn on the basis of our previous discussion:

1. Job title.
2. The nature of work to be performed.
3. A brief description of the job.
4. Working conditions, benefits, hazards and the facilities provided.

5. Future prospects in the job, possibility of promotion and transfers; the relationship of the job with other jobs in the establishment.
6. Equipment and materials used.
7. Emoluments.
8. Qualifications and special qualities required for the success in job.
9. Any special information about the job.

As obvious, this is the bare outline of occupational information. Research and practical experience in counselling has indicated that students need more extended information than contained in this brief description. This being their first introduction with the world of occupations, they are interested in knowing:

1. The history of the occupation, how it developed and how long history does it have. This is especially important in India with the strong prejudices and social prestige attached to various occupations.
2. The pattern of employment, the number of workers employee and the possibility of future employment.
3. The number of people working in the occupation.
4. The importance of the occupation and the contribution it ma to the development of society.
5. Duties
   - *(a)* Specific tasks, other occupations with which this work be related or combined, nature of work, tools, machines and materials used.
   - *(b)* Definition of the job as described by the law and office organizations. This definition should be carefully designed and worded and should

be acceptable to the people working in the occupation.

6. Preparation which includes general education, special training and schools or institutions offering special training.

7. Qualifications, sex, age, community; special physical, men social and moral qualities; skills and the use of special tools and equipment required to work on the job.

8. Duration of training that is the time required to acquire the skills necessary for the job.

9. Emoluments: starting salary, average earnings and the maximum earnings throughout the career.

10. Other occupations with better prospects to which the present job may lead.

11. Methods of entering the job, special agencies like the Employment exchanges and the State Public Service Commissions through which the job must be sought.

12. Yearly duration of work: whether it is a permanent work throughout the year or it closes down during certain months, what are the busy months and what are the comparatively easy months.

13. Advancement: line of promotion and opportunity for advancement.

14. **Health and Accident Risk.** Certain occupations are accident prone and hazards to general health of the employee. The information about the occupation should include these details also.

15. Hours of work, how many hours daily is the worker expected to put in, what is the procedure of overtime, vacations and other requirements.

16. **Employer and Employee Organizations.** Often the status of an employer can be estimated from the type of organizations which he is a member of. Also, the working conditions, the improvement thereof and the professional development of the employee is dependent on the strength of the employee organizations.

17. **Places of Employment.** It is important for the worker to know whether he is to be placed in an office, a shop or a factory. He would also like to know whether the job is transferrable or at one place only.

18. Occupational information would be incomplete without references to other relevant materials on the occupation. Therefore the information collected on various occupations must include references to other relevant materials on the occupations concerned.

An effective counsellor must have all these facts ready at hand. It is not essential that he should have these facts committed to memory but it is expected that he should have it at a place and in a form readily available to him so that he may interpret it to the counsellee any time he needs to do so.

It is important for the counsellor to know the sources from which vocational information is available and he should call upon these agencies from time to time and keep his information library as complete and up-to-date as possible. It is hardly practical for the counsellor to approach each and every agency, factory and organization for information on jobs available with them. The task should be taken up by a central agency preferably with the staff qualified in research methods.

Though there is a real dearth of research in occupational information in our country yet some materials have been produced by the Directorate of Employment through its National Employment Service. Small booklets cover individual areas and give useful information on various jobs available in a particular line. These pamphlets are written in English and Hindi as well as in many regional languages. It is in place to emphasize here the need for further research which can be best and most easily met through a careful planning of the M.Ed. and Ph.D. theses. The research by students at these levels can be coordinated with the practical needs of the profession. Some students can be encouraged to take up the study and collection of information about a set number of occupations; the accumulated output of such researches will be phenomenal and most helpful to the professional counsellor. Precautions should be taken that there is some control on the form in which information is collected and the methods used in collection of the same. Variability in the information available may render it ineffective for use throughout the country. Perhaps the best step would be for a central agency to develop outlines appropriate to our conditions like the one suggested above and for all the research workers to follow it step-by-step.

Information on occupations keeps on changing just as the occupations themselves are subject to change. Therefore, it is essential that the agency or individuals who take up the task of collecting information on occupations should also follow-up the assignment and supplement the information periodically. Once the library of such information is built, it is advisable for the counsellor to keep a catalogue of all the information available with him and with other agencies; to this catalogue he must refer before commencing occupational and vocational guidance with his counsellees.

Occupational information thus collected and reviewed is to be disseminated to the students and there are two methods of presenting this information to them: (1) through individual interviews, and (2) through group contacts. An individual interview is called for when the counsellee is interested in an occupation of little interest to other counsellees or if he has an emotional problem related to a particular occupation. On the other hand, when many students need help in finding facts about various occupations the counsellor meets them in groups and saves his energy and time and funds of the institution.

For individual interviews Baer and Roeber have suggested four principals which should be kept in mind:

(1) The conditions under which occupational information is used in individual interviews. The case of a boy seeking admission to the first year of college will illustrate the conditions. On approaching the desk where admission forms were being distributed this boy asked for a form for admission to the civil engineering course. There is no specific form for admission to the civil engineering course at the first year of college stage. But it was obvious that the boy had decided to take up civil engineer in, course even though he knew very little about the course and its requirements and perhaps about the positions open to him after graduation. Here, the counsellor had the alternatives of either referring him to the sources of information directly or to wait till the counsellee had learnt something about his own abilities and potentialities. It is quite possible that he may be having some personal problems and that this definiteness in his vocational behaviour is a secondary problem. In any case an individual interview is called for during which the counsellee should be acquainted with the information on various occupations especially civil engineering. If necessary, further individual interviews should be arranged during which he may be helped to know himself, his abilities, limitations and potentialities better than he does at the moment. As a result of this work the counsellee would be better equipped with the skill to deal with his vocational problem in a mature fashion.

(2) Selection of appropriate occupational materials for the counsellee is an important responsibility of the counsellor. The counsellor performs this function by studying the interests of the counsellee and determining the level of his reading and comprehension. With the study of his interests the counsellor is in a position to judge what kind of material and which occupations are suitable to the counsellee. Other factors that determine the suitability of the occupational materials are the counsellee's background, ability, experience, his drive to read the available information and his attitude towards his vocational choice.

(3) Evaluation of the use of occupational information is another concern of the counsellor. The counsellor needs to evaluate his own effectiveness he needs to ask questions such as: Is individual counselling helping the counsellee in making a better choice? Does a comparison of this counsellee with the ones who have not had counselling indicate a superior vocational choice and adjustment than those who have not been counselled?

(4) Another principle which the counsellor must look for, before launching on individual interviews, is the amount of assistance which the counsellor should give the counsellee in using occupational information. There are counsellors who feel that having set up the information library, the only duty that they have is to point out the shelves to the student and then it is the student's responsibility or headache to search for the appropriate information, shift it out and interpret it for his use. On the other hand, there are counsellors who believe in reading out each booklet with the counsellee and explaining it to him. The latter may be accused of spoonfeeding while the former are guilty of indifference. The amount of help which a particular case requires is quite different from that required by others. Some students are quite capable of proceeding on their own if the materials are given to them while the others may require help in sifting and following the

materials provided to them. With the latter type the counsellor needs to direct their information by reading and discussing it with them. In doing so he must aim at making the counsellee self directive rather than dependent on the counsellor. The amount of assistance required in each case is to be determined by the counsellor in individual cases according to the type of counsellee and his needs.

Group techniques help the counsellor in imparting occupational information to a larger number of counsellees at comparatively lesser cost of money energy and time. Most of the aspects of vocational guidance can be covered through group techniques; individual interviews are necessary when the individual difficulties or adjustments are involved. Group techniques can be used for:

1. Orientation to occupations—an overall view of the adult work and the world of work.
2. Discussion of the three important steps in choosing an occupation *viz.,* securing occupational information; acquiring information about self and understanding oneself and matching the information about occupations with the specific understanding about oneself.
3. Presentation of information about the various areas of work or specific occupations suitable for school students and the field trips if necessary and appropriate.
4. Introduction to the sources of occupational information.
5. Discussion of occupational trends in the country, the discussion of the availability of jobs in certain areas when an overwhelmingly large number of young adults are getting trained in certain other areas where no jobs are available thus causing the

imbalance of demand for employment and trained personnel.

6. Consideration of the relation between the individual's personality, characteristics and the success in a job.

Some of the typical programmes of guidance in which group methods can be effectively used are:

Courses

A course in occupational choice and information can be useful and effective for high school children who are on the threshold of an important life decision. A well planned course on this topic is not only useful for the students who have not been able to make an occupational decision yet but for those students also who have or who think they have made the final decision on their life career. The course, by offering information on various careers and occupations, helps the student broaden his outlook on work as a result of which the student may choose to change his decision and if he prefers to stick by his original decision then he does so with more understanding and maturity.

Some of our schools may find it difficult to accomodate a full course on occupational information in their curriculum; a compromise may be to earmark some time within the schedule of subject teaching which can be devoted to discussion of job opportunities within that particular subject.

The Career Conference

This is one of the most interesting and worthwhile activities which can be organized effectively both for a school and a college. The organization of a career conference may be simple for a small institution and complex and extensive for a large school or college. During the conference, successful persons from different fields of work are invited to come and talk to the students on their own occupation. Ideally the talk should be followed by a question hour during which each student gets a chance to have his doubts clarified and queries answered; with younger students the teacher can spend an hour followings the talk in analyzing and interpreting the talk to them.

The career conference can cover an array of occupations which can be selected according to the most common interests displayed by the students through their co-curricular activities. The career conference provides an opportunity to the students to attend the talks on occupations in which they are interested.

The College Day

The school can organize college days to which officials and teachers from colleges, which the students of this school usually join, are invited. They talk to the students about what the college has to offer them by way of education, cocurricular activities, social life and the special programmes, if any. As a part of this programme the school students can be given an opportunity to visit the college and witness the class work as well as the work outside the classroom.

While a college day is beneficial to those students only who are planning to enter college an "after high school what?" programme can help even those students who may leave school and join some vocational institution or go straight into a job. The purpose of such a programme is to lead school students into serious and mature thinking and post-high school planning.

Home Room

The home room provides atmosphere for the teacher to discuss educational and vocational planning with the students. The two basic requirements however are that the teacher should be well qualified in dissemination of information and educational and vocational guidance and that the home room period has enough time for discussion of the occupational planning. With an interested and enthusiastic teacher a great deal can be achieved during the home room period.

Displays and Exhibitions

Posters on various occupations and occupational materials can be displayed on most prominent places and most frequented rooms. Student participation can be invited through preparation of posters or collection of booklets and other materials on various occupations. The displays, if effectively arranged, can make a valuable aid to students in choosing their life career. Posters, charts and other materials can be posted on bulletin boards placed at most prominent and obvious places so that they do not escape notice of students.

Student Clubs

Just as most of our schools and colleges have subject clubs for various academic subjects so they can have clubs in which students would discuss occupations, preparation and training for various occupations, institutions which provide training, duration of training, prospects and future of each vocation. The clubs should be built on the basis of student interests and should be run by the students with supervisory help from the staff. Running of the club in itself would be a training for some vocation for many of the student leaders.

Films and Filmstrips

Another attractive way of imparting occupational information to groups of students is through films and filmstrips which are more effective if accompanied by a commentary from an experienced adult. They can be made still more effective by a post screening discussion which would serve the purpose of answering questions, clearing doubts and making the information clear.

Co-curricular Activities

This is another programme during which occupational information can be given to students and their career planning discussed and guided. Many institutions offer career information as a co curricular activity. Most of them organize a career conference as a part of the co-curricular activities. There can be a question as to how effective a Career conference can be as a co-curricular activity but no doubt this is one programme where occupational information can be given to groups.

Field Trips

Field trips are the most practical and realistic source of information on occupations which a student can expect to receive from his school and teachers. During field trips small groups of students are taken to places of actual work *e.g.* a factory, a farm or a hotel and introduced to the various types of work which goes on in each place. This experience is more interesting because there is very little talk in a field trip, its main feature is seeing persons on the jobs, performing their duties which, gives a true picture of the type of job performed, responsibilities, health hazards, risks and the other factors involved in the occupation visited

Subject-matter Approach

Each subject teacher can specify some of his teaching time for information on occupations in his own speciality. The subject teacher is most suited to guide his students about the institutions that offer training programmes, the amount and duration of training required for each job and the future prospects in the line. Sometimes it is perhaps, better to entrust this task to the subject teacher than to the vocational counsellor. The teacher, if interested and dynamic enough, has gone through the course and so has more practical experience and therefore more accurate advice to give to the student than the counsellor.

In vocational guidance both individual and group approaches are useful. One can not replace the other; each one has its own place which the counsellor decides keeping in mind the peculiar circumstances of the counsellee. In an institution where group techniques are recommended the co-operation of the staff members is necessary and they need to use their ingenuity and imagination to discover new and interesting ways of working with the groups and giving them occupational information.

It is in place here to discuss some of the mistakes which students and young adults often make in choosing their careers. Before we start talking of the mistakes it is necessary to remind ourselves that the process of vocational choice requires the individual to be extremely impersonal and objective in studying himself and analysing his own strengths and weaknesses. This is made difficult by the desire for status and idealism—the wish to follow a person we like, adventuresome spirit and the desire to achieve approval of those we love. However, if the student is unable to be objective and evaluate himself in relation with the requirements of an occupation then he is susceptable to making mistakes which would lead to failure and dissatisfaction with the job and subsequent frustration. Some of the common mistakes in vocational choice are:

1. Choosing an occupation which requires higher mental ability than that of the counsellee or does not require as much of it as the counseljee has. To determine whether the job matches the mental ability level of the counsellee, the counsellor should be in a position to use some standardized and reliable test of mental ability. Often it is found that the counsellee aspires for an occupation demanding too high a level of intelligence than he possesses. In such a case, it is the responsibility of the counsellor to advise him in a tactful manner and help him change his vocational

choice. It can also happen that an individual aspires for a job which does not require the mental ability of as high an order as the counsellee possesses. If he is not helped by a counsellor he may take it up and in due course find that the job is not inspiring and challenging enough.

2. Choosing an occupation for which the student can not attain the required standards of skills. Often students who are good at music in school decide to become professional musicians. Unless these students are exceptionally gifted in music, their aptitude in music shown through their proficiency at school level is not necessarily an indication that they would make good musicians.

3. Choosing an occupation for which the student does not possess essential skills in tool subjects. If a student weak in mathematics aspires to specialize in pure mathematics he is sure to be disappointed just as another person weak in spellings would be if he were to decide on taking up a secretarial post. We can help them improve the basic skills required for their jobs and if not, we can work with them and persuade them to change their vocation.

4. Choosing an occupation because of its glamour. Often young persons get attracted by the glitter of a certain occupation without caring to investigate the requirements, the type of work and the duties of the job. An apt example is that of an intelligent and bright girl who walked into the counsellor's office her mind all made up for an air hostess' job. A little exploratory work on the occupation convinced her that that was not be occupation for her.

5. Choosing an occupation for which the student lacks the necessary stamina and physical strength. A boy

with a low stamina and physical strength should not enter the field of engineering which requires hard physical work during training and apprenticeship as well as during ones career. Similarly a student with not too good an eye sight should not aspire to become a pilot.

6. Choosing an occupation for which the student does not have the appropriate personality characteristics. A shy and withdrawn person does not make a good business executive and another one without understanding of human nature and sympathetic attitude towards their problems can not make a good counsellor. Both these types should be helped to plan a vocation suitable to their personality.

7. Choosing a career without considering the financial implications. Often boys and girls start working for an occupation which may involve extensive training spread over a long period of time and involving large funds of money. They need the counselling help in planning their career in line with their limitations and financial status.

8. Choosing an occupation in which there are many more qualified candidates than there are openings. This is illustrative of the situation prevailing in our country at the present moment. The number of graduates coming out of the engineering colleges far exceeds the number of vacancies existing in the field or likely to exist. Inspite of the statistics the students are registering for such courses because of the social prestige which the profession has enjoyed all this time. Counselling help needs to be provided for these students.

9. Choosing an occupation on the basis of the wishes and ambitions of parents and friends. This is the

most common and tragic mistake made by the Indian youth. Our parents play an important and vital role in deciding the vocation of their children which they often do on the basis of what they have themselves wanted to be and have not been able to achieve or what they have always desired their children to be irrespective of their likes abilities and interests. A case in point is that of an engineering student who had invested five years of his educational life and had not yet passed the third year of engineering course. The reason turned out to be the fact that he was not interested in engineering, his interest was in English literature but he was forced by his father to get admitted in the engineering college.

In order to be able to help the counsellee in his vocational planning the counsellor must have the following attitudes:

1. Sincere conviction that each counsellee has abilities and will be useful in the world of occupations.
2. The conviction that the counsellee can be helped to take responsibility of using the information about vocations and himself which he has been helped to acquire.
3. The counsellee should be helped to develop insight into himself in reference to the occupations.
4. The counsellor should refrain from directing and dominating the process of guidance.
5. The counsellee should be helped to develop skills of self-guidance.

❋❋❋

7

Rational Theories and Techniques

Rational theories tend to take a logical and intellectual approach to the counselling process and to the solution of the counsellee's problems or difficulties. These theories are simple in nature, eclectic in approach and likely to accept and adopt a variety of techniques. Rational approaches to counselling are usually based on an analogy between medicine and counselling. Thus these approaches assume that treatment cannot be attempted until some diagnosis can be reached because, logically, the diagnosis would be the basis of differential treatment. Williamson and Thorne both adopt medical models in their counselling approach. Ellis, on the other hand, is not concerned with diagnosis but his approach is rational because it applies logic and rational argument to the solution of the counsellee's problems. One of the goals of such an approach is to help the counsellee in learning problem-solving techniques which he can then apply to other problems. Weitz has also presented this view of counselling in a recent publication. Rational theories present the counsellor as essentially a teacher who applies a rational, problem-solving technique in an individual teaching relationship. None of them limits counselling to intellectual problem-solving; all of them recognize the influence of conation upon the cognitive process but in all, the emphasis is upon counselling as a cognitive process.

Logical approach has a definite appeal in cultures with strong scientific bias but its weakness lies in that the scientific ideal values objectivity and intellectual comprehension and these features may not be entirely advantageous for counselling. They tend to result in an over evaluation of the cognitive aspects. From the counsellee's point of view "insight" in the sense of ability to verbalize self-understanding may be mistaken for genuine attitude change. From the counsellor's standpoint, the scientific attitude may lead to undue stress on the niceties of interpretation and avoidance of frankly emotion-arousing techniques, even though there is universal agreement that in order to succeed, counselling must involve the counsellee's emotions.

Williamson's approach to counselling is, perhaps, the only one which has developed from vocational counselling base, emphasizing problems of educational and vocational adjustment. While this point of view is rational end logical in its approach, it is not associated with intellectualism or essentialism in education. Williamson holds it identical with what he calls "personalism" implying concern for the whole individual. According to Williamson, the basic purpose of education is not only to train the intellect but also to assist students to achieve those levels of social, civic and emotional maturity which are within the range of their potentialities. Counselling, on the other hand, is a concept that embraces and integrates vocational and educational guidance with personality dynamics and interpersonal relationships.

There are five basic questions which every counsellor should try to answer for himself.

1. What is the nature of human motivation? Counsellor must believe that through education, man can become himself in a manner which will bring satisfaction of accomplishment; man continues to strive to become himself. The man is born with the

potential for both good and evil; through life the man tries to seek good and reject or control evil. The degree to which one becomes a full human being is determined by the measure of enlightened self-control attained and deployed in the direction of "full humanity".

2. What is the nature of human development? Since man is born both with good and evil, he is not capable of self actualization or autonomous development. He needs other persons to achieve the full development of his potentiality. Williamson believes that the human self emerges only in the community and has no real existence apart from it.

3. What is the nature of the "good life" and "the good"? The nature of the good life is a question which should not be answered with finality but only provisionally. One dimension of good is the concept of excellence in all aspects of human development.

4. What is the nature of the universe and what is man's relationship to that universe? In answer to this question each counsellor and counsellee must formulate his own conception or personal cosmology.

5. What is the nature of determination of the "good life"? Who determines what is good? parents and teachers, in attempting to dictate the form of the good life, may block the student's search. The search itself may prove to be the good life.

Williamson and the Minnesota approach to counselling works on certain assumptions concerning effective counselling relationships. These assumptions are:

1. The goal of counselling is to help the individual grow through the direction of optimum development in all aspects of his personality. But the optimum

individual development should not be held synonymous with "absolutistic and autonomous self-direction" or autonomous individualism. Counselling should not become a method of freeing individual from his limitations and thus facilitating his development without regard for the development of others. While self-understanding and self-direction are desirable, the goal must be "socially enlightened self-understanding and self-direction".

2. Counselling assumes the desirability, if not the necessity, of voluntary counselling relationship and is opposed to "required" counselling. Nevertheless, Williamson himself has stated that during his own counselling experience, especially with disciplinary cases, he has been able to do much effective counselling even with reluctant or non-voluntary counsellees.

3. Counselling relationship is neutral as regards value orientation and commitment; the counsellor is non-evaluative.

4. Counselling assumes the uniqueness of individuality; individuality is fully realized only within the context of relationship with other individuals.

5. The past concern about vocational choice should be broadened through a series of life stages.

6. Though totality of human development is assumed to be the concern of the counsellor, yet an examination of the counselling practice indicates that it is centred upon the counsellee's own perception of his problem.

7. A most essential and distinctive feature of counselling is its problem-solving dimension with respect to

objective difficulties in the external world and also with regard to associated, subjective, emotional disturbances. Counselling is a "thinking" relationship applying human reason to the problems of human development.

b. A final basic assumption, implicit in the above stated assumptions, is respect for the worth and dignity of the counsellee. Counselling situation may very well be a unique opportunity to accept the individual for what he is potentially worth, rather than what he actually is.

Williamson's approach to counselling views the counsellor as a teacher with the role and function to help the individual learn to understand and accept himself in terms of capabilities, attitudes and interests; to identify his own motivations and techniques of living; to appraise them in terms of their implications or consequences and, when appropriate, to substitute more adequate behaviour to achieve desired life satisfactions that the individual has set as his personal goal. He lists six steps in the clinical counselling which are:

1. Analysis,
2. Synthesis,
3. Diagnosis,
4. Prognosis,
5. Counselling or Treatment, and
6. Follow-up.

Analysis consists of the collection of information and data about the student or counsellee which can be used as valid and reliable basis for the counselling process. The tools for this step of counselling are:

(*a*) Cumulative records,

(*b*) the autobiography,

(*c*) the interview,

(*d*) the time distribution form,

(*e*) the ancedotal records, and

(*f*) psychological tests.

The case history is a method of integrating all the data and consists of a comprehensive record including family history, health history, recreational interests and habits.

Acoding to Williamson Synthesis is as the process of summarizing and organizing of the data from the analysis in such a manner as to reveal the student's assets, liabilities, a adjustments and maladjustments. Diagnosis consists of the interpretation of the data in terms of the problems indicated and the assets and liabilities, the strengths and weaknesses of the student. It is arrived at by a process of logic involving inference and is thus the opposite of analysis. Diagnosis involves three major steps:

1. **The identification of the problem.** This is descriptive and not a mere application of a label.
2. **Discovering the causes.** This involves a search for relationship, past, present and potential, which may lead to an understanding of the causes of the symptoms.
3. **Prognosis.** This can be a part of the diagnosis or a separate step in the process of counselling, depending upon the specific information available.

Where the outcome of a problem or condition is known, the prognosis becomes a part of diagnosis. An example is the diagnosis of too "low intelligence" which will indicate "certain failure if the counsellee tried to take up engineering as a career". Here the diagnosis of low intelligence has led to the prognosis or prediction of the most likely future performance of the counsellee. Both diagnosis and prognosis are a cooperative undertaking between the counsellor and the counsellee; the latter takes the major responsibility in the understanding of himself in so far as he is intellectually able and emotionally willing to do so.

Counselling is the stage at which the counsellor helps his counsellee to answer certain questions for himself, like: how did I get this way what factors and conditions caused this behaviour? What is likely to be the future development if this situation continues? What could be the alternative or modifications, and how can they be brought about? How can I produce the desirable changes? In answering these questions the counsellee becomes prepared to solve adjustment situations before he becomes so involved with self-conflicts and evaluations that deep and complicated therapy is needed.

Among the rational theories of counselling, Thorne has presented perhaps the most comprehensive approach to personality, its disorders and their treatment. The approach is based on the medical model and considers personality disorders as analogous to physical disease. Counselling and therapy, according to Thorne, include all forms of case handling derived from a scientific evaluation of the individual case by competent personnel.

The basic assumption of Thorne's approach is that different conditions require different treatments, depending upon their nature and etiology; the methods or techniques of counselling are thus differentially effective. Thorne discusses various methods under different categories of problems. While there is some logic in this organization, it seems to be more oriented to symptoms than to etiology. Also, some methods are relevant to more than one categories which leads to an overlap and repetition in the pre-sentation. Moreover, his findings are presented more in terms of opinions and experience than on the basis of any scientific or empirical evidence. As a report of one man's reading, thinking and experience, it is valuable; as a scientific basis for counselling practice, it is of interest mainly as an illustration of the inadequacy of an attempt at integrating all information and developing an eclectic approach to counselling.

Learning Theory Approach to Counselling

Counselling is concerned with behaviour change and must, therefore, involve learning and be concerned with learning theory. Learning theory, however, has not been developed to the point where it can be applied widely to practical situations, particularly to situations involving abnormalities of behaviour or deviation from normal behaviour. Also, there is no single theory of learning, but theories of learning. So, it is not clear which theory is most useful, most valid, most comprehensive or most applicable to the kind of behaviour dealt with in counselling. Theories of learning are limited, in general, to relatively simple behaviours of animals or of human beings in laboratory situations.

It is interesting that early discussions are limited to one theory of learning-reinforcement theory—and its relation to or implications for counselling and are further limited to the interpretation or translation of methods of counselling or therapy, such as psychoanalysis, into learning theory terms. The approach of Dollard and Miller is influenced by psychoanalysis and relates psychoanalytic methods to reinforcement learning theory. Conditioning theory has recently being more systematically but differently applied to counselling. These approaches are more manipulative and controlling than the approaches of Dollard and Miller and the Pepinskys.

Eysenck refers to the use of conditioning methods in counselling or psychotherapy as "behaviour therapy". This term has also been used recently in connection with the application of operant conditioning to the counselling interview. Operant conditioning is differentiated from classical or respondent conditioning in that while in the latter a new stimulus is associated or connected with a response which is normally elicited by another stimulus, in operant conditioning voluntary or spontaneous behaviour is strengthened by reinforcement or discouraged by the lack of reinforcement.

The recent work on operant verbal conditioning has not yet been integrated into a learning theory approach to counselling. In verbal operant conditioning 8 is required to emit verbal behaviour as part of a given task and E reinforces a pre-selected class of 8's verbal behaviour by carefully controlled verbal and non-verbal behaviour cues. Thus, an interviewer during the counselling process can, by his reactions to the verbalizations of the counsellee influence verbal behaviour. The counselling process, in this way, is at least in part, explainable and understandable in terms of operant conditioning or the reinforcement of selected verbalizations of the counsellee. The counsellor shapes the verbal behaviour of his counsellee leading him to talk in a particular manner about particular topics. When the counsellee talks realistically, rationally and positively, he is reinforced. The counsellor becomes a "social reinforcement machine". The effectiveness of the reinforcement process and so the effectiveness of counselling can be maximized by the planned, deliberate use of these techniques. While there is little research concerning the use of this technique in actual counselling interviews, there is no question but that such conditioning operates in all approaches to counselling. There are some questions pertinent to counselling and relating to verbal operant conditioning which need to be considered here:

1. Verbal operant conditioning may lead to the "right" verbalizations in clients, but it can be questioned whether this leads to any changes in attitudes, feelings, values, beliefs or changes in overt behaviour. To the behaviourist, attitudes and feelings are unimportant; what matters for him is the overt behaviour. Yet, there still remains the question of whether changed verbal behaviour generalizes to changes in other kinds of behaviour or even to changes in verbal behaviour in real life, outside the interview situation.

2. The effectiveness of conditioning is related to the personality of the counsellor. There is evidence that the subject-counsellee responds best when the experimenter-counsellor is more than a "social reinforcement machine", applying or withholding rewards in a predetermined manner. It appears that to be most effective, he must be interested, attentive, concerned and understanding. These attitudes are expressed in ways that are reinforcers.

3. Even if a change is accepted the question is that of the persistence of the change. What is the duration of the change, how long does it persist or is it a permanent change? The available research on conditioning indicates that when reinforcement is discontinued, the conditioning weakens and disappears or is extinguished.

There is no question, however, about the existence of verbal operant conditioning or its importance in counselling. It is not a simple process, but is influenced in many ways and by many variables in the counsellor, the counsellee and the situation or atmosphere and the interactions among these. Much more study and research is necessary before we can know the extent and limits of the technique and its relation to other aspects of counselling.

Conditioned reflex approach to counselling is another application of learning theory to counselling. It assumes inhibition as a single common element or cause of psychological disturbance. The cure for psychological problems, according to this approach is disinhibition. This approach relies mainly on excitation which consists essentially of encouraging, instructing or directing the counsellee to express his feelings and emotions freely.

Pepinsky propose that the counsellor can and should function both as a practitioner and as a scientist in the counselling situation. He may do this by applying the methods of scientific investigation to counselling—observation, drawing of inferences, formulation of hypotheses involving prediction of future counsellee behaviour and the testing of these hypotheses and observations by further observation.

Pepinskys select a reinforcement theory as a means of illustrating its application. According to this theory, irrational behaviour is learned and it may be changed through learning or relearning. Their key concept is that of anxiety as an irrelevant drive which prevents the counsellee from responding to drive evoking events in ways which lead to drive reduction.

Counselling, according to Pepinskys, is an interaction between the counsellor and the counsellee, the purpose of which is to change the counsellee's behaviour. The counsellor achieves this purpose by creating conditions which consist essentially of the reduction of counsellee anxiety through the counsellor's acceptance and permissiveness and by means of interpretation. As anxiety is reduced in counselling, the counsellee learns to discriminate among stimulus events related to anxiety arousal; there is a reversal of the process of stimulus generalization. Although verbal behaviour initially is anxiety-reducing, it becomes inhibitory since spoken responses are not anxiety-reducing when they are made at the time the anxiety-producing stimulus originally occurred.

According to Pepinskys, within the limits set by native endowment, the culture transmits through social learning, the responses previously learned and generally manifested by its members. The "cultural context" provides conditions assumed to be antecedent to subsequent learning by individual. General definitions of age and sex roles, social class the membership and ethnic and religious identifications influence individual development. Also, the more specific influences of conditions peculiar to a family affect social learning. These antecedent social conditions are beyond our control but the knowledge and understanding of these conditions facilitate the drawing of meaningful inferences about the function of specific events in the life and development of the counsellee.

If counselling is to occur, the counsellee must talk and he must return for further interviews. This is likely to happen if his anxiety is reduced. The counsellor may contribute to the reduction of anxiety by showing liking and respect for the counsellee, by indicating that he understands the counsellee and by being friendly, warm, accepting and permissive.

Anxiety, as a learned drive, is both a product of previous learning—the socialization process—and one of the inferred determinants of present behaviour. A certain amount of "socialized" anxiety is necessary for acquisition of appropriate social responses or of social roles. Some individuals appear to possess too little anxiety to learn or achieve. These may be underachievers, the unmotivated or the socially immature pupils identified by teachers; they are unlikely to come voluntarily to the counsellor. When such a person is referred, the counsellor has the task of arousing enough anxiety to motivate him to continue in counselling.

The reinformcement-expectancy theory of social learning defines personality as the interaction of the individual and his meaningful environment. Behaviour is goal-directed and is determined not only by goals or reinforcements but by the anticipation or expectancy that these goals will be achieved. Under this theory, three basic constructs are proposed to describe and predict behaviour. (1) Behaviour potential is a function of, (2) expectancy and (3) reinforcement value. The same concepts have been stated in broader terms as follows: *(i)* the need potential is a function of, *(ii)* freedom of movement and *(iii)* need value. Maladjusted individuals have low freedom of movement with high need value, that is, they have low expectancies for gratification and high goals.

Counselling is directed towards changing expectancies and reinforcement values to allow for satisfaction and reinforcement. Social learning theory emphasizes the acquisition of new adjective behaviour rather than elimination of poor responses. The emphasis on learning leads to emphasis on rational, problem-solving approach to counselling with possible neglect of feelings and emotions. The reinforcement-expectancy theory of social learning is an advance over the traditional learning theory approaches in at least two respects.

1. The concept of expectancies makes this theory look toward the future rather than the past.
2. The concern with the social aspects of learning and behaviour generates a counselling situation concerned with present behaviour and with its future consequences.

Psychoanalytic Approach to Counselling

Psychoanalysis as a technique of dealing with emotional problems developed by, Sigmund Freud during the first decade of the twentieth century. Through psychoanalysis Freud delved into the unconscious motivation and studied the influence it has on the behaviour of an individual. According to Freud the determinants of human behaviour operate at three levels; conscious, preconscious and unconscious. Conscious level is what in common language we call awareness, preconscious are the experiences which can be recalled easily without much effort. The unconscious is made up of the urges and desires which the individual is born with and on the other hand it contains thoughts, memories and experiences which were once conscious but, due to certain associations, have been repressed or pushed out of memory. They may be pushed out of awareness because they were painful, unapproved by the social milieu in which the individual lives or shocking and shameful.

The principle of unconscious has been used by Freud and other psycho-therapists in the treatment of behaviour problems of various types. The theory behind the psychoanalytic technique is that people are often not aware of their motivation and that a great deal of behaviour is motivated unconsciously. The therapist, through his interviews, helps the client to bring the unconscious motivation to the conscious level. When this is achieved, it is believed that the patient develops an understanding of the causes of his symptoms and that helps him in modifying his behaviour Though psychoanalysis in too is not accepted by all therapists yet some of its basic principles especially the unconscious motivation is widely accepted and applied in psychotherapy and counselling. The therapists who use psycoanalysis as psychoanalytic therapy differentiate between the two the latter is not only shorter, it is less intensive, being on a once or twice-a-week basis instead of daily. It is conducted in a face-to-face setting instead of with the client on the couch. It is more active, directive or manipulative than orthodox analysis. It is with psycho-analysis that the study of the role of feelings and emotions in psychological experience originated, as a reaction against the rationalism and intellectual emphasis of the then current psychology.

Bordin's psychological counselling, while somewhat eclectic in nature, is probably the only approach in general counselling which utilizes psycho-analytic theory and principles. According to Bordin, the distinction between counselling and psychotherapy is quantitative lather than qualitative. Counselling relationship is characterized by much less intensity of emotional expression and relatively more emphasis upon cognitive and rational factors than is the relationship in psychotherapy. Psychological counselling includes educational and remedial counselling that is not simple information giving or teaching but involves emotional and motivational aspects. Counselling is closely related to education, since both share the same general goals.

There are a number of assumptions a bout personality theory underlying psychological counselling. Behaviour is organized in a net work of interdependent systems which includes nuclear attitudes, emotions and impulse systems. While certain aspects of behaviour may include only the periphery of the net work, most of the behaviour involved in problem situations taps far reaching systems of motives and emotions. The larger the system involved, the more extensive the change of behaviour which occurs.

No definite sets of diagnostic categories are useful for counselling but it is important to understand the counsellee in terms of basic impulses and satisfactions. The greater the total knowledge the counsellor has about the counsellee, the deeper the understanding he can have about what he is feeling. Care must be taken that intel est in the counsellee's history and his potential feelings does not lead to neglect of the significance of his current behaviour.

The process of counselling is initiated when the counsellee faces a problem which he feels inadequate to handle without assistance from a professional person. Usually the counsellee perceives his problems as pretty much outside himself. He must recognize and accept the fact that his own feelings have been an important factor in his problems and he must take responsibility for himself and his problems. Counselling is not an abstract, rational discussion of external problems, but a relationship which includes some emotional commitment and involvement on the part of both the counsellee and the counsellor. Psychological counselling does not attempt to bring unconscious conflicts into consciousness and resolve them, it is concerned with the ways in which these conflicts appear in conscious and preconscious actions. In counselling increased insight into ego defenses is won through the counsellor's interpretation of omissions, contradictions, denials and forgetfulness as these appear in the coumellee's story. Through this process the counsellee is helped to approach his situation realistically, control some of his tendencies towards self-defence and to become more effective in controlling the distorting effects of the conflict.

Client—Centred Counselling

The counselling approach which was at first called non-directive is now called client-centred and is best represented by the writings of Rogers. The non-directive or client-centred counselling does not aim to do something to the counsellee or for the counsellee. Neither does it purport to induce the counsellee to do something about himself but it assists him in his development, in maturity and thus enables him to cope with his problems effectively. The client-centred counselling hypothesizes that man is rational, socialized, constructive and forward moving and that each individual has the potential for development and self-actualization. Counselling releases the potentials and capacities of the individual. This approach is based on the personality theory which is called self-theory because of the central importance of the self or self-concept in it. It is essentially a perceptual, or more specifically, a phenominological theory. Phenomenology assumes that although a real world may exist, its existence cannot be known or experienced directly but is felt or inferred on the basis of perceptions of the individual.

The phenomenal field is the person's own unique world of experience determined by his own individual and personal perception of his environment. These experiences and perceptions may stay at the unconscious or they may become symbolized by virtue of some striking association and thus may continue to operate at the conscious level. Another and related element in the self-theory is the organism which is the total individual and functions in the following ways:

(a) Reacts to the phenomenal field as an organized whole to satisfy its needs. Its one main objective is self-enhancement.

(b) Denies symbolization to some experiences that are inconsistent with the self-concept, so that they remain unconscious, it can also give them a distorted symbolization.

(c) Ignores its experiences when they lack perceived relationship to the self.

(d) Organizes its experiences into some relationship to the self and in doing so it symbolizes its experiences so that they become conscious.

Still another element in this theory is the self which is a symbolic elaboration of a part of the personal and unique experiential world of the organism's interaction with the environment, particularly as a result of evaluational interactions with others. It is an organized; consistent conceptual "gestalt" composed of perceptions of the characteristics of the "I" or "me" and the perceptions of the relationships of the "I" or "me" to others and to various aspects of life, together with the values attached to these perceptions. Thus defined, the self is modifiable, it is not rigid, it may change as a result of maturation and learning. The values which are a part of the self are either acquired through experience and learning or they may be passed on to the individual through traditions, social customs and mores. In a way the latter also ultimately amounts to learning through conditioning. As learnt behaviour these values are also modifiable and like to change.

Interaction of Organism with the Self

According to Rogers, there are two behaviour-regulating systems: the self and the organism. These two systems can operate in the following alternative ways:

(a) In opposition to each other—when the organism denies symbolization to significant sensory experiences which have failed to get organized into the self-structure. The result of this denial is tension and maladjustment. Under these conditions both the organism and the self strive together for the satisfaction of the basic needs of the individual but once this aim is achieved, the self and the organism go their own different ways. This causes a real discrepancy between the actual experiences of the organism (usually operating at the unconscious level), and what the self is conscious of—the self-concept.

Awareness of this discrepancy on the part of individual makes him feel unsure of his direction which may lead to insecurity and anxiety. It often leads to vague fears, vague unfulfilled needs and lack of decision. Persons under these conditions describe their problems thus, "I cannot decide on anything", "I don't know what I want to do", "I am afraid of something, I do not know what". According to Rogers, the person who denies some experiences must continually defend himself against the symbolization of those experiences. As a consequence, all experiences are viewed defensively as potential threats rather than for what they are. In inter-personal relationships words and actions may be perceived as threatening when in reality they are not. Such an attitude proves a hindrance to acceptance of others but encourages fear of attack from others.

(b) Work together—if all sensory and visceral experiences of the organism are assimilated and integrated into a consistent relationship with the self-concept then the consequence is well adjusted behaviour. Rogers has theorized that self-concept is not static; it is a dynamic concept the structure of which can be modified and revised so as to assimilate and include new and so far threatening experiences.

By adopting a non-threatening attitude the counsellor helps his client to feel accepted and secure so that he does not feel the need for defences he had built around him to safeguard and protect his "self". If this accepting attitude on the part of the counsellor is consistent then very soon the counsellee experiences that even the new facets which he reveals of himself are accepted by the counsellor. With support given by the accepting attitude of the counsellor, the client ventures to explore the new experiences. Just like a child frightened of dark places can venture to explore the darkness when accompanied by and holding the hand of his father and discover that there is nothing frightening about it, the counsellee also ventures to explore the new and frightening experience with the support of the counsellor's accepting and assuring attitude during the counselling process. Gradually, he starts feeling free from the frightening threats, feels more secure and sure of himself, is able to take his own decisions and feels responsible for such decisions.

Client-centred counselling has proved helpful because it respects human dignity, freedom and rights. It aims at helping the counsellee grow, learn how to solve his own problems and thus be self-reliant in facing life. Client-centred counselling has been criticised because, it is believed, it is useful for only slightly disturbed counsellees; it is insufficient to modify behaviour of the seriously disturbed patients. One needs to remember, however, that not all techniques can be handled effectively by counsellors. The counsellor must adopt the technique which is best him and his counsellee.

Existential Approach to Counselling

Existentialism is in part an outgrowth of the phenomenological movement in philosophy. Existential philosophy is concerned with nature of man, with the existence in the modern world and with the meaning of his existence to the individual. The man as a subject can never be separated from the object which he perceives or experiences. The objective fact depends upon the subject's relationship to it. Existentialism focuses upon the individual's experience particularly the non-intellectual modes of experience, and upon existence in its total involvement in a situation within a world. Its frame of reference is in man, with the full range of his fears, hopes, anxieties and terrors.

There is no single existential psychotherapy; rather there are numerous approaches. Existential philosophers do not constitute a single school; there are differences and conflicts among them. All the same, there are some common aspects or elements basic to all existential approaches to psychotherapy and counselling:

1. Human beings differ from all other animals in their capacity for being aware or conscious of themselves as well as of the events that influence them and of the past, present and future as a continuum. This makes choices and decisions possible, and man is thus responsible because he can choose. Man is free. He is what he makes of himself; heredity, environment, upbringing and culture are alibis.
2. It is impossible to think of the subject and the world as separate from each other. Man lives in three worlds simultaneously:

(a) The biological world without self-awareness.

(b) The world of inter-relationships or encounters with other persons, involving mutual awareness.

(c) The world of self-identity or being in itself.

3. The human being is not a static entity, on the contrary, he is in a constant state of transition, emerging, becoming and evolving. Man actualizes himself or fulfills his potentials by continually participating in a world of things and events and always in encounters or dialogue with other men. Counselling is a dialogue in which the client is enabled to develop certain human qualities. The "being" is not something given once and for all, but is constant by developing.

4. "Being" implies the fact of non-being and the meaning of existence involves the fact of non-existence. Man is aware of the fact that he must die and that he must face this fact. He is conscious of isolation, loss of individual identity, alienation or emptiness.

5. "Being" is not synonymous with the introjection of social and ethnic norms. The self-esteem based on a sense of being is not simply the reflection of others' views of onc. Individual is not a carbon copy cut from social pressures and norms but is unique, singular and irreplaceable and thus significant.

6. The threat of non-being, because it is always present in all individuals, is a source of "normal" anxiety, hostility and aggression. Anxiety affects the very core of the individual's self esteem; it involves a conflict between being, on one hand, and the loss of present security on the other. Guilt is the failure to fulfill one's potentialities.

7. Man has the capacity to transcend and rise above his past. He exemplifies transcendence in bringing the past and the future to bear upon the present, in thinking in symbols, in seeing himself as others see him and, most characteristically, in the capacity to be aware that he is the one who is acting.

Three concepts of existential psychotherapy are especially significant:

(a) The concept of existential neurosis, according to which emotional disturbances are a result of an inability to see meaning in life rather than repressed drives, a week ago, life stress or trauma.

(b) The concept of therapeutic relationship as an encounter, a new relationship opening up new horizons rather than a transference relationship repeating the fast.

(c) The concept of readiness for therapy. There are critical points when the client is ready for therapy, and when rapid change and improvement are possible.

Though these elements and concepts seem to characterize most of existential therapies, yet, they are not sufficient to develop an existential psychotherapy or counselling. The existential approach is not a system of therapy, although it makes important contributions to therapy. It is not a set of techniques either, though it may give birth to them. It is a concern with understanding the structure of the human being and his experience which should underlie all techniques. The centeral task and responsibility of the counsellor, according to existential approach, is to understand the counsellee as a being in his world, technique follows rather than precedes understanding.

While existential therapists appear to use many of the techniques common to other approaches, six aspects or emphases seem to characterize existential therapies and distinguish them as a group from other approaches:

1. Existential therapists are flexible and versatile, adapting their techniques with individual clients and with different phases of treatment of the same client, depending on what is necessary to best reveal the existence of this particular client at this moment of his history.

2. Existential therapists utilize psychological dynamics such as transference, repression and resistance but in terms of their meaning for the existential situation for the patient's own immediate life.

3. Counselling aims at helping the counsellee experience his existence as real which includes becoming aware of his potentialities and being able to act according to them.

4. In counselling situation the counsellor concentrates on the "present" ; the past and future are involved in so far as they enter into the present experience which includes not only the counsellee's experiences outside counselling but also the relationship with the counsellor.

5. Emphasis is placed upon the reality of the counsellor-counsellee relationships in which the counsellor is concerned not with his own problems but with the understanding and experiencing the being of the counsellee through entering and participating in his field.

6. The counsellor tries to avoid behaviour which would impede or destroy the existence of full presence in the relationship.

7. Existential therapy helps the client to develop the attitude or orientation of commitment. Such an attitude involves decisions and actions with commitment to a specific point in one's own existence.

These aspects of existential psychotherapy are hardly sufficient to base practice on. It is necessary that the concepts be implemented by methods or techniques and it would be supposed that the concepts and principles of existentialism are different than other theories so as to suggest different methods and techniques. No thorough and systematic statement of existential therapy, its procedures, methods and techniques, however, is available anywhere.

There is a striking similarity between existentialist concepts and client-centred therapy which has been increasingly emphasizing the immediate experiencing of the counsellee. The phenomenology represented in existentialism is probably developed and implemented in client-centred therapy better than in any other systematic approach to psychotherapy. Clientcentred therapy is most concerned about the counsellee's perceptions and the importance of the counsellor's participation in the counsellee's internal frame of reference.

Techniques of Counselling

Different theories and approaches suggest techniques of counselling which are commensurate with their individual philosophies and best suited to the achievement of aims and goals of counselling as defined through their specific orientation.

Williamson proposes five categories of counselling techniques: (1) forcing conformity, (2) changing the environment, (3) selecting the appropriate environments, (4) learning needed skills, and (5) changing attitudes. He goes on to say that there are no techniques appropriate to counselling of all students so that no text can give complete directions for counselling a particular individual case. The counsellor's techniques must be adapted to the individuality and uniqueness of the counsellee.

The only generalization that can be drawn is about the techniques to be used during the interview, which is the mainstay of the counselling process. These techniques have been discussed by Williamson under five headings:

1. **Establishing Rapport.** When a counsellee comes to the counsellor, the first thing to do is to put him at ease by greeting him cordially and avoiding any semblance of impatience or ill-humour. The factors, which provide a foundation for rapport include the deserved reputation of the counsellor for competence, respect for individuality and keeping confidences and relationship with the student prior to the counselling interview.

3. **Advising and Planning a Programme of Action.** The counsellor begins with the counsellee's choice, goal, point of view or attitude and points out the favourable and the unfavourable data; he weighs the evidence and explains why he advises the student in that particular way.

   Williamson is "directive" enough to suggest that the counsellor should state his point of view with definiteness. He should avoid being dogmatic but he should not appear indecisive. The counsellor is not afraid of direct advising because the student often is not able to recognize the implications of the data or is unwilling to recognize them. He suggests three methods, which can be used in advising the counsellee after the presentation of the data: *(a)* Direct advising in which the counsellor frankly states his own opinion. This approach may be used with tough-minded students who persist in an activity in spite of the danger of failure. *(b)* The persuasive method is useful when the data clearly indicates a definite alternative.

3. **Cultivating Self-understanding.** The counsellee must have an understanding of his assets and liabilities before he can be helped to want to utilise his assets and overcome his liabilities. This requires the counsellor to be experienced in test administration and interpretation of test scores. Test scores provide a firm basis for diagnosis and prognosis in the counselling process.
4. **Referral to other Personnel Workers.** Since no counsellor is competent to work with all kinds of student problems, he must recognize his limitations, know the sources of specialized help and advise the students to seek the help from appropriate sources.
5. **The explanatory method is the most desirable method in counselling.** In this the counsellor carefully and slowly explains the diagnostic data and points out the possible situations, which will utilize the student's potentialities. It involves a careful and detailed reasoning of the implications of the data.

   Carrying out the plan. Following the choice or decision of the counsellee, the Counsellor may provide direct assistance in its implementation.

Williamson believes that the counsellor is an available role model for youth to consider. As a possible model, the counsellor should express a hopeful and optimistic philosophy in his behaviour. His behaviour should exemplify reason and intellect and should indicate that he is carrying on his own independent intellectual life, that he is a "broadly informed and cultivated educator" as well as competent in his own field. The use of intellectual analysis and reason, however, should not be formal and impersonal. Williamson's approach therefore, though rational, does not ignore feelings and emotions.

Techniques of counselling are highly important in Thorne's personality counselling approach. He has organized counselling methods under five headings, which represent the types of problems and stages of the counselling process. They are: *(a)* Methods for dealing with presentation of complaints, *(b)* Dealing with emotional factors in maladjustment, *(c)* Methods of influencing the counsellee for therapeutic purposes, *(d)* Maximizing intellectual resources, and *(e)* Methods for intellectual reorientation. As a general rule, Thorne advocates that passive methods of counselling should be used unless definite indications exist for more active methods. Specifically, the plan of counselling is determined by the following factors and criteria:

1. **Specificity of Action.** A specific method is the one which acts directly on the etiologic factors in the disorder.

2. **Economy of Action.** That method which is most quickly and economically effective should be preferred.

3. **Natural History of the Disorder.** The pattern of development of the disorder must be understood for the most effective choice of method of counselling. Specific methods need to be applied at the optimum time in order to achieve maximum effects.

4. **Failure of Progress.** When a counsellee fails to respond to counselling more drastic methods are applied. When no rational approach is possible, when plans have failed, every possible method is used.

5. **The Distributive Principle.** In distributive counselling the Counsellor directs the treatment actively and according to a plan, adapting to the course of treatment and counsellee progress.

6. **Total Push.** Every possible influence and technique should be brought to bear in a concentrated manner.

Counselling methods, according to Thorne, may be placed on a continuum from directive and regulatory at one extreme to passive and non-directive at the other. He believes that the distinction between active or directive and passive or non-directive counselling is an artifact, they are methods to be used according to the indications of the case. They should not be treated as dogmas of different schools or systems of counselling. Thorne makes the following suggestions for their use:

(a) In general, passive methods should be used whenever possible.

(b) Passive techniques are, usually, the methods of choice in early stages of counselling in order to permit emotional release.

(c) Active methods should be used only with specific indication and with the minimum of necessary directive interference.

(d) Complicated methods should be used only when the simpler methods have failed.

(e) Directive methods are usually indicated in situational maladjustment requiring the cooperation of other persons.

(f) Some degree of directiveness is inevitable, even if it is the decision to use non-directive methods.

(g) All counselling should be client-centred, that is, the counsellee's interests are paramount.

(*h*) Every counsellee should be given the opportunity to resolve his problems non-directively; inability of the counsellee to do so is an indication for more directive methods.

Methods of directly and actively influencing the counsellee have been in disrepute but this is so, according to Thorne, mainly because they have been abused and inconsistent with the prevailing orientation of counselling. Nevertheless, there are counsellees who are unable to move towards goals by their own efforts alone and who require active intervention and direction. Some of the methods that directly influence the counsellee are the following:

1. Suggestion is the process of influencing of the ideas, feelings or actions of another person without direct command or appeal to intellectual functions. The technique of suggestion is facilitated if, *(a)* it is kept to a minimum and used where indicated, *(b)* is not used too early, *(c)* positive ideas are emphasized, *(d)* negative suggestions are avoided, *(e)* benevolent rather than dictatorial authority is used, *(f)* suggestions are repeated often, *(g)* the counsellee is prepared to accomplish the suggestion, *(h)* the truth is adhered to, and *(i)* the counsellor is cheerfully assuring.
2. **Pressure, Coercion and Punishment.** Modern counselling rejects the use of any punitive methods but there may be situations in which the suppresive methods of pressure, coercion and punishment are useful. Such techniques should be used with a firm, kind and under-standing authoritarianism. Restraints and punishments are necessary in dealing with the behavioural excesses of immature and a social personalities. Indications for the use of pressure and coercion include the failure of other methods, the

presence of uncontrolled emotionality, the need to face reality, the need to establish dominence-submission ratios and the need to regulate or control a social behaviour where the counsellee cannot act or where he is indecisive. They should not be used unless indicated and they should be abandoned if they stimulate frustration, defensiveness or aggressive reactions.

3. **Persuasion and Advice.** Where some directive action is indicated, persuasion and advice may be useful in obtaining cooperation from the client persuasion and advice imply dependence and lack of responsibility in the client. These methods have fallen in disrepute because they tend to limit themselves to symptom removal and ignore emotional elements. Persuasion includes pointing out the facts of the situation to the client, explaining causal relationships, showing why the client should change his attitudes or habits, pointing out future consequences of maladjustive behaviour, encouraging the facing of reality and introducing alternatives for action.

Techniques Suggesed by Learning Theorists

While Pepinskys give no systematic discussion of techniques, Dollard and Miller believe that from the point of view of the counsellee, the novelty of the counselling situation lies in its permissiveness. He is allowed and encouraged to talk, his statements are received by the counsellor with an even warm attention. The counsellor is understanding and friendly; he is not shocked by what he hears and does not evaluate or criticise. The permissiveness, applies to thoughts but not to actions. There are definite restrairits on the counsellee's actions while he is under counselling. He is not encouraged to take significant decisions, such as change of job, change of courses or marriage, while counselling is in progress.

Free association is used to get as much information from the counsellee as he has to give to the counsellor. The free associations are not interrupted with questions from the counsellor but whatever gaps may be left after the primary sessions, are filled through the questions of the counsellor. By that time he can ask appropriate questions in context with the information the counsellee has already released.

On the basis of the materials provided through free associations, the counsellor develops an understanding of his counsellee and is able to empathize with him. The counsellor sorts out this information, makes his own diagnosis and interprets the counsellee's problems to him. The skilful counsellor makes well thought out interpretations and does not base them on mere hunches. He waits until he has strong evidence for his hypothesis before be attempts an interpretation. The fewer ill-founded notions the counsellor utters, the greater his authority when he does speak.

Finally, the therapist or the counsellor teaches discrimination to his client. He calls his counsellee's attention to a problem area in order to evoke new discriminations. He also discourages certain responses by labelling them fake or doubtful. The counsellor is thus an operator in the field of language, exciting learned drives, administering learned rewards and eliciting adequate sentence chains to guide instrumental responses. Generalization to similar sets of stimuli can be facilitated if their similarity is pointed out.

According to the social-learning theory structuring continues throughout counselling and consists of a discussion concerned with the purposes and goals of counselling, the plans of the counsellor, the respective roles of the counsellor and the counsellee and the attitudes of each. The purpose of structuring is to get the counsellee to attend to, react to or concern himself with the appropriate things, rather than leaving the situation ambiguous or leaving counselee-learning to mere chance.

In structuring, the counsellor attempts to make it cleat to the counsellee that while counselling includes understanding his attitudes and reactions and discovering alternatives to them, this is not sufficient as the counselling process; the counsellee must be motivated to change and be willing to try out new bebaviours. Limitations of counselling are also made clear to the counsellee.

During the process of counselling, the counsellee must feel that the counsellor is concerned with him, interested in him, wants to help him and likes him. The acceptance of the counsellee as he is, without judgement of moral inadequacy, on the part of the counsellor, is necessary for successful counselling. Reassurances such as:

1. The counselee's problems are real and that seeking of counselling help is not an indication of weakness.
2. Counselling can be successful and can lead to satisfying alternative behaviour.
3. The counsellee is capable of achieving specific goals, are required in counselling.

Catharsis as the recall and reliving of earlier painful experiences without the original punishment, occurs and is useful in some cases. Catharsis as ventilation of feelings to a warm sympathetic, accepting counsellor reinforces the counsellee's defences but with proper direction from the counsellor, it may result in insight. Positive results of catharsis are outcomes of guided new learnings and the direct reinforcement provided by the counsellor. Insight can be intellectual and emotional; the former is usually verbalization of understandings without any influence on behaviour. Verbalization or understanding of the underlying bases of behaviour, on the other hand, may lead to the development of new expectancies through the recategorization of previous experiences.

During the process of verbalization the counsellor helps his counsellee by guiding him through interpretations. Interpretations consist of focussing the counsellee's attention on particular aspects of his experiences or by directly suggesting explanations of relationships. Almost, all the verbal responses of the counsellor may be considered is interpretations. Thus, the question of how much the counsellor should interpret is essentially the question of how active the counsellor should be. The social learning therapist/counsellor would be fairly active in order to provide new experiences, ideas and relationships.

Techniques Used and Psychological Counselling

Since many people with vague conflicts and problems come for counselling, the counsellor needs information before committing himself to any specific course of action. He may obtain this information in the initial interviews. The counsellor is alert to the implications of the sequence of the counsellee's communications, the relationships between topics and the connections between persons discussed under succeeding topics. He may use psychological tests to aid in obtaining a diagnostic understanding as a basis for decisions about acceptance for counselling and about the conduct of the counselling process.

In opening the initial interview many counsellors try to establish rapport through small talk and general socialization. The counsellee may be impatient to talk of his problem and thus may resent this small talk. The counsellor should be sensitive to the feelings of his counsellee and should handle the interview accordingly. Sometimes the counsellee comes with an urgent problem, which cannot be postponed until he has acquired the capacity to meet it. In providing the solution, however, the counsellor must be careful that he does not underestimate the resources of the counsellee and must not provide more help than is necessary. The counsellor should be sensitive to the counsellee's ability for interaction in counselling relationship. He should be able to maintain just the right distance so that he can help the counsellee to adapt to the counselling relationship. In the beginning the counsellor feels the need to understand the counsellee.

After information has been gathered through interviews and psychological testing, the counsellor proceeds to interpret the data with the counsellee. The aim of interpretation is to review the information with the counsellee so that he may understand his feelings, emotions and may be able to see the alternative feelings and actions under the peculiar situations that he is living in. Interpretations can be for clarifications, which try to crystalize the counsellee's thoughts and feelings, to focus his attention, to pick out a theme or to summarize. These interpretations are usually in the form of questions and simplified restatements. Interpretations are also given through comparison when two things are placed side by side to show similarity or contrast-past behaviour may be compared with the present to underline the similarities or differences. Interpretations may also attempt to interpret the wish and defense the two components of the conflict. This type is labelled "wish-defense" interpretation. The counsellor's role is that of suggesting partial interpretations while the coumellee makes the final and complete interpretation. Awareness of relationships does not automatically change reactions or behaviour; the various contexts of the impulse-defense conflicts need to be brought to awareness which leads to a generalized awareness and to a less distorted action on the impulse. Intellectual and rational grasp of a single interpretation is not enough, an integrated under-standing, termed insight is required. The process of achieving insight is called" working through".

Psychological counselling is concerned with the personality of the counsellee and not only with a specific decision or situational problem. Thus, the counsellee's personality is dealt with only as it effects the decision or the problem situation and the counsellee is not encouraged to stray away. The counsellor controls the relationship by keeping close to the reality problem. More cognitive emphasis on the interpretation also limits the relationship; rational analysis rather than the communication of feelings can be encouraged. There is, however, a danger in this that the counsellee's efforts to inhibit his feelings may be reinforced by this emphasis on the rational analysis.

Synthesis of Various Approaches to Counselling

Every counsellor considers himself unique in some respect. A study of various approaches to counselling reveals a picture of complete diversity. The various points of view differ considerably in philosophy, goals and in techniques. The theoretical orientation of counsellors is based upon widely divergent hypotheses, theories and ideologies. Nevertheless, the one redeeming feature is that all approaches, given favourable conditions, achieve favourable results: the counsellee gets relief and is often enough able to find suitable solutions to his problems.

The numerous specific differences among theories of counselling relate to the nature of man and the nature of emotional disturbance; these may be reduced to a single basic difference in what Allport refers to as the image of the nature of man. He describes three models: 1. Man as a reactive being. He is viewed as a bilological organism reacting to stimuli in his environment. He is determined by his past experiences, by his past learning or conditioning and by potential reconditioning. The concepts used in this point of view include reaction, reinforcement, reflex, respondent, reintegration and reconditioning. Man as a reactive being is the image of man assumed by the behaviour theorists and by counsellors who take a learning or behaviour theory approach to counselling. 2. Man as a reactive being in depth. This is the view of depth psychology, including psychoanalysis. The man is viewed as reacting to his drives motives and needs and influenced by their past frustration or satisfaction. Concepts used in this view of the nature of man include repression, regression, resistance, abreaction, reaction-formation and recall and recovery of the past. This point of view also sees man as reacting to stimuli, but these stimuli, as contrasted with the first point of view, are from within the individual. These two models can be combined and the man considered as reacting to stimuli in the external and internal environment. 3. In contrast to these images is a third model, the image of man as a being—in-the-prccess-of-becoming—a view of man as personal, conscious and future-oriented.

These three models form the general basis of all differing approaches to counselling. Behaviour theory, learning theory approaches and psychoanalysis fall in one group-viewing man as a reacting being-and client-centred and existential approaches in the other-viewing man as a being—in-the process-of-becoming.

The counselling process is viewed by different approaches. Psychoanalysis stresses insight in relation to the past, achieved by skilful interpretation. For Kelly counselling is the process of loosening old constructs and reconditioning personal constructs. For Ellis, it is a matter of convincing the counsellee that he has been functioning irrationally and teaching him a more rational structure by which to live. The client-centred approach conceives of counselling process as the experiencing, in a psychologically safe relationship, of feelings, which have previously been too threatening for the counsellee to experience freely and fully. Behaviour therapy views counselling as the process of eliminating undesirable behaviour through desensitization, extinction and reconditioning.

The various concepts of counselling process can be interpreted, by a lay reader, as forming a continuum with highly rational approaches at one end and the strongly affective approaches on the other. In the rational approach the counselling process tends to be planned, objective and impersonal. In the affective approach it is considered as being warm, personal and spontaneous. The former approach emphasizes reason and problem solving while the latter affect and experiencing. In fact, the various current approaches tend to indicate two divergent trends in counselling; one towards a. more cognitive approach and the other towards a more affective approach.

London makes another differentiation of approaches in terms of process, which he calls insight-action dichotomy. He includes client-centred therapy, existential analysis and the various forms of psychoanalysis under the insight therapy. The differences among the insight approaches, according to London, are insignificant compared with their commonalties. The two major commonalties, which London considers sufficient for categorizing the insight therapies together are: 1. is the major instrument of counselling and the counselling session is so planned that the counsellee does most of the talking and decision-making. 2. The counsellor does not reveal his own personal life to the counsellee. He helps the counsellee to express himself and expose his repressed and unconscious thoughts which are then responded to by means of reflection, empathetic understanding or interpretation of the counsellor leading to insight or the part of the counsellee.

Action therapy or behaviour therapy, on the other hand, is not concerned with verbalization or talk but with behaviour, action or symptoms. The action therapist does not care for what the counsellee says or does not say about himself or even know about himself unless such behaviours have concrete and demonstrable value for producing change. According to London, two characteristics of the counsellor working under this approach are: 1. The counsellor assumes a much greater influence over the detailed conduct of the counselling session and, possibly, over the outside life of the counsel1ee than a counsellor with insight therapy bias would do. 2. The counsellor is much more responsible for the outcome of counselling and whatever changes take place in the counsellee than are the counsellors with insight therapy orientation.

The same dichotomy is proposed by many other writers with different titles and with different inter-pretations of the categories. Ullmann and Krasner talk of the evocative or expressive and behaviour dichotomy. They recognize that there are over-lappings in techniques, while learning theory concepts are present in expressive therapy, they are systematically applied in the behaviour therapy. In terms of rational-affective classification both insight and action counselling may be considered as rational approaches. In insight counselling, the process or approach is rational in terms of the theory of personality and its disorders; the techniques tend to be rational discussions of problems. In action counselling also, the approach is rational in terms of its underlying theory of the causation of behaviour disorders through faulty learning which must be corrected by application of specific techniques rather than by consideration of affects or feelings in a personal relationship.

An analysis of the goals of different approaches also reflects an amazingly vast range and variety. Some of the important interpretations of goals are:

1. Counselling aims at achieving the personality reorganization for the counsellee through the counselling process.

2. Counselling helps the counsellee feel better by removing disturbing symptoms.

3. Counselling aims at helping the counsellee acquire independence and develop a sense of responsibility. Or assist him to explore and fully utilize his potentialities and to actualize himself.

There are obviously many differences among the various approaches of counselling, in methods or techniques, goals or purposes and philosophy. A number of research studies conducted to study the differences in orientation of counsellors and psychotherapists support the existence of differences among counsellors. A study conducted by Sundland and Barker provides evidence for the rational-affective continuum or dichotomy. Another study conducted by McNair and Lorr also tends to support this classification of approaches or techniques. In addition, the authors of this study found a factor (D) which may indicate support for London's dichotomy. Neither the Sundland and Barker nor the McNair and Lorr study, however, would support London's classification of client-centred and existential approaches with psychoanalysis in a homogeneous insight therapy group. None of these studies included behaviour-therapists and it is certain that the results would have been different if they were included. Behaviour-therapy has added a new dimension to counselling and psychotherapy.

It seems difficult to find a common philosophy, or even a single common concept, among the various points of view regarding counselling. The concepts relating to the nature of man and the nature of emotional disturbances vary considerably. Nevertheless, as minimal as it may appear, there is agreement in the view of man as capable of changing, or at least of being challged. A learning theory approach may even assume that man is infinitely susceptible to change. Though other approaches may not be so optimistic about the changeability of personality or behaviour, clearly they assume this is possible; otherwise there would be no point in practising counselling or psychotherapy. At least one other common element lies in the recognition that, *(a)* neurosis, disturbance, maladjustment, conflict or the presence of an unsolved problem is unpleasant and painful for the counsellee, and *(b)* such a state of affairs is undesirable and warrants attempts to change it. Yet another common element is the recognition of the influence of the future, or of anticipations, hopes or expectations related to the future, on the present behaviour. In other words, the recognition that behaviour is not entirely caused by the past but is also influenced by future consequences or expectation of consequences seems to be accepted by most points of views.

In the process of counselling all approaches utilize the private interview in which verbal interaction is the major component. Conditioning, considered as a major aspect of behaviour therapy, may be used outside the interview situation but the counsellee's environment outside the interview situation is much more difficult to control than the interview environment. Moreover, the behaviour-therapy also utilizes the interview technique. A few studies conducted on the commonalties among approaches to counselling in terms of process, have found that counsellors from different schools agree upon the importance of the ideal counselling relationship in counselling process. It appears that a relationship characterized by interest, acceptance and understanding is basic to influencing others therapeutically.

Besides interview, there are a number of other aspects of counselling which most, if not all, schools and approaches to counselling share. Some of these are the characteristics of the counsellor and the counsellee and can be listed as below:

1. The counsellor must have a genuine interest in and concern for his counsellee. The counsellor should have a strong desire to help and influence his counsellee and change his behaviour.

2. All counsellors realize the importance of acceptance of and respect for the counsellee as a person and as an individual. This acceptance and respect is unconditional, and is there in spite of his problems,

difficulties and the disagreeable characteristics. In other words, a counsellor does not accept and respect the counsellee because be is behaving in a pleasant and agreeable manner but he does so because the counsellee is a person and an individual with whom the counsellor is working on a specific problem.

3. All cousellors expect their counsellees to change. The degree of this expectation may vary with different counsellors but it is always present. Counselling is possible only if there is the attitude of expectation of change.

4. The counsellee's perception of the counsellor determines the latter's characteristics and contribution. The crucial aspect of the counsellor's impact or contribution is not his actual personality or behaviour, not even his intent in the relationship, it is how the counsellee perceives him and his behaviour. Thus the counsellee's characteristics, his attitudes and set are important aspects of the relationship.

5. Another element common to all approaches is the "sincerity", "honesty" or "openness" of the counsellors. Different approaches designate this characteristic by various labels but the basic element is the same. The client-centred approach refers to it as "therapist genuineness" or "self-congruence". The existentialists use the term "authenticity". Some approaches do not refer to it in their theory but the acceptance of this element becomes obvious in their discussions.

6. Each counsellor believes in and has confidence in the theory and method which he uses. It might be hypothesized that success bears a strong relationship to the degree of confidence the counsellor has in his

approach. The failure or inability of the counsellor to commit himself to an approach tends to limit his effectiveness.

Having discussed the commonalties regarding the counsellors, it is in place to discuss here some of the common aspects of the coumellees which are accepted by all counselling approaches:

1. The counsellee when he approaches a counsellor is "hurt"—he is suffering and is unhappy because of conflicts, symptoms, unfulfiled desires or aspirations, feelings of failure or inadequacy or lack of meaning in his life. He is therefore motivated to change.

2. The counsellees also believe that change is possible and expect to change through counselling help. According to some, this is a complex factor, which may include belief that improvement will occur, belief in therapist as the major source of help, belief in the techniques or procedures and belief in the counsellee himself.

3. The counsellee must participate in the counselling process. He is not a passive recipient, as the physician's patient is considered to be, but he is active and participates in the process of counselling. As counselling is considered a learning process and all learning requires, activity—motor, verbal or intellectual—on the part of the learner. The counsellee activity in the counselling process includes self-analysis or self-expression.

4. Like the counsellor, the counsellee must also be genuine, open and honest with the counselling process. He must be keen to receive help with his problems and should be willing to cooperate with his counsellor.

The above discussion clearly indicates that there are a considerable number of factors in common among the diverse approaches to counselling. To some extent the various theories or points of view represent different ways of describing or explaining the same phenomenon. An integrated approach to counselling can be developed in view of the numerous commonalties between the various approaches. The essential nature of counselling, as universally accepted, is that it is a relationship. It is not simply a cognitive, intellectual and impersonal relationship but an affective, experiential and highly personal relationship. The counselling relationship always involves conditioning aspects. The accepting, understanding, non-threatening atmosphere of the counselling situation offers the opportunity for the extinction of anxiety or for desensitization of threatening stimuli. In this relationship when external threat is minimized, anxiety arousing idea, words, images and feelings are free to appear. The most powerful influences of behaviour are the respect, interest, concern and the attention of the counsellor. Many, if not most, of the problems or difficulties of clients involve interpersonal relationships. It is being increasingly recognized that good interpersonal relationships are characterized by honesty, openness, sincerity and spontaniety.

The counsellor is most effective when he is a person, when, in the client-centred terms, he is genuine in relationship. Counselling cannot be reduced to the essentials of technique as some of the behaviour therapists have attempted to do. The most effective influence on the counsellee is that of another person offering a genuine human relationship. When an experienced counsellor decides to eschew technique and just be "himself" with the counsellee, then he is accomplishing the following things: 1. He provides a condition, which elicits real-self-being and is spontaneous, un contrived self-disclosure in his counsellee. This can be treated as a parallel to showing the rat in a maze how the lever works. 2. He provides a strong and powerful reinforcement to real-self being in his counsellee. "Real-self-being begets real-self-being". 3. By spontaneously responding to the counsellee the counsellor also helps to extinguish many of the sickness-fostering responses made by the counsellee. The counsellor provides the counsellee with a role-model of honest healthy behaviour.

The available research evidence points out that the establishment of a particular kind of relationship between the counsellor and bis coumellee is the crucial element in counselling process. The techniques, which the counsellor uses are not so important in this relationship as what he is. What he does is not so important as the way he does it. Rogers reviews the research on this point thus, "Some of the recent studies suggest that a warmly human and genuine therapist, interested only in understanding the moment-by-moment feelings of this person who is coming into being in the relationship with him, is the most effective therapist."

***

8

Elementary Education to Vocational Guidance

It is generally recognized that vocational guidance in a school system is primarily a problem of the secondary school, including in this term the junior and senior high school and the college. Most of the remaining chapters will deal with techniques and methods used in performing the various services which make up a comprehensive programme of vocational guidance in secondary schools. But before taking up a detailed discussion of these services it seems desirable to consider what contribution, if any, organized elementary education-education for which provision is made in elementary schools-should be expected to make to vocational guidance.

In the discussion that follows, the term "elementary education" will be used to include the work the first six grades only. The seventh and eighth grades will be considered as belonging, with the ninth, to the junior high school period of education, even though in many school systems the junior high school organization has not yet been perfected.

Objectives of Elementary Education

Any attempt to determine the contribution that elementary education should make to vocational guidance must be undertaken with the objectives of elementary education clearly in mind.

Most, of the well-known statements of educational objectives were formulated in terms of organized education as a whole rather than in terms of the work of elementary schools, secondary schools, and higher educational institutions separately. This is true of the seven cardinal principles (or objectives) of education enunciated more than twenty years ago in United States, by the Commission on Reorganization of Secondary Education of the National Education Association: "(1) health, (2) command of the fundamental processes, (3) worthy home-membership, (4) vocation, (5) citizenship. (6) worthy use of leisure, and (7) ethical character." It is equally true of the more recent grouping and elabouration of educational objectives under four heads by the Educational Policies Coin-mission, namely:

1. The objectives of self-realization.
2. The objectives of human relationship.
3. The objectives of economic efficiency.
4. The objectives of civic responsibility.

Obviously, certain objectives are applicable alike to elementary school, secondary school, and higher educational institutions, though with varying emphasis at different levels. On the other hand, some, including the vocational objective especially, do not appear at the elementary level. The objectives of education as provided for in the elementary school period itself have been variously stated by different authorities. These objectives may be summarized briefly as follows: to help all children acquire common tools with which to work (command of fundamental processes) and to develop in these children fundamental habits, ideals, attitudes, methods of procedure, and appreciations that will be useful to all as individuals, as citizens, and as consumers.

Thus elementary education deals with those things which are the common need of all without regard to sex or occupation. It is concerned primarily with the things that tend to unify or integrate people rather than with those that tend to differentiate them.

Relation of these Objectives to Vocational Guidance. Accepting the validity of these objectives, the way is cleared for consideration of the subject of this chapter. On the surface it may appear that no contribution from elementary education to vocational guidance should be expected. Vocational guidance is not mentioned in any way in the objectives. Since the elementary school is concerned with the common needs of all, its function is to help all students toward the same general goal. As noted in an earlier chapter, some may travel faster and go farther than others but all are headed toward a common destination as far as the elementary school is concerned. Vocational guidance, on the other hard, while part of an educational programme, consists of a group of specialized services which are based upon individual differences and is concerned with helping individuals toward different goals. True, elementary education also takes account of individual differences. But it is interested in these differences primarily from the point of view of methods and content of teaching in order that each student may progress as rapidly as possible in the direction desired for all.

A more careful examination, however, gives rise to the question: May not some of the materials used in the elementary schools for the purpose of helping all to obtain what for want of a better term is called "general education" on the elementary level have important vocational guidance values?

Why Study the Industries in Elementary Grades? In attempting to answer the question of the last paragraph, it seems wise to consider at some length the place of one group of man's productive activities in accomplishing the purposes of elementary education. Let us take the group known as the industries, defining this term in its narrower sense as including only those occupations devoted to making changes in the forms of raw or partly manufactured materials in order that they may be more useful to man. Agriculture, mining, trade, transportation, and the professions are, for the time being, left out of account.

A Scientific Element Added to the Humanistic Element in Elementary Education. In addition to the "three R's," or the tool subjects as they are sometimes called, education long ago introduced a humanistic element into the schools for the purpose of developing the child in the direction of adjustment to his social environment. This consisted of literature, history, geography, music, art, and the like. Later, with the wonderful development of science, it became necessary to introduce a scientific element for the purpose of helping to adjust the child to his physical environment. Among the subjects included in the scientific element introduced into the elementary schools are nature study, hygiene, and elementary general science. For example, as long as it was the accepted belief that sickness was an act of Providence, hygiene had no place in the schools. But when medical science revealed the real nature of sickness and disease, particularly of the communicable diseases, such as typhoid fever and tuberculosis—showing that they are caused by germs, how they are transmitted from the sick to the well, how to avoid contracting them, and the like—then a body of subject matter in hygiene, of vital importance to the child in his relations with his physical environment, found its way into the schools.

An Industrial Element Necessary Also. Along with the scientific development, and partly as a direct result of it, has come the most remarkable industrial development the world has ever seen. Work that formerly was carried on in the home or in the little village shop, where children could see what was done, how it was done, and under what conditions (in many cases helping to do it), has been transferred to great manufacturing plants employing thousands and even tens of thousands of workers. From processes performed slowly and carefully by hand, industry has changed to processes performed by intricate and powerful machines with tremendous rapidity.

Take, for example, the manufacture of woollen clothing. In colonial times, and even later, most children saw sheep feeding in the pastures and saw them taken to the brook in the spring of the year to have their fleeces washed. Later they saw the fleece sheared from the sheep and saw the wool carded, spun into yarn, woven into doth, and made into garments, some of which kept them warm in winter. What does the average boy or girl know today, from actual observation, about the making of woollen clothing? He knows how it looks, how it feels, that it is purchased at the store, and that it keeps him warm. He knows little or nothing by experience about where wool is grown or how. He knows nothing of the processes of washing the wool, carding, combing, spinning, weaving, and finishing, as these are carried on in the great woollen mills of today, nor of the modern methods of making the woollen goods into garments. He knows nothing of the conditions under which the work is done, little of the importance of the woollen industry in the life of his time, and very little of the artistic or wearing qualities of products of the woollen mills and clothing factories. The same is true of other industries.

Social and Political Significance of Industrial Element. And while the modern factory system has deprived our children of the opportunity to see how the industries are carried on, these same industries have come to occupy a larger and more important place in the social, economic, and political problems of the city, state, and nation than ever before. The big questions that occupy Congress and the state legislatures and enter into the political campaigns are largely questions growing out of modern industry. Among them are the tariff on manufactured products in order to protect against foreign industrial competition; antitrust laws to prevent big industrial organizations from becoming too powerful and stifling competition; workmen's compensation laws; factory inspection laws; child labour laws; unemployment compensation laws; laws governing hours of labour, minimum wages, strikes, lockouts, and housing conditions in centers growth congested because of industry; and so on through a long list.

There is, therefore, abundant reason why, in order to help adjust children to the large and tremendously important industrial environment which surrounds them, an industrial element should be added to the humanistic and scientific elements already introduced into elementary education. Most children will find this industrial material, when properly presented, quite as interesting, quite as easily mastered, and quite as worth while, from the point of view of general education, as much of the material now offered in other school subjects. For instance, a study of the automobile industry, its place in the development of the country, of dependence upon it today, the principal automobile manufacturing centers, the processes of manufacturing automobiles, conditions under which the men work and live, uses of the different kinds of automotive vehicles, etc., can be made very interesting and valuable to a boy of ten years.

The Purpose: General Education. It should be understood, however, that the study of the industries under discussion has for its purpose general education. It does not aim to make electricians, or carpenters, or plumbers any more than the, study of art or music in the elementary schools alms to make artiste or musicians. It seeks to give an understanding and appreciation of the most essential things involved in the work done by large numbers of our people—work out of which arise many social, economic, and political problems. The product sought is more completely developed individuals, better citizens, and more intelligent consumers, not skilled mechanics. This general educational purpose is well expressed by Bonser and Mossman:

> The materials, processes, conditions of production and the purchase and use of the products of the more important industries may be studied for the values which such study affords in one's everyday life, regardless of his occupation. Such a study of Industrial arts, we describe as "general." To realize its purposes, we make no attempt to develop any considerable degree of skill in any of the several industries studied. Productive skill is not included in its purposes as it is in vocational education. The field includes numerous industries, not limiting itself to one industry as in vocational education.
>
> The purposes or outcomes of the general study are realized in the degree in which it helps one to become efficient in the selection, care, and use of the products of industry and to become intelligent and humane in the regulation or control of industrial production. This study is from the point of view of the problems, opportunities, and obligations of the consumer and the citizen.

Principles Governing Selection of Industrial Material for the Elementary Grades. When one attempts to select the industries that should be given attention in the elementary school, he finds himself confronted with an embarrassment of rich material. His problem is not to find enough but to select the best from the wealth before him. His guiding principles in selection must be relationship to the objectives of elementary education. Bonser and Mossman have expressed this well.

> That field of industry comes first which has the largest relationship to the common needs of life. Those industries having least relationship to the common needs of life would be omitted, judged constantly, as they must be, from the point of view of the consumer and

citizen. By this standard, industries devoted to the production of food, clothing, and shelter would stand at the top of the list, those concerned with the making of walking sticks or artificial limbs would be omitted.

It should be noted, also, that not all parts of any industry are of equal value for educational purposes. Selection within the industry becomes necessary.

It follows from what has been said concerning the relationship of the material that is chosen to the common needs of life, that the best basis both for selection and organization of this material is the uses of products of the industries.

The large uses of material products center very conveniently for classification about the needs of man for six kinds of service which are respectively: food, clothing, shelter, utensils, records for transmitting experiences, and tools and machines. The subject matter making up such an organization is found largely in answer to two questions: (1) What are the changes made in materials which increase their values to make them most useful and satisfying in meeting these six respective forms of need? (2) What are the problems relating to these changes which concern us as consumers and citizens?

What Provision for such Study of the Industries? The question naturally arises: Does not such a study of the industries require departmental teaching in the elementary school? Is it not necessary to have a teacher for the industrial arts work who is so well trained in the manipulative and art sides of her subject that she cannot adequately be prepared to teach other subjects of the elementary of school also? It is, of course, important that the teacher should be well trained in the manipulative and art sides of industrial arts. It is equally important that she should understand the economic and social aspects of this subject. But it does not follow that industrial arts in the elementary school should be taught by a specialist who teaches nothing else. As most elementary schools are now organized, the subject should have its time allotment in the curriculum in the same way as do the historic three R's and the other standard subjects of the elementary school, and all may be taught, and generally will be, by the same teacher.

If, however, the platoon system of elementary education is accepted, with departmental teaching of some subjects, then a special teacher of industrial arts may be provided. The important thing is that this subject, which touches all others so intimately, should be a unifying factor in the curriculum and full advantage should be taken of the many opportunities to correlate other subjects with it. This is more likely to be done when one teacher has responsibility for all the work of a class, provided this teacher is properly prepared to teach industrial arts as well, as the other subjects. A number of school systems have demonstrated the practicability of this procedure in elementary schools by using projects which combine study of industries with reading, writing, arithmetic, geography, and other subjects.

However, details of organization and method need not be considered, further. They may safely be left to those whose special field is industrial arts in elementary education. What does concern us here is the place that study of the industries should have and gradually may be expected to attain in organized elementary education and the general character of such study.

Under the names of manual training and household arts, some of the aspects of industrial arts as discussed above have long been accepted as part of elementary education. But the manipulative and process aspects in a very limited number of industries have claimed nearly all the time and attention. Often the work has had little relation to other subjects of the curriculum and less relation to life. In recent years, the tendency has been in the direction of a much broader and more genuinely educative treatment of the subject.

Relation to Objectives of Elementary Education. It is apparent from this discussion that study of the industries in the elementary school not only harmonizes with the objectives of elementary education, but is essential to the realization of these objectives, provided the study is so conducted that it results in desirable changes in behaviour.

> ....In one's selection, use, and enjoyment of the products of industry; in one's participation in the securing of just and fair treatment for producers in industry and for consumers of products; and in one's taking an intelligent interest in the processes, products, and workers in industry as changes in these result from the use of new materials and methods.

It has been noted that there is a wealth of material for this kind of study from which selection must be made upon the basis or relation to the needs of life. It has been noted that the tendency today in elementary education is strongly in the direction of this type of study of the industries, in place of the older type which emphasized chiefly manipulation in a very limited range of activities, some of which have little relation to the life of the average individual.

Similar Study of Other Fields of Activity Desirable. There is no good reason, however, why such study should be limited to that field of human activities, broad as it is, which is known as the industries. Agriculture, mining, transportation, trade, the professions, and the other large groups of occupations also have a close relationship to the lives of all of us, as well as have those activities which bring about changes in raw materials in order to fit them for human use. A similar study of these other fields along with the industries is essential to full realization of the objectives of elementary education.

The growing of cereals such as corn, wheat, and oats; of fruits, of vegetables, of fibre crops such as cotton and flax, and of livestock; the extraction of minerals such as Iron, coal, copper, oil; lumbering; the transportation of these raw materials of farm and mine and forest· the manufacture of these materials into finished products for human use; the distribution and sale of these products as they came from the factories; and the many kinds of professional, public, and personal service—all these are involved. The extent to which they are involved is determined only by the time that can be devoted to this kind of study and the way the subject matter is organized and presented.

Taken together, these constitute the world's work at which humanity spends more than one-third of its waking hours, be means of which it subsists, arid through which are provided the products and services humanity uses and enjoys.

Surely nothing is more closely related to the needs of life than this material. And, if treated in its broader aspects, nothing is richer in value as material of general education. Here, in the world's work, history, geography, community civics, and elementary sciences find their applications and, to a large extent, their motivation. Here also arise the problems of arithmetic and the need for reading; and writing. It would be quite possible to make the world's work the integrating factor of elementary education.

Significance of such Study for Vocational Guidance. When elementary education gives to boys and girls such an acquaintence with the world's work as is needed for purposes of general education, it will make all the contribution to vocational guidance that may be expected of it. While the objective throughout is general education, a background of information concerning occupations will be builtup which will be of distinct value later when a decision concerning the vocation to be pursued/must be made, or when a more comprehensive study of occupations is undertaken for vocational guidance purposes. The information will not be detailed or complete concerning any occupation. It will not deal with requirements for success or opportunities for advancement. It will place different occupations in the scheme of the world's work for the child. It will give him some idea of the nature of the work done in different occupations and of the history, the social status, and the contribution to society of many of the more important occupations.

Occupational Information for Guidance Purposes. In his earlier writings Brewer expressed the view that definite provision should be made in the elementary grades for supplying occupational information to children for vocational guidance purposes. To be sure, he was thinking in terms of an educational and social situation quite different from that of today. Thirty years ago students left school earlier to enter employment. Also there was somewhat less disposition then than now to make provision for study of the world's work for purposes of general education in the elementary school.

That Brewer's views have changed with the passing years is shown by the fact that his only reference to this subject in his more recent book is, "Vocational guidance may be faint in the picture for the elementary school, but it should be clear for later education". The writer would go further and say that study of occupations in the elementary grades for vocational guidance purposes is neither essential nor desirable. Choice of occupation is a differentiating factor in the lives of children. The elementary school is concerned with those elements of study and experience that are of common value to all, regardless of sex or future occupation. Let the differentiating factors be reserved for a later period of education.

It may be argued that some children leave school at the end of the sixth grade and will have no help in choosing an occupation unless it is provided in the elementary school. Where compulsory education laws are enforced, the number of normal children who leave school without completing the sixth grade is extremely small. Subnormal children constitute a special problem and should be handled in special classes, as they are in most city school systems. What vocational guidance they need, and they need some even though most of them will engage in unskilled work all their lives, can and should be provided in their special classes. In systems too small to maintain special classes for subnormal, the problem should be handled individually without modifying the elementary school work as a whole in order to meet the needs of a few.

Records of Students in Elementary Schools Valuable for Guidance Purposes. Another fact that should not be overlooked in considering the contribution of elementary education to vocational guidance is that an adequate record of the student's responses to his experiences in the elementary school will provide information concerning his achievements, aptitudes, limitations, and personality traits that should be of value in counseling him later regarding his 'vocational plans. Information from this source will, of course, be considered by the counselor in relation to information of similar type derived from the pupil's secondary school record. Especially important will be the consistency or lack of it between the pupil's elementary and secondary school records. Effective counseling, as will appear more clearly later, depends so much upon adequate significant data concerning the one counseled that the counselor cannot afford to neglect the rich contribution of the elementary school in this respect.

Education in the elementary grades, aimed chiefly at development of the individual along lines of good citizenship and good consumership, is concerned with the common needs of all regardless of their future occupations. All are traveling toward a common goal though at different rates of speed and with different degrees of success. Vocational guidance, on the other hand, is concerned with helping individuals toward different goals.

For the purpose of helping children to understand and appreciate the ever-expanding industrial aspects of their environment, an industrial element has been added in elementary schools to the older humanistic and scientific elements. Material included in this industrial element is, of course, selected on the basis of its relationship to the common needs of all. The aim is not to make better artisans or to help in choosing an occupation but to make better individuals, citizens, and consumers. Similar material related to other occupational fields-agriculture, mining, transportation, trade, the professions, and the rest-must be used also if the objectives of elementary education are to be realized.

However, the information and experiences acquired by children in the elementary schools as a result of this study of the world's work will serve as a valuable background when those same children later face the necessity of choosing an occupational field for themselves. Thus, while study of occupations for vocational guidance purposes has we place in elementary schools such study for purposes of general education may make an important contribution to vocational guidance. Elementary schools make a valuable contribution to vocational guidance also by means of carefully planned, well-kept cumulative records which follow the children as they advance through the secondary schools and are available for the use of counselors.

***

9

Phenomenon of Transfer of Learning

The skill, knowledge and attitudes acquired in one subject or topic or type of situation influence skill, knowledge and attitudes in another situation. The influence may be positive, *i.e.,* facilitation; or it may be negative, *i.e.,* inhibition. When the effect is positive, we have positive transfer of learning: when the effect is negative we have negative transfer of learning. The influence may be little or great but it there is. When learning one task makes learning a second task harder we speak of negative transfer. Learning to drive a scooter is inhibited by learning to drive a motor cycle. Gears while driving a scooter are changed with hand; whereas while driving a motor cycle gears are changed with feet.

The use of the result of previous learning in situation (B) that differs in some way from that in which the original learning took place is transfer of learning. For positive transfer, it is necessary that one must be able to recall previous learning at least in situations so similar to those in which learning originally occurred.

Educational Importance of the Phenomenon

If there is any formal education as that we have in schools, it must be for transfer. Schools are established only with one purpose in mind that they should prepare children for meeting situations different from those met in schools. It is not enough to learn to remember the first course in chemistry or the primary principles of hygiene. Learning these courses should help the child in solving problems in daily life. Learning should transfer. The study of chemistry should help the child in studying biology. The study of hygiene should help the child in improving his health habits.

Without transfer the preparation of children for adult life would be just as the preparation of animals to perform tricks. Without transfer education would be specific, limited and duplicative. Without transfer knowledge would not expand. Without transfer there would be no creativity, no productivity and no expansion of education. Without transfer the teacher's job would be just like that of a trainer of animals. In education transfer is a pervasive factor. All our educative efforts are directed to learning that can be transferred to other new areas, from the present to the immediate or remote future.

We teach something solely because we want they should be adopted, modified, or transferred to other similar situations. We teach art, music, literature to our students so that their daily lives may be enriched. We teach art because want our boys to become skilled in working with colours, because we desire that they should apply that knowledge or skill to everyday matters of dress and decoration. Transfer of learning is a factor that is found everywhere and in an indefinite number of places at the same time.

Why do we educate our children? It is because we want them to meet the problems of life effectively. Some of these problems we can realize beforehand quite accurately, but there are hundred and one problems that we cannot so easily anticipate. If the problems of life cannot be anticipated in advance correctly, then we cannot prepare our children to meet them successfully. If a solution cannot be found out to a problem that our children will meet in adult life, we can devise an approach to that problem when they are still in our schools. We can formulate a set of guiding principles now, which they may use at a later date. Therefore, we teach things so that they may be used, adopted, modified, or transferred to other similar situations later.

Problems of Transfer

The phenomenon of transfer of learning is essentially significant to the teacher, that be has to consider specifically: What transfers? Under what conditions? To what?

In simple terms we may put the same questions as follows. To what extent and in what way will the acquiring of skills, knowledges, understandings and attitudes in one situation affect the acquisition of skills, knowledges, understandings and attitudes in another situation? Do such subjects as mathematics or foreign languages have potency for developing in a student habits of attention, consistency of thinking, etc., so that their study will help him to meet any intellectual problem more effectively than if he had not read them? To what extent does skill acquired in Mathematics transfer to life? To what extent does the study of Sanskrit roots and conjugates increase vocabulary in other Indian languages? To what extent does training in simple addition help one in subtraction? Do laboratory experiments in biology help the general understanding of biological phenomena or do they sometimes leave the students confused?

The student of educational psychology is mainly concerned with the following types of problems about transfer:

(a) How can we get more transfer values?

(b) What teaching methods facilitate the occurrence of transfer?

(c) What subjects are more likely to stimulate transfer?

Various Theories of Transfer of Learning

Under what conditions transfer takes place? To what? How can we get the maximum transfer? These are the problems which psychologists have tried to study and have offered several explanations. Each of these explanations or theories has a great educational significance.

The Theory of Mental Discipline. The first forerunner in the field was the theory of Mental Discipline. At one time it was believed that mind is made of certain faculties. For example, there is a faculty of memory, a faculty of reasoning, a faculty of judgement and so on. There is nothing very wrong in this belief. There are generalized areas in the brain that function primarily in certain mental activities. The second aspect of the theory of Mental Discipline is that these faculties can be sharpened by exercises or by mental discipline just as the muscles of the body are made strong by physical exercise. This aspect was questionable. The educational practice then emphasized the necessity of developing the faculties of mind by vigorous mental exercise. It was believed that the more vigorous the exercise, the more disciplined the faculties became. Different subjects like Mathematics, Greek or Latin were taught for their disciplinary value. It was believed that their study in some mysterious way trains the faculties of the mind.

A great importance was laid on training. There was no attempt to make school work pleasant. Students were given multiplication tables to memorize and it was held that memorization of these tables would develop reasoning. No consideration was given to the utility of the subject so long as it provided strenuous mental activity. "How did such a strenuous mental activity train the mind?" Nobody was allowed to also. Even now we have parents and educators who believe in formal discipline theory and hence like to keep such subjects in the curriculum for their disciplinary value.

The concept of mental discipline is now not so popular with teachers and psychologists because experimental studies have shown that memory is not improved by memorizing *sutras* of Panini nor is reasoning automatically improved by studying Algebra or Geometry or by memorizing the multiplication tables. 'How did this change come about? is a long story not to be related here. But a salient feature of the research findings may be indicated in brief that led to discarding of the old theory of Mental Discipline.

The following four types of researches had been made to shelve the doctrine of mental discipline:

(i) Training in a subject or activity to improve performance in it.

(ii) Training in school subjects to improve mental function.

(iii) Training a faculty to improve it.

(iv) Training in school subjects to improve life adjustments.

It is an indisputable fact that training in a subject will improve learner's performance in it. Training a faculty to improve it was the major concern of William James and others who showed that memory could not be trained by memorization.

Researches had been made to find whether training in school subjects improves mental functions. Does training in Algebra improve problem solving ability? But impartial evidence could not be obtained. The researches conducted to find whether training in school subjects improves life adjustments fail to provide adequate data because of the difficulty in adequately measuring life adjustments. The net result of all such studies is that the concept of mental discipline has become unpopular with psychologists.

Theory of Common Components. In ninety's Thorndike stated on the basis of his experiments that: "Learning is facilitated in a second situation to the extent to which it possesses factors that were present in the first situation."

What he meant thereby is that the amount of positive transfer is directly proportional to the presence of the identical elements in the two situations. The theory has now been modified and states that the amount of positive transfer from one situation to another depends on the extent to which the new situation resembles and is recognised as the practical one. We have now common components in place of identical elements. The two situations are said to have common components when they are similar in content, have similar methods and procedures, and possess the common aims. Thus, the study of Sanskrit may facilitate the learning of the vocabulary of modern Indian languages to the extent that similar or identical roots are a planned part of teaching and are recognized by the student. Transfer depends in part upon the extent to which there are similarities between two situations and also upon the extent to which the learner perceives similarities between them.

It means that there is some transfer when the two situations are similar. But for maximum transfer to occur it is necessary that the learner should perceive the similarity. The perception cannot occur unaided. It occurs most likely, when the teacher makes an effort to indicate what the common components are. He can prompt students to discover and enumerate the common components and the similarities between the situations. It means that, however similar the two situations may be, maximum transfer would not occur unless there is a teaching for transfer.

Transfer of Learning through Generalizations. The theory of Generalizations states that generalizations learned previously are applied to a novel situation resulting in more rapid learning then that which occurs without previous practice. In other words, the theory says that the degree of transfer depends upon the extent to which experiences in one situation are consolidated into generalizations.

An illustration of the theory of generalization is given in the report of a pioneer experiment by Charles H. Judd. The experiment was made to inquire into the relation of special training to General Intelligence. One group of boys was given a full theoretical explanation of refraction. The other group was left to work out experiences without theoretical training, These two groups began practice with a target under 12 inches of water. In the first series of trials both groups gave the same results. The learning of theory seemed to be of no use to the first group. Now the 12 inches of water were reduced to 4. The difference came out very strikingly. The boys without the knowledge of the theory of refraction were very much confused. The practice gained with 12 inches of water did not help them with four inches. Their errors were large and persistent. On the other, hand, the boys who, had the theory, fitted themselves to 4 inches very rapidly.

Thus, there is a greater possibility of transfer from one situation to another when generalizations are so mastered that they can be applied with facility and ease.

The theory emphasizes the importance of generalizations in learning process. But it must be remembered that the learner should realise that the possibility of further application exists. If the learner does not realise this, transfer will not be maximum. It is the teacher who can make the boy feel that there exists a possibility of further application of a principle learnt. If he wants transfer he has to teach for transfer. For example, a student can be made to memorize certain principles, but if maximum transfer is to be achieved, the teacher should give numerous examples of the principles. Such a method will increase the possibility of application of the principles to new situations.

Materials in the classroom should be so taught and learnt by children, that they are related to subsequent experiences. For example, the principle of refraction of light was so taught in the experiment just quoted above that the experimental group of boys adjusted more readily to a change of depth. As it is not possible to educate children and youths for all future situations, it is the teacher's duty to stress upon learning that contains principles and broad generalizations to a greater extent than mere recitation and memorizarion of facts. More than that, if the student formulates his own version of the principle, it is more productive and superior to having the teacher give it.

The basic teaching consideration is: if you want transfer, teach for transfer. Transfer must be a planned objective. Ideals, generalizations, principles should be the conscious objectives of the teacher who wants maximum transfer. Generalizations in the classroom are generally made from a limited number of specifics. They involve inductive and analytic process. But it is the duty of the teacher to get them tested and retested in various other situations.

Gestalt Theory of Transfer. This theory does not differ essentially from the theory of common components or from the theory of generalizations. It gives much more needed emphasis to understanding as an aspect of transfer. It states that transfer from an old to a new situation occurs when the learner (individual) recognizes them as being similar or when he understands the common principles. It is not enough for transfer to take place that the two situations should have common elements or there should be an existence of all pervading generalizations. It is the learner's response to the total situation that matters. For example, students who learn neatness in drawing geometrical figures do not, in general, transfer neatness to other situations because they do not perceive the similarity between the two situation. It is the perception of common elements in two situations that aids in transfer being maximum. So we conclude that the amount and kind of transfer depends upon the existence of common elements, the possibility of formulation of generalizations and their application, the teaching methods and the response of the individual.

The theory of mental discipline is outmoded and psychologically unsound. The theory of common components and the theory of generalizations offer better explanations of the amount and kind of transfer. They provide a framework for educational practice. They suggest that if the teacher wants maximum transfer he should do the following:

(i) Formulate clear-cut objectives.

(ii) Challenge pupils to formulate their own principles.

(iii) Point out both facts and processes that are common in various situations.

(iv) Encourage the understanding of principles.

(v) Encourage overlearning that makes facts and principles more readily availahle to new situations.

(vi) Show how these principles can be applied in various situations.

(vii) Help students develop a desire to search for opportunities for transfer.

Experimental Findings on Transfer

The experimental finding in the field of Transfer of Learning arose out of investigations made to attack the Theory of Formal Discipline. It was believed that the study of certain subjects trained the mind in some mysterious ways. By giving exercises in thinking, attention and remembering, these faculties of mind could be improved. The best exercise ground was the study of languages and mathematics. Greek and

Latin and Euclid were regarded as the main subjects to improve mental functions.

Investigations have been made to show that no subjects as such can strengthen the muscles of the mind and enable children to learn to think. In one investigation E.L. Thorndike gave to a group of students course in mathematics and to the other group course in cooking. At the end of the courses, both groups were given test material consisting of analogies, absurdities, problems in arithmetic reasoning to find the relative influence of a year's training in increasing ability in thinking. He found that the differences between the scores were so small that the influence of the subject studied seemed quite unimportant.

The inference of this finding is that when good thinkers studied Latin and Greek, these seemed to make good thinking. When good thinkers are studying physics and chemistry, these subjects then tend to make good thinkers. If, however, good thinkers begin to study dramatics and physical education, these subjects again will make them good thinkers. So it is not the subject studied that can improve thinking, but it is the original ability which is an important factor in the development of thinking.

The educational implication of the findings of such investigations is that general training in methods of work, attacking a problem, and thinking can be obtained in almost any subject in proportion as teaching is intelligently directed to this end. Every subject can serve the purpose of general training. No subject has a disciplinary value and hence a subject should be taught in the classroom for its intrinsic worth and not for the fact that it trains the mind.

Other experiments conducted in the field infer that if we want transfer we must teach for transfer. The most economic way to master any arithmetic skill is to practise it consistently, and not practise some other skill and hope for transfer. In

1927 Starch investigated the problem to determine how practice in mental multiplication spreads to other arithmetical processes, such as, addition of 3 place numbers, addition and substraction of fractions, multiplication of 4 place numbers and division of 3 place numbers. The trained group was given practice in multiplication of a 3 place number by a one place number 50 questions a day for two weeks. At the end of the practice session the trained group made scores 29% greater than made by the control group. Similarly, it has been found that drill in arithmetical computation appears not to transfer to problem, solving in arithmetic. In an experiment two groups of 36 boys were equated on the basis of a pretest. One group practised arithmetic computation 30 minutes a day for 10 days: the other group practised drawing. At the end of the practice session both the groups were tested in arithmetic reasoning and both of them obtained the same average score.

For transfer the method of teaching is very important. When there is teaching for transfer the amount of transfer can be greatly increased. The lack of transfer from school room situation to practical life so far as instruction in mathematics specially is concerned is mainly due to poor instruction and lack of student motivation. If the teacher shows the applicability of general rules and procedures and develops them systematically, transfer is greatly increased. For example, Curtis demonstrated that the trained group on a test of scientific attitudes after getting a training for four months showed definite superiority over the control group and thus illustrated the fact that in teaching science there should presumably be a special effort to develop and generalize an understanding of scientific methods and to achieve a broad scientific outlook.

The reason why transfer does not take place from learning of mathematics to real life situations lies in the fact that mathematics teaching is specific and the similarity between the classroom and the life situations is little. The theory of Identical Elements or the Principle of Similarity states that the greater the similarity between two situations the: greater is the amount of transfer. Taking both the conclusions together we can say that Transfer takes place in proportion to the similarity of situations and it increases in magnitude if there is teaching for transfer, *i.e.,* if the teacher lays emphasis on the similar elements in his teaching.

A growing interest has been shown in the studies of transfer in the less formal classroom situations chiefly with a view to discovering the degree to which learning in one subject area advances or retards learning in another.

Two studies were made by Thorndike and his assistants. Both dealt with the transfer effects of various school subjects. The purpose of these studies was to find out the effect of a year's training in a particular subject on rational thinking. Thorndike inferred from the results that the influence of the subject studied seems unimportant. There have been several interesting investigations to find out the transfer value of generalization in problem-solving and reasoning.

Teaching Methods and Transfer

In a previous section we have tried to answer the above question in part, because certain suggestions have been given cursorily. It should be remembered that no subject in itself has transfer value. Those, who defend the place of mathematics in the improvement of reasoning, forget that it is the method by which mathematics is taught that improves reasoning and not the subject itself.

Subject matter, of course, has to be learnt (and overlearnt even) before it can be transferred. So subject-matter is important. But subject-matter without transfer has no value. The teacher should know what is to be transferred and to what. For example, the knowledge or skill gained in simplifying an arithmetical fraction will facilitate (or transfer to) learning of the same process in Algebra. Hence, we must, as teachers, consider while determining instructional techniques, what is to be transferred and to what. In general, certain habits, skills, ideas and ideals are to be transferred. To what they are to be transferred the teacher has to determine himself.

The following are the instructional techniques that faciliate occurrence of transfer:

(i) Establishing clear-cut goals.

(ii) Challenging students to formulate their own principles.

(iii) Encouraging understanding of principles, processes, relationships.

(iv) Emphasizing ideals and attitudes.

(v) Encouraging overlearning.

Establishing Clear-cut Goals. The learning in the first situation can facilitate learning in the second situation only when the previous learning has been effective. For previous learning to be effective it is necessary to have clear-cut goals before the learner. He should know where he is going. The teacher also should know where he is leading the learner to. Stated simply, your objectives may be development of knowledge, habits and attitudes. Every teacher wants to give knowledge and every learner wants to gain new knowledge. But he should be led to develop a desire to gain new knowledge every day. He should feel that he is worthy and able. He should develop confidence in himself. There are some of the desirable attitudes the teacher may aim at developing. Similarly, he may develop in the learner good work habits which include system, thoroughness, perseverance and determination. So, for effective learning and consequent transfer both the teacher and the taught should have clearly defined aims.

Understanding of Principles and Processes. The teacher has to adopt such instructional techniques in his day-to-day teaching that encourage the understanding among pupils. 'Learning by doing' is a teaching method which develops understanding. So learning by doing has a greater transfer value than learning by drill. If the teacher wants that his pupils should learn the role of citizenship in human life, he should encourage them to participate actively in student government.

Activity projects, field trips and T.V. lessons are ways to check mere verbalization and improve understanding. But their use in teaching can be justified only when the method of presenting subject matter facilitates transfer. Common elements in Solving problems in Arithmetic and in actual life situations, for example, may be found out and indicated.

The student should be encouraged to understand the principles, processes and relationships well. A principle is a statement which compresses many factors and conditions. For example, the Principle of Conservation of Energy states that energy can neither he created nor destroyed. It is not sufficient to simply state it, memorize it or read it from a Text-Book on Higher Secondary Physics. It is necessary for the student to understand the many factors and instances that have gone into its formulation.

Understanding processes is also very important for effective learning. It is not enough that a child should be able to solve a mathematical sum or give an answer to a question. Teachers should ask their students to explain why and how they got a certain solution. They must be able to discuss the steps they have taken in getting a certain answer.

Understanding of relationships is also very useful. A teacher teaching a modern Indian language, for instance, should try to indicate relationships between the vocabulary of that language and Sanskrit from which it might have descended. The teacher of mathematics or science should relate these subjects to everyday life.

Encouraging Self-study. Giving principles, processes, facts, and skills readymade to pupils is nor enough. Let them try to give their own version to a principle. Let them try to search out a process. Let them study facts themselves. Let them discover something for themselves. It has been experimentally found that self-discovery shows more transfer than instruction in which the teacher gives the facts, principles of skills himself.

✸✸✸

10

Tests in Guidance and Counselling

Tests are used to serve three main purposes, namely, prognosis or prediction, diagnosis and research. Tests are used for selections in which the tester tries to predict the suitability of a particular candidate with respect to the specific purpose in mind. Tests are used by employers to select suitable candidates for various job situations, we use tests to select students who should be admitted to a college or university, we also administer tests to predict the job or career in which the individual will make a success. In all these situations we are predicting future success of an individual in a particular position; test results are a prediction of the future performance of an individual.

Tests are also used for diagnosis especially in guidance and counselling situations. A student who starts failing in school is referred to the counsellor whose main concern is to find out the causes of this failure which could not and had not been predicted from the student's previous record or the test results. In his effort to locate the cause of this behaviour the counsellor would start with a number of hypothetical causes. The boy could have failed because of lower intellectual level than required for higher studies, he could have failed because of lack of basic knowledge which he should have acquired through earlier schooling or he could have failed because of poor study habits and many similar reasons. The counsellor who begins with the above hypotheses will administer the tests which purport to test these aspects of human behaviour and make comparisons between the performance of the student on these tests. In his mind the counsellor would be trying to answer the question, "Does he perform better on intelligence test or reading test? How well does he measure on the background knowledge which he is expected to gather during his school days?"

While in predicting future performance the tester compares the test scores of the individual with those of the others who took the test under similar conditions, for diagnosis the counsellor compares the same individual's scores on various tests given to him under different conditions. The emphasis is on studying the performance of the individual under different circumstances and tracing the difficulties and causes of these difficulties. Only after he knows the difficulties and their causes is the counsellor in a position to help and guide the person. On the accuracy of diagnosis will depend the precision of prediction and the effectiveness of guidance and counselling.

As samples of human behaviour in controlled and standardized situations, tests are of great help in research. When used for research, tests must be treated as completely valid measures of certain human characteristics. Knowing the drawbacks of tests, it is hard for any good research worker to believe that they are infallible, yet the researcher must treat test scores in his experiment as accurate quantification of real and useful variables. Tests can be used as control variables, descriptions of human behaviour or to verify hypotheses about relationships among behaviours, only if they are treated as accurate and dependable measures. In con" elusion one may say, tests are intended to contribute to the analysis and description of individuals, evaluation, prediction and guidance of their behaviour and education.

The applied psychologist uses the test for prediction purposes and encourages all those working with human behaviour in one way or another to use test scores before making decisions. Decisions especially in case of selections need reliable and valid information about differences among people and in specific behaviour of the same person at different times. Every test tells about the difference in performance of people at the moment. These differences would not be very meaningful unless they were related with variation in some other behaviour pattern. For example, let us take the case of a personnel officer. Before he makes selection for a particular post he requires information about the people seeking that position. Let us further suppose that he flashes a few letters for them to remember and recall; in the results he finds that one man is able to grasp and recall correctly only four letters while another has given him eight correct letters. The difference hardly means anything unless he is able to relate this ability with the accuracy with which the two persons will be able to register correct signals or the efficiency with which they will be able to promote a reading programme in an educational institution. If this relationship between the test and the practical situations is established, then the personnel officer can rightly predict the better scorer to make a better traffic policeman or a better helper in the reading programme of a primary or secondary school.

The reader must have guessed from the above statement that the test results are not final and complete in themselves. On the basis of the test scores alone the personnel officer, mentioned above, can come to two conclusions about the same person, he can be a good traffic policeman or a primary teacher in charge of the reading programme; surely there is a great deal of difference between the two professions. His final decision has to be made after he has considered many other factors about the person including his academic qualifications, personality characteristics, likes and dislikes, interests and aptitudes. For many of these factors he can use other tests while for some he can look up the history and school records of the person concerned. Thus we can conclude that no test should be used alone.

Tests are used in higher education also and with time and research their use is becoming progressively popular. Test results serve two important purposes for the institutions of higher education:

1. Help in making selective admissions to colleges.
2. Work as a criterion for placement in various classes and courses.

With independence, the philosophy of education in India has undergone a significant change. While previously only a few select persons could aspire to go on for higher education, now everyone who passes the high school examination wants to be admitted to a college. In effect education for the elite has come to be the education for the masses. Though every one aspires to go to college, yet to maintain the standards and the value of our degrees we do need to adopt certain selection procedures which would ensure that only the right and the most qualified persons go for higher education. If we do not resort to selective admissions, we run the risk of diluting higher education and making the graduate degrees so commonplace that they would serve no selection purpose.

Once the issue of admissions is decided we need to classify people into various levels of study, pass course, honours course, special classes and the like. Test scores can be helpful in these selections and placements also. Selection of courses, in our society, is hardly ever based on scientific findings. Usually the parents decide on the college the youngster should join and also the courses which he should take. The selection of courses is based on the likes and dislikes of the parents, the social prestige attached to various professions and sometimes the unfulfilled ambitions of the parents and other relatives who may have influence on the child's life. Interest inventories and aptitude tests are a great help in correct placement in different courses.

A great deal yet remains to be achieved in testing for selection in higher education. Testing for this purpose is far from universal in India but it is encouraging to find it being used for admissions to more and more of professional and technical colleges. Use of tests in clinical situations is common in schools and higher education. Child guidance centres and counselling centres in higher education lean heavily on tests of various abilities and characteristics. The behaviour of a student in a test situation, besides his scores on that particular test, is revealing in telling us how he works against odds, what is his reaction to failure and finally how he compares with the performance of other persons like him when placed under exactly the same conditions. A counsellor needs this information before he attempts to help the student with a problem.

Selection of Tests

Tests are standardized instruments designed to measure objectively ore or more aspects of a total personality, through samples of performance and behaviour. The standardization and objectivity of a test provides it with the scientific quality which is absent in an individual's subjective estimate of the same psychological traits and characteristics. Each standardized test is required to be administered under set conditions; standardized instructions are to be given and there is a set procedure of when the instructions are to be repeated. Sometimes each item is to be stated, in a particular manner to each candidate, time limits are set, the procedures for answering questions asked by the subject and the use of practice exercises are also indicated. The score ratings derived from such tests are not dependent upon the subjective judgements of individual examiners; the scores thus given by one competent examiner are comparable with those given by others. In selecting a test, therefore, the first and the foremost consideration is the objectivity of the test and its administration. Before we use the test we want to be sure that the objectivity, which is the main advantage of a test over the subjective judgement, is established beyond doubt.

Every test is designed and intended for use with a specified population. A test of intelligence, for example, may be meant for the ages of two years to adulthood, a scholastic ability test may be suitable for the sixth, seventh and eighth grades only. Similarly, personality tests may be meant for different age groups, sex, educational level or for particular clinical types. In selecting a test our main concern is to see that the subject answers the precise description of the standardization sample for the test.

Another consideration for selection of tests is the validity of a test. Tests are designed to measure specific traits, skills or characteristics of human behaviour. Validity is not an absolute measure, it is a relative concept. Therefore, it is wrong to ask "How valid is this test?" No test can be valid or invalid in general. The right question to ask is "How valid is this test for my purpose?" or "How well does this measure the trait that I have set out to measure?" A good test manual usually reports the validity studies which are an attempt to check how well a test measures, what it purports to measure. If not well constructed, an intelligence test can easily be reduced to a test of scholastic ability. Without proper investigation of its validity, therefore, it would be wrong to treat this test as a measure of intelligence.

The most simple procedure to study validity of a test is to conduct a follow-up study. A test score predicts the future performances of the individual but if the predictions based on the test do not correspond with what happens in actual life, the test was worthless in its predictive value. A follow-up and a careful record of the subjects who have taken the test will give a reliable index of how validly the test predicts the future performance of people. The procedure followed for such studies is to administer the test, make predictions, try the treatment suggested by these predictions and wait for the reactions and results. After suitable time interval, a record of the outcome can be obtained which may consist of the teachers' report, the counsellor's ratings and diagnosis or school grades. These records are used as a 'criterion' to measure the prediction with. This is a straight forward empirical check on the accuracy with which a particular test measures a skill, trait or characteristic of human behaviour and is known as its predictive validity.

While predictive validity involves comparison with the criteria obtained at a later date than the date of the administration of the test, there is another type of comparison made between the test results and an outside criterion. In this case the criterion is predetermined and the test and the criterion are applied to the subject at the same time. An example will be the case in which for clinical diagnosis the test results and the judgement made by the psychiatrist are compared to arrive at the final diagnosis. In this case no prediction or waiting for results is involved, the application of the criterion is immediate and concurrent with the test administration.

In achievement testing still another type of check for validity is given. Teaching aims at bringing about a change in behaviour, therefore, when measuring educational achievement we are interested in measuring the same type of behaviour and nothing else. For example, if the test is administered to measure achievement in history, it should measure only history and not political influences or the geographical facts about the country under reference. Whether the test measures the behaviour we are interested in cannot be established by comparison of the test performance with an outside criterion. Analysis and minute study of the content of each item included in the test is required for this purpose. The process of study involves examination of individual items against the purpose we have set for measurement of achievement. In the above example the worker will require to take up each item and ask himself whether the item measures history and nothing else. When he is satisfied with the analysis of one item he moves on to the next for similar analysis and study. This procedure of analysis is known as the 'content validity'.

There are times when the tests are used for no other purpose than pure research. In testing validity, in this case, the tester is interested in investigating the concepts which may rightly be used for interpreting test results. The questions which he asks himself are, what causes the subject to score a certain test score? What does a test score mean psychologically? The research worker works with the theoretical constructs and the process of validation or test interpretation is known as the 'construct validity'. To prove that a certain construct applies to a test, it is necessary for the tester to derive hypotheses about test behaviour from the theory related to the construct and to verify them through carefully designed experiments. One of the hypotheses, for example, may be that the subjects exposed to the threat of electric shock will work under acute anxiety which will reflect itself in their test scores. The effect of anxiety as a construct on the test performance needs to be proved through careful experimentation.

No test manual is known to test all these types of validity for a particular test. It is more common for the test developers to predetermine the purpose for their tests and examine the validity relative to this particular purpose. The professional demand on the test developer is limited to assume all responsibility for providing proof for the recommended use of the test. The manual should report the validity of all inferences for which the test is recommended. A user who wants to use the test for any other purpose than prescribed is expected to conduct his own validity studies.

Besides measuring accurately, the test must also give reliable measures of the ability or trait. While validity is an index of internal consistence, reliability refers to the extent to which an instrument yields consistent results on re-test. On the consistency of measurement depends the accuracy of the prediction. Reliability is a question of degree; no test is perfectly reliable. Test and re-test have never given perfectly stable scores. It is normal for individuals to differ in their performance on two different occasions; the differences can be due to chance or are the expected variations as a part of the process of growth and development. While selecting a test we need to look for a high degree of reliability.

Reliability plays an important role in influencing practical judgement about people. For example, the decision whether a student has successfully completed a course or not and whether a borderline case has improved enough to be classified as slow learner or does he stay with the trainables only, should not be decided on tests with low reliability or chance errors or variations in performance due to occasional factors. A positive decision based on chance variations may not be so serious but a negative decision based on chance factors can cause serious damage to the individual concerned.

Reliability is calculated and expressed in terms of a reliability coefficient which is a correlation between the two measurements obtained in a standardized manner, or in terms of the standard error of measurement. The standard error is calculated estimate of the amount of variation in scores on a series of measurements of the same trait. If a large number of measurements of the same object, on the same test are taken and placed on a normal curve, then the standard error is the standard deviation of these measures, *i.e.* the variation which can be attributed to chance factors such as the physical condition of the subject on the day of the test, fatigue and the difference in interpretation given, on two different occasions, or to the language used in the test items. The hypothesis is that the ability of the person remains constant from one test to another but that his obtained scores vary because of the chance factors operating on him. The concept of "true scores" assumes calculation of a typical score of the subject from a large number of samples of his behaviour. When we want to know how well a typist will type during the next six years or so, usually, we test his performance in one test administered on one particular day. This is a judgement based on a very small and inadequate sample of his behaviour and may not be reliable. The true score is the average score of a very large number of sample trials given to the subject. Error is defined as the variation or fluctuations in the performance of the individual on test and retest. The reliability calculated from such errors and fluctuations is called test-retest reliability and is calculated by finding out the correlation between the scores on the first and the second testing of the individual.

The test-retest method, however, does not answer all problems related to reliability. All variations in test performance cannot be attributed to error. Fluctuations are known to be due to growth and development or learning and forgetting process. If the retest takes place after a long enough interval, the subjects may have been learning or forgetting in the meantime. On the other hand, if the retest occurs too soon, practice effect may inflate the scores.

Parallel forms of tests have been used to overcome this drawback. Instead of using the same instrument for retest, the counsellor may use another test which is supposed to be measuring exactly the same trait, under precisely the same conditions and on the same population. As it is impossible for the same population to take two tests at exactly the same time and under identical conditions, it becomes difficult to establish that two forms are parallel. The method for estimating reliability from parallel forms is the same as the one used for calculating test-retest reliability. The only difference between the two is that the scores on the parallel forms are used instead of the retest with the same instrument. The question can be raised that the scores on two parallel forms were different because the two tests were not exactly equivalent. Since different items are used in the two forms, it is possible that the same item may be more difficult for one person and at the same time slightly easier for another. Under these conditions both time to time and form to form or sample to sample fluctuations are called errors.

'Split-half reliability' is used to overcome the difficulty of calling real fluctuations in the trait error. As two tests cannot be administered to the same subject at exactly the same time, the split-half method administers the complete test and then divides the items into two equivalent parts, each to be scored separately. The correlation between the scores obtained on one part of the test with those obtained in the other may represent a measure of form to form fluctuation only. It is often known as the coefficient of equivalence'.

Like in the cases of parallel forms there is the question of whether the two parts can ever be exactly equivalent. To establish this, item analysis can be conducted and the items can be paired according to their difficulty, content and discrimination value. One item of each pair thus formed can be assigned to each part. An easier and more commonly used procedure is to split the test according to odd and even items. All even numbered items can be placed on one half while the ones bearing odd numbers can constitute the other half. For reliability estimate the correlation between the scores on these two forms can be calculated. One problem which the test user has and that is peculiar to split-half reliability is that the length of the test is an important factor in determining its reliability. The longer the test, the more accurate will be the estimate of the typical behaviour of the individual on that particular trait. In split-half reliability when we divide the test into two parts we reduce its length and so affect its ability to measure precisely. Since split-half gives correlations on only half of the fest, a correlation is required to determine the reliability of the entire test. Spearman-Brown prophesy formula is used to achieve this estimate. In using the formula, however, it is assumed that the items added to make the test longer measure the same trait and further that the variance of the scores on two half tests is equal.

Another classical method of considering variable error is in terms of inconsistency of performance on the items within in the test. If the test is rightly arranged according to the difficulty value of the items, then a particular subject should be able to reach a point on the test before which he could answer all items correctly and beyond which he could not attempt even one item right. Clear and definite lines of this type are, however, very difficult to achieve on any test. Usually, there is an overlapping area in which the subject is able to correctly answer some of the more difficult items and unable to do the easier ones. This is where, according to Kuder and Richardson, the error occurs and the reliability of the test is lowered. Usually, our tests cannot be measures of more than one variable at a time. For example, a test of arithmetic can very easily be a test of speed in dealing with arithmetical concepts and facility with language. Reliability calculated by Kuder-Richardson method, therefore, is known as the measure of homogeneity.

Hoyt defines the variable error in a slightly different way, though his results turn out the same as those obtained from Kuder-Richardson formula. Hoyt does not consider item to item variation as error; according to him, it is all real difference, an intra-individual difference and the one which should not be involved in the estimation of reliability. This variation, he thinks, is made up of three components: true inter-individual differences, inter-individual differences measured by item variance, and error inter-individual differences.

A number of factors cause variations in the reliability of a test. While studying reliability as a criterion for selection of tests, it is appropriate to discuss some of these factors here. The specific procedure used in calculating reliability causes its own peculiar effect on the reliability of a test. The split-half reliability is bound to be higher than the parallel form reliability simply because the former has scope for practice effect and memory carry-over which is successfully eliminated by the latter. Because the parallel forms give a conservative measure, the parallel form reliability is to be preferred; that is to say, the true reliability of the test is not going to be any lower than this estimate. Split-half reliability, on the other hand, is considered to represent the upper limit of reliability. The true reliability is likely to be no higher than this estimate. Research findings indicate that any single trial method of estimating reliability results is an overestimate if applied to tests having a large speed component.

Length of the test is another factor which affects its reliability. Items on a test are a sample of all possible items which represent a given content universe. Ideally the entire universe should be included in the test but that is impractical became that would give the test an infinite length, though a person's score on such a test would be his true score. Because only a sample is possible in practical situations, the score observed is only an estimate of the true score. The sampling principles indicate that the larger the sample, the more reliable the estimate and smaller the error is likely to be on any testing. Thus, when a larger sample is taken the test becomes longer and more reliable.

The nature of the group is the third important factor effecting reliability of a test. As a ratio of the true score variance and the variance of the observed score, reliability is a relative measure. Suppose that the actual amount of error in the test remains constant but variation in the observed scores changes considerably, it is obvious that a decrease in the observed variance (which can be obtained by restricting the range of ability in the group tested) will sharply reduce the reliability of the instrument. To overcome the flaw many test publishers are reporting separate reliability coefficients for different subgroups included in the sample.

Yet another method to meet this problem is to report an index which, while a function of reliability, is independent of the variability of the group on which it is computed. This index is called the standard error of measurement, and represents an estimate of the standard deviation of the errors obtained in repeated samples. The basis and rationale for calculation of this index lies in the assumptions that it is possible to put in one group all persons having exactly the same ability. If so, their true scores should be the same but their observed scores will differ and that difference will be due to the errors which vary from person to person. If the observed score of this sample were arranged in a frequency distribution then the error components should be normally and independently distributed with a mean of zero, the mean of the observed score will be the true score and the variance of this distribution will be the error variance for reasons of this level.

Another factor which influences the reliability of the test is the extent to which the instrument is a measure of speed rather than power. A test of pure speed is the one in which the subject is sure to score right on an item if only he could reach it. The examples are tests of clerical ability in which the subject is expected to mark out every "t" or "e" that he comes across in a passage given to him. These tests are usually timed, so if he can read fast, go through the entire passage and hit at every "t" or "e" contained in it, his score will go higher. The quality of performance does not affect his score in speed tests as it does in power tests. The single trial estimate of reliability especially the split-half reliability does not allow much variation. The maximum possible difference in the split-half is one. If the time permits the subject to end his performance on an even item he will have one more score on even items, and if he ends his score on an odd item he will have one extra score on that half. Because the quality of performance does not count in these test, there is not any p08sibility of other variation. As such the reliability reported is bound to be higher than the true reliability of the instrument. Also, since, in a pure speed test, no errors are made on the items reached there are no inconsistencies in the item to item performance of the subject. As such, with methods of estimating reliability, which define error in terms of such item score fluctuations, the reliability would be increased spuriously.

General attitude of the subject is important in determining his score on the test; it would decide the variation in his performance and so the reliability of the test. His motivation, the set to respond positively or negatively and the tendency to guess affect his score and so the reliability of the test. Establishment of proper rapport and use of standardized instructions for administration of the test can take care of this factor to a great extent. Usually, physical condition of the subject is considered an important factor in determining his scores. The experiments, however, have proved that feeling unwell or headaches and mind indispositions do not affect the score of the individual in any significant measure. The individual feels that he has not done well but this feeling is the only thing which is affected by the indisposition of the subject and not his actual score on the test. The only differences observed under these conditions have been the ones which can be attributed to normal expected fluctuations.

Finally, the conditions resting in the person administering the test influence the reliability of a test. If the tester is unable to establish rapport or emphasize enough the importance of responding honestly, then the personal attitudes, referred to earlier in this section, multiply and affect the reliability of the instrument. Insufficient and varying directions, a misreading of the stopwatch, a lenient attitude of letting the subject finish an item even after the assigned time is over and a special hint in answering an item right, are factors within the test administrator which affect the reliability of the test. In view of all these, it is necessary that standardized instructions are adhered to, without allowing even minor alterations.

Evaluation of Tests

Evaluation of tests becomes important when one is setting up a testing centre or is conducting research in testing. The specific tests for evaluation can be marked after the aims and purposes of the testing programme or the research are defined but a general format for evaluation can be designed which would be useful for every test we need to evaluate. While using the test, it has been mentioned earlier, one must look for a test which serves our purpose and not just a "good test of intelligence" or a "good test of reading." Any test manual, therefore, should be approached with a definite purpose in mind; the purpose may be as specific as selecting candidates for clerical positions or as general as gathering information for future reference in counselling practice.

Next to the purpose of testing, the tester and his status determines the kind of test which should be chosen. On the tester and the time available to him depends the choice between the individual and group test, whether age or ability range should be the criterion and what level of interpretative skill should be used. For example, a test for later reference in coumelling will have to be a group test because large numbers are to be tested, it will have to cover the whole range of normal ability and should involve the level of interpretation which is suitable to all teachers and counsellors.

With general principles and purposes in mind, one approaches standard yearbooks on testing and makes a list of tests which should be considered for evaluation. Until 1967 counsellors in India had no yearbook or catalogue of tests giving precise and detailed information about the quality of tests, their standardization and subsequent research findings. In 1967, under the editorship of Dr. Leuis Long, the National Council of Educational Research and Training has printed the first Indian yearbook of testing. It is a valuable reference material for students of testing, counsellors, research workers in testing and the interested teachers. It lists Indian tests up-to-date and gives brief description of their content, the method of standardization, the norms available and validation studies, if any. It also gives information about the manual, whether it is available or not, what kind of instructions are given and whether administration is simple and unambiguous. The counsellor can hope to make a wiser selection if he consults the yearbook before using any particular test.

A definite measurement problem determines the test that may be considered. It determines the choice between the individual and group test, the age, the range of ability to be measured and the level of interpretative skills to be employed. A test, for example, to be given for later reference in the counselling centre will be a group test because individual tests for the entire school population are not feasible; it will have to cover the entire range of normal population and should be such that its interpretation and practical application are meaningful to counsellors, teachers and administrators.

Interpretation of Test Scores

The raw score obtained by an individual on a particular test, by itself, has no meaning in indicating his status in a particular group. The same raw score on three different tests may mean completely different positions for the individual tested. Let us take the example of a raw score of 150 on a test of mathematics on which the average score of a particular group is 140; on another test of history, meant for the same group, which has an average score of 100 the raw score of 150 will certainly mean an entirely different position. For selection, guidance and clinical use of the test we arc constantly making comparisons of different individuals with the group performance of the sample of equal ability and standing on a particular trait. Individual comparisons are not possible in each case under study, therefore, sound psychological tests provide test users with norms which may be in form of age norms, grade or class norms, percentile ranks or decile ranks, standard scores or any other measure depending upon the nature of the test.

Norm is an average or a typical score made on a particular test by a specific population; the score of an individual when placed next to this average will give us an idea of how far removed he is from the average or typical score. This position is not very meaningful unless we know the variation in the group. Let us take the example of a test with 100 as its mean and a standard deviation of 10 and another test with 100 mean but a standard deviation of 15. In the first case the middle two third of the cases will rest between the scores of 90 and 110 while in the second case the middle two third cases will spread between the scores of 85 and 115. As such identical score on these two tests will place the individual in a significantly different position with reference to the standardization samples. Both the mean and the standard deviation of the distribution of scores of the standardization sample are necessary for any meaningful interpretation of an individual's score on the test.

A number of indices have been commonly used to indicate the relative rank of a particular individual. It is in place here to briefly consider some of these indices. Percentile and decile ranks are med to indicate the percentage of the standardization sample that scored below the individual under consideration. If the subject is given the 50th percentile rank, then it is right to assume that 50 per cent of the sample, on which the norms were developed, scored lower than this person. The advantage of using percentile ranks is that the nature of the curve of distribution does not affect them. The only indication which they give is that of the relative position of this particular person with reference to the specific sample used for standardization of the test. His position in another sample will depend on the nature of that particular group. Deciles perform the same function as percentiles; with the difference that deciles indicate the one-tenth part of the group in which any tested person is placed by his score. Deciles are useful when the number of scores in a distribution is small; in such cases it is meaningless to make too fine distinctions in ranks.

Standard score is another index used to indicate the relative position of a person in a specific group. It indicates, in terms of standard deviations, how far a particular score is from the mean of the group. The formula used for calculation of standard scores is:

$$Z = \frac{X - M}{SD}$$

in which X is the individual score, M the mean and SD the standard deviation of the group constituting the norms. To make the position of the subject meaningful, the standard scores need to be translated into percentile ranks. This is easy to do because the number of cases, within a given number of standard deviations, in a normal distribution, is fixed and known.

T-score is a variation of standard scores in which the mean is assumed at 50 and the standard deviation of 10 while for standard score the mean is zero and standard deviation 1. To calculate T-score the standard score is multiplied by 10 and added to or subtracted from the mean T-score of 50. In this process the standard score of + 1 becomes 60 and that of – 1 becomes 40. Each standard deviation in case of T-scores is divided into 10 equal parts; this avoids the possibility of negative and fractional scores.

Stanine is a variation of standard score technique which came into use during World War II and was coined by the psychologists working with the army and the air force research units. According to this method, the entire population is divided into nine groups. The rank of Stanine 1 indicates the lowest group and includes all scores below – 1.75 standard deviations. All other units except the Stanine 1 and 9 are equal to one half of a standard deviation. A score of 5 represents the median group defined as those scores which fall between ± 0·25 standard deviations of the mean; or a range of half standard deviation at the centre of the curve. A rank of Stanine 6 represents the section of the group whose scores fall within ± ·25 and ± ·75 standard deviation. The meanings of other stanine rankings can be calculated in terms of the standard deviations. Being a single-digit system, the Stanines have certain advantages for machine calculations and eliminate plus and minus signs; other than these, the Stanines can hardly claim any special consideration over the other indices of relative ranking described above.

In review of the indices of variation discussed above, it is necessary to realize that the ultimate interpretation of all scores is based on the percentile system; the various techniques of standard scores and variants also derive their significance from the relation to the percentile system. The psychologists and test users, while interpreting test results, will always want to answer the question: "What is the percentile equivalent of a given standard score, T-score or a Stanine?"

Mental age and intelligence quotient are the indices used to indicate the developmental status of an individual on a particular scale of intelligence. The concept of mental age was introduced by Binet in 1908 with the first revision of his scale. For calculation of mental age the items are grouped according to the age levels of the subjects. While scoring, the age level at which the subject can answer all items correctly is marked and treated as the basal age of the subject. Thereafter he is given credit, in terms of months, for every additional item which he can answer correctly. The sum of the basal and additional credit, in terms of months, is the subject's mental age.

Mental age norms are also used with scales that are not arranged according to age levels; such instruments are called point scales. In these tests the subjects are given straight scores for every item attempted correctly, the total raw score is converted to mental age according to the norms provided and relevant to specific tests. Thus, on a Point scale, an individual who, irrespective of his chronological age, earns a score equivalent to the norm of ten-year old sample population, will be given the mental age of ten. In determining mental age, an individual's performance on a standardized series of test items is being compared with the performance of the average group of representative sample at successive age levels. Hence, mental age can be defined as the level of development of mental ability expressed in terms of equivalent chronological age at which the average group of individuals reach that level.

Mental age alone, however, does not adequately represent the mental capacity of an individual; it has certain drawbacks which prevent it from giving absolute measures. Experience has revealed that it is possible for individuals of widely different chronological ages to reach the same mental age on a particular intelligence test. For accurate interpretation we need to know the difference between the mental ability of a ten-year-old and an eight-year-old both reaching the mental age of ten at the same time. The concept of intelligence quotient was introduced to meet this need and consists of the ratio of mental age and the chronological age multiplied with 100 to iron out the decimal and the fractions. To make the interpretation further meaningful, the various categories or brackets of IQ need to be described in terms of the practical functions which the person in each level can perform. With his 1916 version of the Binet scale, Terman provided a table giving the percentage of children performing at each of a number of IQ levels. The person whose test performance is normal for his chronological age, earns an IQ rating of 100. The test user must be warned that the limits of these categories are arbitrary and that during interpretation the categories must be used as guidelines only. The significance of each category lies in the relative rank it indicates and its psychological, educational and vocational connotation for the individual tested.

Besides its quantitative meaning, the IQ has its qualitative significance because it indicates the subject's position in the hierarchy of intelligence. If the measure of intelligence is valid then a person with an IQ of 50 is seriously retarded and is in the lowest one per cent of the population in terms of the tested functions; a person with an IQ of 100 is the typical average individual while a person scoring an IQ of 150 is definitely superior and belongs to the top percentile rank of the group. The qualitative significance of the intelligence quotient can be illustrated by asking the question: Is the brightest of these persons three times as intelligent as the retarded one and one and one-half times as bright as the average scoring one? It is obvious that this question cannot be answered in terms of numbers; it is impossible to say how many times one person is brighter or duller than other persons tested on the same trait. But each of these intelligence quotients has certain connotations from which the trained clinical psychologist will be able to draw important inferences regarding the rate and quality of school learning, level of educability, vocational possibilities and types of interests of the person concerned. A superior and bright boy, for example, will have almost unrestricted scope for vocational placement, education and interests; a student with average IQ will have numerous job opportunities available to him, a reasonably high level of education and achievement and a range of interests but the dull child will have limited educability, a narrow range of interests and limited scope for vocational placement. These inferences are useful for educational and clinical guidance of the person but there are no psychological or statistical techniques through which one can calculate the precise proportion of superiocity or inferiority of a person.

It must be realized that the above inferences should not be based solely upon the numerical value of the intelligence quotient; due importance must be given to the clinical and other features in the test performance not accounted for in the numerical index. A bright and superior person, for example, may be of unstable personality who is failing in almost all the school subjects, a student with average score might have worked under language handicap and his lower score may be due to this handicap and not the accurate estimate of his mental ability. An experienced psychological examiner should be alert to the influence of these factors but should not infer that all or most test ratings are affected by the external factors influencing the test performance.

The educational age is often used as an index of a pupil's average level of achievement in a group of school subjects, measured through standardized tests and in terms of the average for various chronological ages in school. Some of the drawbacks of this index are: (1) There is no uniform list of school subjects for which educational ages are obtained and as such the various EAs are not necessarily comparable. (2) Even when achievement in the same school subjects is measured but with different tests, the EAs might 110t still be comparable because of the differences in the process of standardization. Educational age is used to determine the grade placement for the student; this practice, however, is doubtful in view of the inaccuracies discussed above. The most reliable index for grade placement are the grade norms which are provided with most of the tests on the market. As expected, educational age is accompanied by educational quotient which is the ratio of the educational and chronological age; its purpose is to measure whether a pupil's knowledge of a group of school subjects is commensurate with his chronological age, above or below the level to be expected of him. The formula used to calculate educational quotient is:

$$EQ = \frac{EA}{CA}(100)$$

The value of the obtained educational quotient is dependent on the reliability and validity of the achievement tests used.

Achievement quotient is another index used to indicate the educational status of the individual pupil. Achievement quotient is the ratio between the educational age and the mental age of the subject. Mental age is used as the denominator because it is considered to be more valid indication of the pupil's learning capacity. The ratio between educational and mental age is supposed to tell whether the individual is working at the level expected according to his mental age. The achievement quotient as an index of the learning capacity of the individual has the following drawbacks. All mentally superior children cannot be expected to achieve equal to their mental age. Let us take the example of a superior child with a mental age of 10 and suppose that he has passed the first class at the age of seven. In order to obtain an AQ of 100 he must have an EA of 10 which he can only have if be can learn in one year as much as the other average children are expected to master in four years. This is just not possible because the superior child, especially at the lower class levels, has not had the time and the length of schooling necessary to make EA and MA equal.

A second drawback of the AQ is that the sample population on which the achievement test is standardized is different from and not comparable with the population from which the norms for the intelligence test have been derived. Generally, the former is less representative of the population and is dependent upon the equivalance of the schools ill which the standardization was carried out. A third defect with this index is that usually, the achievement tests do not differentiate so well among the pupils as a sound test of intelligence does. This tends to reduce the variability in the former and its correlation with the latter.

Interpretation of tests is necessarily based on norms which have already been defined as average scores or values determined by actual measurement of a group of persons who are representative of a specified population. Norms, thus defined, do not necessarily mean the optimum performance of the individual. On the other hand, norms are the performance of a group of persons under prevailing conditions and reflect all the effects of omission and commission in the development of people included in the sample population. To derive reliable norms the sample must include persons with as varied background and conditions of nurture as possible. Norms must be distinguished from standards which are the desired goals or objectives which may be far higher than the achieved norms and can be achieved only under the improved conditions of development. Psychological tests measure traits and functions as they exist under present conditions; they do not aim to provide the psychologist or the educator with "what ought to be."

The complete interpretation of a person's performance on psychological tests cannot be based on his raw or converted scores only. The various aspects of standardization process discussed so far are concerned with the performance of groups of persons with normal relationships and the statistical treatment thereof; for their clinical use, the test needs to be applied to individuals under varied conditions and situations in order to prove its discriminative value among individuals at several levels of ability. Modern psychologists are placing increasing emphasis on the "patterns" of performance during test administration as clinical aids to psychological diagnosis and counselling.

A person's responses can be analysed to explore whether he possesses any special ability or disability, to diagnose the maladjusted and abnormal personalities and for discerning the mentally defectives. Persons with numerically equal scores are known to have given entirely different patterns of responses on the test performance having thus indicated an entirely different "mental organization." The objective and numerical scores and the comparative status of the individual, in the group, are no doubt important but also important to study is the attitude of the subject during administration of the test, his cooperation, apathy, degree of confidence, the manner in which he attacks a particular item, any negativism or resentment and the richness or paucity of his responses. The individual test situation can thus be turned into an opportunity for general psychological observation or a penetrating psychological interview. A psychologist or a test user must develop the skill to assess and interpret responses and to evaluate the individual's behaviour during test besides the ability to score the test and give its statistical analysis; the former he can develop through his work with individuals only. A thorough understanding of the psychological and statistical foundations and hypotheses upon which the tests are based must make the basis of qualitative analysis of the individual's performance on tests.

Ethics in Testing and Measurement

Interpretation of test scores gives the psychological examiner personal information about the individual's status in a particular group with reference to specific psychological traits and abilities which the examiner is required to guide carefully. The psychological examiners work under certain codes of ethics which, unfortunately, are not given much importance in India. As a matter of fact, no code of professional ethics has been developed by rest developers or test users in India. Some of the precautions which the test users must take and which will definitely improve the testing services are:

1. The test score must not be disclosed to outsiders without permission of the client. His score, together with other confidential information may need to be discussed with other persons in the profession but this should be done with minimum identification. Sometimes for referral purposes it may be necessary to share this information with the teachers and other agencies which is permissible, provided the teachers and the officers of the agencies are also conversant with the ethics involved in testing and measurement. The counsellor should seek permission of the pupil for this purpose; if he permits, the score can be disclosed to and discussed with parents, teachers and others who can be of help to the client. Under no circumstances should it be available to the client's relatives and others on request.
2. In the absence of any code of ethics, it has become a common practice with the test users in India to give samples of test items to the prospective testees. This is unethical. Actual test items should never be

disclosed to any person. In our psychological and educational meetings, it is common to see tests on display. This amounts to revealing the test items. For display purposes it should be sufficient to have the directions for the test administration and a few sample items but not the actual tests. During interpretation of the test with teachers, guardians and others, they should not be permitted to examine the test; only the interpretation of scores should be shared with them.

3. The tester must use only the tests which he is trained and competent to administer. It is unethical to administer and interpret tests which he is not competent to use. Often psychologists and counsellors overlook this aspect and, embarrassed to admit their limitations, they go ahead and use the instruments. Professionally it is prestigious for a counsellor to know the limits and to clearly state these limits to his client.

4. While it is permissible to provide candidates with sufficient information about the test, the traits it: measures, how to prepare for it, etc., it is unethical to provide practice or coaching for the test. In ignorance, parents have often approached the psychological examiners to give training or prepare their children for a test they are due to take. It should be an accepted practice for the tester to refuse this request. Sometime the administrators have asked the psychologists or counsellors to take up such responsibilities; it is unethical for the administrators to do so. When the students are absolutely unfamiliar with the items and the nature of the test, it is legitimate to show them some multiaptitude tests and the information booklets prepared for various testing programmes.

5. It may be considered an ethical responsibility to continue research in testing. A counsellor who keeps up with the continuing research work by others and plans his own experiments, definitely improves the quality of his testing and counselling procedures. This research may be very informal but without it testing and guidance tend to go down in quality.

Classification of Tests

Tests can be classified along three different dimensions, namely, Form of the Test, Purpose of the Test, and Content of the Test. Cronbach adds another dimension which is dependent upon whether we want to measure the maximum performance of an individual or his typical performance. We measure maximum performance of the individual when we are testing for ability. The question we try to answer is bow best can he perform under a given situation. His scores on intelligence tests, scholastic ability tests and other special ability tests answer this question to a great extent. This is the reason why modern test users insist that the client be told in specific terms that he is taking an intelligence test. Older psychologists made it a practice to introduce intelligence test, especially for younger children, as play. The modern tester argues that such an interpretation leads to misguiding the client. When we are testing him for his maximum performance, he must know and be given an opportunity to show his best. While testing for typical performance, we are interested in knowing the typical behaviour of the individual. This we do through interest tests, personality tests, aptitude tests, study habits, etc. In these tests he is not pressed to show his best performance but the counselleei is expected to show his natural and typical behaviour.

According to form we can divide tests into two distinct categories: individual tests and group tests. Tests, whether of intelligence, aptitude, ability or personality, can be administered to the individual singly and also to a group of them together. In guidance programmes for a school, the latter type is more useful and popular. The testing programme for the entire school requires testing of large numbers within a limited period. This necessitates testing in group though the individual tests are known to have certain advantages over the group tests.

The classification of tests based on purpose is the most extensive one. Depending upon the purpose of test users, we have tests of intelligence, tests of scholastic ability and other special abilities, achievement tests, aptitude tests, interest tests, attitude and value tests, personality tests, and situational tests.

Intelligence tests ale often confused with the tests of scholastic ability. In reality the intelligence tests should purport to measure the various factors which define the total general intelligence of the individual while tests of scholastic ability measure the specific performance of the individual on academic tasks only. The two are very closely related with each other which is the reason for many of us to consider them identical. Beginning with Binet the Western psychologists, especially in America, have achieved outstanding level of research in its development. Numerous reliable tests are available to measure intelligence and special aspects of intelligence and other abilities. In India, on the other hand, the literature does not exist in such an abundance yet it is difficult to claim a paucity of test materials suitable to various regions anti language groups. For up-to-date information on tests the reader is referred to Mental Measurement Handbook for India compiled and published by the National Council of Educational Research and Training, New Delhi.

The function of achievement tests is to measure the educational achievement of the clients according to age or class placement. As such, achievement tests are very closely related with the syllabus followed by schools and therefore, are dependent upon the type of school and the teaching thereof. Standardized achievement tests in various school subjects are useful for the testing programme.

Aptitude tests are expected to measure the potential for specific abilities and skills such as music, graphic arts, medicine, law, engineering, teaching, etc. Aptitude tests are different from interest tests. While the interest tests measure the liking that an individual may have for a particular skill, the aptitude tests tell us how well the individual is equipped to excel in that skill. Cases are common when a person is interested in a certain field but does not have the aptitude for it. He may excel through sheer hardwork but not because of the potential talent. Considering the fine distinctions between the different types of tests, the test developer has to be careful in defining his goals and in preparing items for various tests.

Attitude is a pattern of response to certain persons, situations and objects. Attitudes are learnt so well that they become a typical mode of response with a particular person and attitude has a well defined object of reference. Some of the examples are attitude towards education, attitude towards special kinds of food and drinks, attitude towards various communities and provinces. Values are closely related with and influence our attitudes. If our values accord a certain person, place or situation a high status, our attitude towards them would also be positive. Conversely, if our values place anyone of these low, our attitude is also likely to be negative. Though a learned behaviour, attitudes involve the process of generalization. After contacts with a, b, c and d belonging to a particular group, we generalize some of their striking characteristics and apply them to the entire group. Hereafter this learnt impression or attitude becomes a typical mode of our behaviour.

Personality is defined in terms of individual's behaviour, *i.e.*, perceptions, reactions, attitudes and opinions, and his feelings about external world which are not apparent or discernible in his overt behaviour, and in terms of one's feelings about himself. The individual's feelings may be at the conscious or unconscious level. The reasons for these feelings also may be known to the individual or he may be completely unaware of them. All these aspects of personality are dynamic in nature and are inter co-related. They are dynamic in the sense that continuous development takes place in them. The development does not merely take place within the personality but the individual's behaviour is characterized by an interaction with the environment. Personality, thus defined, is the product of interaction between the individual as a developing organism, having certain psychological and biological means on the one hand, and on the other his environment which nurtured, influenced, satisfied or in certain cases failed to satisfy those needs.

Personality tests aim to assess this totality of individual's behaviour. There are numerous techniques suggested for personality measurement. Rating scales have been used to collect rated opinion of people who have known the individual under various conditions. Personality inventories have been used to gather individual's direct response to certain questions related to various traits. Inventories have been used (1) to assess specific traits, (2) to evaluate adjustment to various aspects of environment, such as home, school and community, (3) to classify clinical groups like paranoiac, psychopathic, etc., and (4) to screen subjects into two or more groups. Inventories like Minnesota Multiphasic Personality Inventory, have made significant impact on research and practice in personality assessment.

Projective techniques are an important method of assessing personality. They are based on the concept of projection which is a psychological term meaning the unconscious process through which an individual attributes certain thoughts, attitudes, wishes, emotions, and feelings to objects or persons in his environment. It also takes the form of attributing one's own needs to others in his environment. In projective techniques the individual is presented with semi-structured or unstructured materials and is asked to talk about them or what he perceives in them. In giving his reactions to these materials, it is hypothesized, the individual gives expression to or projects his own needs and feelings. Expert interpretation of his responses can provide us with valuable insights into the individual's personality. Thematic Apperception Test, Children's Apperception Test, Symonds Picture-Study Test, Blacky Pictures and Rosenzweig's Picture Frustration Study are some examples of projective tests. Most of these tests have been tried under Indian conditions and many of them have been adapted to Indian population.

The situational tests are comparatively a recent development; they test the individual in action or confront him with situations related to his own life in response to which he gives expression to his feelings for other persons. Situational tests are more structured than Rorschach or TAT but they still have scope for projection. Socio-metric tests and psychodrama are examples of situational tests. Moreno, as the inventor of these tests, has defined the socio-metric tests as techniques which reveal and evaluate the social structure of a group through the measurement of the frequency of acceptance or rejection between the group members. It is an approach to the study of inter-personal relationships. It permits the analysis of position and status of each individual within the group. In psychodrama the individual is required to play spontaneously an assigned role in a specific situation. It may involve two or more persons and it deals with a situation significant in the life of one or more participants. The individual may be required to play his own part or that of some other personality with whom he may be in contact.

The classification based on content gives us two distinct categories of verbal and non-verbal tests. The former has a heavy loading of language. Whether tests of ability, personality or interest, these are the tests that are difficult to transfer to a population with facility in other languages than the one in which these tests have been standardized. Verbal tests of intelligence standardized in English and in Western countries are inadequate for use with Indian population. Besides the language loading, the content of these tests varies from culture to culture. A non-verbal test serves the dual purpose of measuring the practical performance of an individual and providing the psychological examiner with culture-free materials to test various traits. These tests have very little of language component which consists of instructions for administration of each section. The performance on these tests when combined with the score on verbal tests measuring the same ability, give us a composite score of the individual on a particular ability.

❋❋❋

11

Research and Evaluation in Counselling

Research and evaluation are basic to the development and success of guidance and counselling programmes. Like any other applied discipline, the principles, philosophy and practice of guidance and counselling require research findings and periodic evaluation to verify and support them. The impression prevails that the guidance and counselling services being a new development in Indian education, should be given a few years to establish themselves before any demands for research and evaluation are made. For most effective research programmes, on the contrary, it is essential that a plan of research and evaluation be built into the very proposal of the new programme. With the multiple responsibilities of a guidance worker and counsellor, the research is very likely to slip by unless it is planned as an integral aspect of the profession.

If we refer to the historical development of guidance movement in the United States of America we will notice that the research and evaluation in guidance-personnel work first became important during the 1920's. In India research in this area still remains to be organized; whatever research has been conducted has been mostly in the disciplines related to guidance and counselling such as education, psychology and sometimes sociology. Very little research has been conducted by the persons actually working in the area of guidance and counselling. The research topics and findings, therefore, are rather scattered. Most of the research has been undertaken as part fulfilment of requirements for the Master's or Ph.D. degree in one of the above mentioned disciplines.

As earlier discussions have pointed out, counselling requires an interdisciplinary approach. Therefore, the researcher should feel free in borrowing techniques, plans and even points of view from other disciplines. These borrowings when adapted to the special needs of counselling, provide an accurate understanding of the counsellee behaviour. A review of the research conducted so far reveals that the researchers have relied heavily on psychology and education for methodology and research techniques but have borrowed very little from sociological and anthropological methods which might cast light on group and peer society problems.

There is possibility of a great deal of research if we recognize the assumptions underlying some of the problems. For example, we work under the assumption that occupational information is useful for students in planning their future careers but the amount of information required, the kind of information most helpful for the purpose, the ways in which this information can be most effectively given to the students and the amount of it actually assimilated by the students need to be investigated. Before any research is designed, there is need to develop clear cut concepts and the definition of what constitutes research.

Types of Research

Research has been defined in many varied ways but two types of research have been universally accepted. (1) Quantitative research and (2) Qualitative research. Under the quantitative research, survey type of studies predominate; they are most familiar to and popular with the student researchers. Surveys are based on the results of questionnaires or interviews and usually explore the existing practices, needs and opinions. The two most appropriate examples of such studies are:

1. The survey of guidance needs of Indian students conducted by the All India Vocational and Educational Association in 1960-62; and
2. The survey of student problems of adjustment conducted by Pasricha at the Maharaja Sayajirao University of Baroda in 1960-64.

The other type of quantitative research in which a problem or hypothesis is stated and tested is less frequently undertaken and is most often labelled as " classical research". It is less popular especially with student investigators because it involves setting up of hypotheses and devising appropriate research methods before any data can be collected. Using analysis of these data as the basis the hypotheses are either proved or disproved. Both of these types rely heavily on the statistical methods; within these two types the researcher rarely has an opportunity of expressing his own opinions, judgment or his conclusions, other than those based on the statistical calculations.

The qualitative type of research, on the other hand, includes bibliographical studies, historical research which can provide significant insights into the counselling practice. Research using the longitudinal approach, such as case histories of individuals or of groups also falls under this category. An important possibility under qualitative research is the study of protocols of counselling interviews. Guidance and counselling work, because it deals with human beings and abstract concepts, needs more of qualitative research than the pure quantitative conclusions. The quantitative approach to research has a limiting effect upon the kinds of research endeavours that can be undertaken and it precludes the less traditionally sanctioned types. It restricts the research efforts to only those areas which lend themselves to quantitative measurement and analysis. Some aspects of counselling, vocational guidance, occupational information and testing can be investigated through quantitative research but many other phases of counselling and guidance work get completely neglected.

Using application as the criterion, research can be classified as pure or basic and practical or action research. Pure research seeks facts and the relation between these facts. The purpose of this type of research is the pursuit and the advancement of knowledge itself to satisfy the insatiable curiosity of the scientist. Practical research, on the other hand, is directed towards the solution of some particular problem which has arisen during the course of practice. The enquiry into a practical problem may lead the researcher to investigation of the more general and abstract problems and to scientific generalizations but that is never the primary aim of practical research. The nature of pure or basic research is greatly different when conducted under the discipline of physical and natural sciences than it is under the social sciences especially the social science of guidance and counselling. Physical and natural sciences can deal with such questions as, how a cell operates, what an atom is like or what elements remain to be discovered but the applied social science of guidance and counselling does not deal with such simple units. Its" elements" are human beings passing through the most formative period of human life and operating in the most specialized but complex environment of the school or college campus. If basic research implies dealing with the simplest indivisible elements under highly controlled situations then guidance and counselling research is far removed from basic research. It will be meaningful to define basic research in guidance to include studies which throw light on the development of the human individual or on the nature and activities of the society in which he lives. It would also include studies of individuals reacting to each other and interacting amid the forces, pressures and movements of their environment.

Action research, however, seems more suitable for the problems central to the field of guidance and counselling. This is an investigation conducted by the persons engaged in a particular type of work the findings of which are to be eventually used in their own practice. The evaluation studies of the guidance programme, for example, are best planned as action research; these are sometimes also called "self-surveys". Since guidance is an applied science, its research should be for the purpose of evaluating and thereby improving its functions.

Evaluation

Though recognized as basic to the success of any guidance organization, evaluation is seldom taken up by the guidance workers. It is rarely taken up by the researchers in the related fields of psychology and education. There are two basic questions which the evaluative research in guidance and counselling tries to answer. These are: (1) Does counselling do any good? (2) Do persons who experience counselling get along any better in life than those who did not have an opportunity to use such help? These simple questions give rise to another important question of whether counselling success should be judged on the basis of satisfaction of the counsellee or the adjustment he makes as a result of counselling. If satisfaction of the counsellee is taken as the criterion then there are certain social conventions which may determine the responses of the counsellee. The only way one can find out the satisfaction of the counsellee is to ask him if he feels better after counselling. It will be observed that when a person is asked whether he feels better or worse as an experience of counselling, it is more likely and natural for him to report an improvement than deterioration. The result of such a study, therefore, will be biased and not objective; it is easy to get favourable evidence through the use of this technique.

If, on the other hand, we decide to use adjustment as the criterion for the success of counselling, we face new problems. Should adjustment be judged on the basis of objective estimates or subjective evaluations. The change in the test scores and class marks or the number of job changes which a graduate makes can be good objective criteria easy to use for statistical computations, but experience indicates that anyone of them can be misleading in a particular case. Often enough job changes are an indication of healthy vocational development than otherwise. In general, however, one would expect the counselled student to maintain a higher average of school marks than the non-counselled student and a counselled worker to be more stable on his job than the non-counselled individual. The subjective evaluation of adjustment involves someone else's ratings on the adjustment of the counsellee. The ratings are either based on the case materials given to the raters or on the follow-up interviews which the raters hold with the counsellee. This method also has the difficulties which the other subjective techniques are known to involve. The ratings are someone's estimates of adjustment of an individual and these estimates are influenced by their own attitudes and judgements of what constitutes adjustment and success in our society. Often two or more raters have been appointed to raise the reliability of the evaluations, still the bias remains. We would, perhaps, achieve the best results if both subjective and objective criteria are used together; they tend to correct the defects of each other and ultimately give a more balanced estimate of adjustment than either one is capable of giving.

Evaluation requires the following conditions:

1. Definition of the aims and objectives of the programme or activity to be evaluated.
2. The design of techniques and instruments through which this progress can be measured.

3. Establishment of criteria against which progress towards these aims can be judged.

4. Judgement against the criteria about the quality and quantity of the progress towards achievement of the stated goals.

5. Collection of complete information from all sources.

Evaluation is a more complicated process than the research which it contains. Perhaps the greatest difficulty in carrying out an evaluative study centres around the problem of defining the aims of the work and selecting criteria by which to judge progress toward those aims. This leads us to the issue of the philosophy of guidance and counselling and what the various workers consider to be the aims of guidance work. Mere statement of the aims is not enough, for the evaluation studies it is essential that these aims should be converted into concrete terms so that criteria can be established and the progress toward the aims measured in quantitative terms.

Often guidance workers can detect changes in counsellee behaviour without being able to determine the factors which could have caused these changes. Such changes may result from a new environment, new teachers, different friends and many other factors that have very little or nothing to do with the guidance programme as such. Unless the changes produced by counselling are more pronounced than the spontaneous changes tend to be, one cannot be sure that counselling has been very effective. Hence, the process of evaluation requires very careful examination of all variables to insure that there is a relationship between the aspect of the programme which is under study and the desired results. The only way we can be sure that the changes are produced by counselling is to compare the changes with the behaviour of a similar group where no counselling was lives. It is not easy to find a control group. The very fact that the individual voluntarily seeks the help of a counsellor shows that he is different in some aspects of his motivation and personality than another person who seems to be like him in age, intelligence and general environment under which he lives. It is difficult to match cases or groups on the motivational characteristics which may have a more important bearing on behaviour change than any other trait. One way to solve the problem is to compare the results of a new programme of guidance with those of an already existing one and thus evaluate the significance of the new aspects introduced in the existing programme.

Follow-up

Follow-up, an integral part of guidance and counselling work, forms another important type of research activity in this area. Through the follow-up the counsellor and the counsellee learn the nature and extent of the progress the latter has made. Follow-up helps them determine the areas of life in which the counsellee has made successful adjustments and the ones in which he needs to make further adaptations. Counselling is incomplete without proper follow-up because without it the counsellor is unable to find out whether the counsellee behaviour showed any improvement after counselling; follow-up answers one of the questions raised in evaluative research that is, does counselling do any good? Follow-up is, perhaps, the best technique for evaluative studies.

One of the mistakes which a counselling set-up is likely to make is to provide less or no time for the follow-up of past counsellees. Usually, the administration is so keen on showing results, and the results of counselling are usually assessed by the number of cases worked with, that work with current and new counsellees is given preference over the follow-up activity. Difficulties of establishing contacts with the counsellee once he has graduated from the school or college have added to the neglect of follow-up work. As long as the counsellee is attending the educational institution, follow-up is convenient and easy but once he has graduated, the counsellor and the faculty need to make extra efforts to establish contact with him.

The need for follow-up can be met through a well organized system which would try to resolve the above mentioned difficulties. It is possible to meet this need because all the cases which approach the counsellor would not require a follow-up. Practice reveals that a large number of students come to the counselling centres for information or problems which are simple in nature and can be helped easily; the effectiveness of such help given to the counsellee is easy to evaluate because the effects are immediate and obvious. Follow-up is most essential, and must be planned on periodic basis, for the cases that come with serious adjustment problems. Let us take examples to illustrate the follow-up method used with different types of cases.

Suppose that in the beginning of the academic session twenty students seek interviews with the counsellor and among these he finds ten with educational difficulties, their academic achievement is not as high as their intellectual status indicates. He arranges another interview with these ten and during this interview he discovers that they require help with study methods—how to read fast with comprehension, how to take notes, how to prepare for examinations and how to write examinations. The counsellor then would explore the possibility of arranging special classes in study methods for these students. If special classes are arranged then the students may follow special work for a few weeks, at the end of which the counsellor calls for another interview with these students to check the progress they have made in their learning methods. It is quite possible that during this third interview the counsellor may realize that the underachievement of three of them is not due to poor study methods but is connected with some emotional and personal difficulties which they are trying to resolve for themselves. He will now hold individual interviews with these three and arrange the counselling help which each one of them may require. After the counselling sessions are over and the counsellees have had an opportunity to be on their own for some time, the counsellor will need to arrange another series of individual interviews with these three to assess the progress they have made after individual help was provided for them.

Even the cases which come with a seemingly simple problem such as choice of career, need a follow-up interview because without it the counsellee may continue to struggle in a wrong choice which he might have made as an outcome of the initial interview. The choice of a career can not be finally determined as a sequal of a single interview. The counsellee needs to try the suggested career in which he may stay happily ever after but it is quite possible that he may have certain difficulties in this choice which can be reconsidered during a follow-up interview and an alternative choice suggested. In summary, it may be said that follow-up is an integral aspect of counselling and if well planned and organized, it is the most useful technique for evaluation of the effectiveness of guidance and counselling.

Ideally, the counsellee should come to the counsellor for the follow-up. When the counsellor starts work with the counsellee he can explain to him the process with emphasis on follow-up and can suggest a definite interval after which he must come back to the counsellor for an interview. It is possible and common, however, that once the counsellee feels satisfied with his decision or adjustment he stops coming to the counsellor. Under such conditions, the latter has to take the initiative and find appropriate ways of arranging a follow-up interview with the counsellee. As counselling is an individual service and each counsellee is unique and his problems are unique, the follow-up also needs to be organized on the individual basis. The main aim of the follow-up programme is to provide each individual counsellee with appropriate opportunity to review his situation at regular intervals and also whenever such a review is called for.

While the counsellee is still in school the counsellor should plan to meet him at the end of each term or at least once at the end of the school session. At these meetings the counsellee can review his progress since the counselling sessions and can plan his programme for the coming term or year. If the counsellor foresees certain difficulties which the counsellee is likely to encounter with his courses or educational programme then he can fix further meetings with him and try to forestall these troubles. If the counsellor finds that the student is having personal problems then he should find the best and the most appropriate time and methods for the follow-up work. In case the counsellee is having a number of difficulties, it is advisable not to list them all in anyone interview. While it is difficult for the counsellee to concentrate on all of them at a time, a listing of them all is likely to create panic in him. It will be helpful to space them out and discuss two of them at a time-one of which is relatively easy to cope with.

When planning the future programme of the counsellee, the counsellor needs to be sure that the objectives of the counsellee are realistic and possible for him to achieve. After he is sure of the realistic nature of the objectives, the counsellor can proceed to consider the factors which effect the progress of the counsellee towards these goals. These factors reside both within the counsellee and in his environment.

The purpose of all follow-up activities is to seek answers to questions such as:

1. How well is he adjusting to his present situation?
2. In the light of new developments, does he need assistance in modifying his plans or in making further adjustments?

3. How well is the counsellee following the plans developed during earlier interviews?

The answers to these questions form the criteria for evaluation of the effectiveness of the counselling process.

When the counsellee is about to leave school he requires special attention of the counsellor who first helps him to explore all the possible ways in which he can employ himself. A large number of our students leave school unobserved now; they require help from the counsellor who works with them and tries to help them understand the reasons for leaving school. He explores with them the possibility of their staying in school or resumption of studies at a later stage. If the counsellor finds that the counsellee is absolutely determined to leave school then the counsellor arranges an interview during which he tries to get information regarding matters such as:

1. The immediate reasons for withdrawal from school;
2. The various effects of the student's withdrawal on his earlier and present plans and decisions;
3. The changes, if any, in the student's educational and vocational plans;
4. The possibility of the student resuming his studies at a later stage;
5. Any definite steps taken by the student to find work and their outcome;
6. The consideration of ways, other than withdrawal, to meet the student's situation.

The purpose of this interview should not be confined to the collection of such information only but the opportunity can be used to help the counsellee to understand himself better, strengthen his belief in himself and his plans, reconsider his earlier decisions and review the possibility of new solutions which may be more appropriate to the counsellee's present situation and current interests and abilities. The exit-interview, as we may call this conference with the outgoing student, under no circumstances, should end on a negative note; it should be an opportunity to make positive and encouraging suggestions to the counsellee about his future career, it should also be used to assess the need for referral and, if indicated, the counsellee should be sent to the specialist with an appointment for a follow-up interview later.

As a research technique, the follow-up of the students leaving school before they can complete their studies is a source of abundant data on wastage in our schools, its causes and the possible preventive measures. It is important for any educational system to know the amount being spent on education and the national gains and wastage thereof. These interviews with the" drop-out" students can suggest many a useful research plan to the interested research worker.

The follow-up of the final year student who is about to pass the school examination and will be looking for a full-time work in the very near future, is different from the other follow-up interviews we have discussed so far. When the school has a well organized counselling service then it is the responsibility of the counsellor to initiate the placement procedures. Ideally, the counsellor or the placement bureau of the college or the university which works in close co-operation with the counsellor—has information about various employment opportunities available in the field of specialization of this particular counsellee. The counsellor would discuss these possibilities with the counsellee and would assist him in making contacts and applications to the suitable agencies. In the process of placement of the graduating counsellees the absolutely close and continuous cooperation between the counsellor and the placement bureau is important.

Such follow-up would yield valuable data on the status of the alumni, their progress in various professions and the attitudes they hold about the school and its counselling facilities. Furnished with this data the counsellor can plan studies to review and suggest modifications of the procedures and techniques used by the counselling and the placement units of the institution.

The follow-up of the former student is important in as much as it yields information about the educational institutions he attended since graduation, the curriculum he followed, the degree or the degrees he obtained, the honours he received, the career he has taken up and the kind of success he has made in this career. Such information is important to the school because it gives them an idea of how its graduates are placed which, in a way, is indicative of the quality of training which it imparts to its students. On the basis of this information, useful research can be designed to explore the relationship between the training and its practical application in the later life of the student. These studies can lead to a review of the training curriculum and changes, if necessary, therein. If objectively followed, such studies help the institution determine the effectiveness and suitability of its course offerings. The experiences of the former students can be helpful to the counsellor in working with his current counsellees. On the basis of his experience of work with the former students, the counsellor progresses in his understanding of the younger generation; this contact continuously fills the gap between the two generations. Contact with the former student is more difficult than the current or graduating student.

The counsellor has to use varied methods to establish contact with the former students; some of these methods are: Questionnaire. The questionnaire sent to the former students purports to collect two types of information (1) where and in what position is the former student stationed, and (2) what further education did he receive after he left school. Each institution will need to develop its own questionnaire but one principle must be remembered in preparing this instrument i.e. it should be short and precise. Sometimes the research workers have made the mistake of developing questionnaires which require the respondents to write short notes or express their opinions on certain controvertial subjects. Such instruments tend to defeat their purpose because the respondents, who are busy with their positions and jobs, feel reluctant to answer these lengthy and time consuming questions. In preparing a questionnaire the counsellor or the research worker needs to do all the thinking and the work related with the responses. In the final form the instrument should be so precise that the respondent may complete it by making a few tick-marks at the appropriate places.

Ideally, the returned questionnaires should be analysed and preserved in form of a study. This would require a sufficiently large percentage of the returns; in practice, this has not been possible in India. The counsellees or their parents and other relatives do not realize the importance of follow-up and so they do not care to return the questionnaire and provide the important information which the counselling service calls for.

If available, the telephone can be effectively used to establish follow-up contacts with the former students. Though informal, this is the most friendly and the quickest mode of communication with the past students. The drawback of this device is that unless the counsellor knows them personally, the former students may not be willing to give him the information he requires. But if the counsellor has been habitually using the telephone to talk with them and exchange greetings, he may be successful in collecting the information. Telephonic talk can be helpful in still another way and that is to explain to the former student the purpose of the follow-up before the questionnaire is despatched. Sometimes it so happens that the alumnus does not send back the questionnaire on his own, in that case the telephone can be used to remind him to send his response and provide the valuable data for research.

Letters can also be sent for follow-up purposes. They do not, however, provide quantitative information; they are best used when the counsellor requires qualitative information. A letter has two distinct advantages; it is confidential and as such it protects the former student as well as everyone else concerned; being personal in nature, it is likely to draw many more responses from the persons queried than any other method used for follow-up.

Interview is the most appropriate method for collection of objective and detailed information but has many drawbacks. The former students are presumably well settled in full-time occupations; they may, therefore, have little time to spare for detailed interviews. Even if the time is available, an interview needs to be taken in a standardized manner with all the former students interviewed by the counsellor. An interview can be standardized if the questions and the mode of asking these questions is reviewed ahead of time and used in the same manner with all the interviewees.

For the collection of data in an objective manner, it is necessary to take detailed notes of the interview. At this point the counsellor is faced with a problem of whether to take notes during the interview or after it is over. If he decides in favour of the former, he runs the risk of disturbing the student and thus creating an adverse effect on the data. On the other hand, if he opts for the latter then he runs the risk of missing many useful details of the interview. The solution of this problem lies in the discretion of the interviewer. If he is sensitive enough he can let the personal discussions proceed undisturbed and write subject he reports later. The use of mechanical aids such as tape recorders and the stenographic help through the one-way vision screen has become common in counselling techniques. When these mechanical devices are used it is essential and moral responsibility of the counsellor to consult the interviewee and obtain his consent to their use.

The need for further research in follow-up technique is obvious from this discussion. Progressive evaluation of follow-up techniques is essential for their improvement and development of new methods. Research is one guidance activity which, under the pressure of other demands, can be allowed to slide. Counsellors and guidance workers can hardly be blamed, if in the midst of their multitudinous duties, the time for research is devoted to other activities. It is possible that certain institutions may not lend themselves to evaluation, their attitudes and emphases may not favour evaluation. Yet, it is important that the guidance workers and educators have practical and meaningful information on which to base their plans for the future. Therefore, the guidance workers as individuals, should be able to make their own studies which may lead the way to far reaching institutional evaluation.

The overcrowding in schools and colleges, lack of finances, shortage of staff, time and facilities indicate two distinct types of research possibility in the future:

1. Government, University Grants Commission or philanthropic organizations may support the broadly conceived research or evaluation studies.
2. Individuals who are more interested in guidance and counselling research may take up more specialized problems and narrow aspects of the programme for investigation.

Individuals with limited resources-financial and in terms of time may concentrate on specific areas within the vast field of guidance and counselling. There exists a definite lack of understanding of the assumptions and the philosophical concepts basic to guidance and counselling work. There is also a need for the study of how guidance and counselling work is allied to psychology, sociology and anthropology. A study of the relationship between guidance and psychology may lead to interesting sociological and educational developments. There is also a need for studies of the organization of guidance work. What organizational pattern enables students to derive the greatest benefits from guidance and counselling? How does the organizational structure enhance or impede the efforts of individual workers in the field? There is also a need to discover what is going on inside the individual student or inside the student groups. The peer group has great influence in the development of young people; the counsellor also assumes that he exerts an influence upon the student. The comparative study of these influences will be of interest and of great importance to the guidance workers. A study of various influences and their effects upon student behaviour, it is hoped, will give important information to the guidance workers and will provide answers to such questions: how to combat certain influences, if necessary? and how to work with groups to direct their energies into constructive channels? This type of research is necessary for the guidance worker to feel sure about the efficacy of his programme.

Guidance and counselling being interdisciplinary in approach, draw upon many academic fields for ideas and techniques. It is not sufficient for the guidance worker to keep himself informed of the research in his own area, he must follow up research in education, psychology, testing and measurement, sociology, social anthropology and group dynamics. It is practically impossible for a post-graduate guidance student or for a newly trained guidance worker to be able to keep up with the current literature in all these areas so basic to his work. A synthesis of research is obviously called for. Studies need to be made in which the authors select and describe pertinent research from many areas, combine the information into a unified system and show the implications for guidance and counselling. A synthesis is not a collection of material similar to an annotated bibliography, it is a combination of materials that preserve the original findings and yet produce new conclusions which provide directions for future study. Synthesis involves perceiving and establishing relationships. As clear from its description the synthesis of research can not be undertaken by anyone individual; it is a type of institutional research. A number of departments need to cooperate in order to make this type of a study successful, it requires a large number of personnel and a sufficiently large budget.

Closely allied to the synthesis of research is the problem of dissemination of information about the current research and evaluation. Synthesis of materials is a good technique for dissemination of research findings and their application but the worker must be aware of the drawbacks of synthesis also. Poor understanding of the materials, inadequate coverage of topics, misinterpretation of results and combination of unrelated materials are some of the errors that can occur in synthesis of research. These errors can be avoided or corrected, if objective criticism stays a constituent of research and evaluation.

Criticism is usually interpreted as bad, negative and destructive. Most critical remarks are dismissed on the basis that the point of view of the critic or evaluator is negative and often the critic himself is condemned as an unhealthy influence in the profession. While some criticism may stem from a wish to destroy, we must remember that much of it originates from a sincere desire to improve something that is already good but could be better. In a sense, criticism is the highest praise which a study, person or work can receive; no one cares to waste his time, energy and effort in criticizing something that is of no value. The best way to improve research and evaluation is through the critical analysis of the studies already conducted. Such criticism provides a check on research and its conclusions and, if properly conducted, it should suggest new ways of studying problems.

Two conclusions can be drawn from the above discussion:

1. The training of the guidance and counselling workers should give them good grounding in research methods and techniques and should provide them practical experience in conducting research.
2. The training programmes should give the same importance to research as the profession is likely to attach in practice.

A review of the training programmes, will reveal that no programme offered in India includes research methods and an opportunity for the student to apply this knowledge about research to actual problems in the field of guidance and counselling. The situation in other countries looks no better. In the United States of America also those students who have not completed a doctoral programme, have had very little training in conducting research or applying their knowledge of research methods to the problems of guidance and counselling. Almost all the courses offered in India include a paper in statistics which is usually theoretical and unrelated with the practice of guidance. Opportunities of applying statistical techniques to research data are conspicuous by their absence. Action research is almost unknown to the guidance workers and those who are familiar with the need and importance of such research can not devote time and effort to it because of the overloaded teaching and counselling schedule which they have to keep. The existing situation can be summed up by saying that research in guidance and counselling has not yet acquired its proper place and importance in the profession. Yet some research, though theoretical, has been taken up by the guidance workers or under disciplines basic to guidance and counselling which needs to be reviewed here.

***

12

Motivated Behaviour

It is an accepted fact that behaviour of an individual is very much guided by instincts and accompanying emotions. In the present set-up, there is also a school of psychologists who do not accept the instincts as the cause of the behaviour of the individual. Psychologists of this school put forward a theory that the behaviour of an individual is guided by motive and drives. Here we shall try to discuss about all these things.

According to M. Jolmson, "Motivation is the influence of general pattern of activity indicating and directing the behaviour of the organism." "The influence of the general pattern of activity, initiating and directing the behaviour of the organism, goes by the name of motivation."

According to H. J. Klanmesier, "Motivation is an integral component of learning and a critical problem in educational settings. Educational psychologists and educators use such terms as needs, interests and goals in treating the motivational aspects of teaching learning processes; in other specialities in psychology primary drives, secondary drives and incentives appear frequently."

According to N.L. Munn, "The inner control of behaviour as represented by physiological conditions, interests, attitudes and aspirations."

Meaning of Drives

As mentioned above, R.S. Woodworth suggested the

term "drive" for urges. In the beginning 'drive' meant the energy that sets things going. But lateron, its meaning was expanded and "drive" stood for "energy" or action arising from physiological needs like hunger, the rot, sex, fatigue, elimination of bodily wastes, maintenance of constant temperature and barometric pressures." L.F. Shaffer has defined drive as a "stineubes, usually internal, that arouses persistent mass activity" and a mechanism as "an acquired response tending to the reduction of a drive."

On the basis of these definitions Shaffer point out that many drives may be innate, and all mechanisms are the results of learning processes. But as we have seen, Woodworth has a slightly different view, for according to him every mechanism has the power to become a drive. Woodworth stated that drives can be acquired also. That is why, some psychologists suggest that there are primary and secondary drives. Primary drives are nature and secondary drives are acquired.

Element of the Drive. There are following three elements that drive or stimulate persons to take to some work:

1. The excitement, which inspires a person to do some work.
2. This power is stimulated from within.
3. The hope, that if the work has been completed there shall be some peace and satisfaction.

Causes of Motivation

Following are the various causes that bring about motivation:

1. The desire of the person to survive and live.
2. He feeling of safe-guarding against pain and unhappiness.

3. He feeling of self-preservation or security.
4. Desire for pleasure.
5. Sub-conscious mind.
6. Sex instinct.
7. Internal love or affection.
8. Various circumstancial or environmental factors that direct the movement of the body.
9. Emotions, instinct, thinking, feeling, etc.
10. Power of determination of desire to do a thing. It may also be termed as will.

Importance of Motivations in Education

Motivations play a vital role in the field of education. M.K. Thomson is of the opinion that motivation is that education, by which interest is created in a person, who does not have it. Due to interest the students concentrate their attention on studies. If an interest is created for a particular subject in the child, then he shall learn it easily and quickly. By motivation, the development of the character and the personality of the child is also possible. In short it can be said that motivations have important place in education in this regard, it is necessary to see to the following:

(a) The teacher should try to develop the spirit of cooperation in the students.

(b) The teacher should try to create group feeling or the feeling of working and living together, amongst the students.

(c) The teacher should try to present good examples before the students. These example shall inspire the children.

(d) So far as possible, the teacher should try to awaken the motivation.

(e) The strongest motivation of the child should be awakened to the maximum.

(f) The teacher should be enthusiatic and zealous. Every individual has an aim or goal. It is necessary to make efforts to reach that goal. The students should be encouraged to set a goal and make purposeful attempt to reach it.

Characteristics of Motivated Behaviour

The analysis of place of motive in experience and behaviour as given above, clarifies the general characteristics of motivated behaviour. Roughly speaking, these characteristics are as follows:

1. Energy Mobilization. Even the most peaceful animal becomes frightening in times of emergency. This is due to the mobilization of energy. This process of the mobilization of energy is chemical as well as physical. It cannot be perceived directly, but when there is some difficulty in the instilling in him love towards good habits, hatred for bad ones, anger for injustice, curiosity towards nature, *etc.* Once there emotions are conjoined to the right object, his behaviour takes a good turn. Sublimation does not destroy the emotion, it only changes the mode of its expression. It achieves the necessary control while avoiding all the damage that is the inevitable corollary of repression. It also avoids the formation of emotional complexes. As psychoanalytic studies have revealed, most of the great poets, authors, scientists, leaders and saints could contribute to human well-being only through the sublimation of their emotions. The compositions and creations of both Tulsidas and Kalidas clearly show the results of sublimation of their love for the opposite sex, as a result of which their sexual instinct was sublimated into love of God.

Attainment of the object of motive, it is seen in the form of extra energy. The animal tries to attain the object with as much power as is the urge of the motive behind it. A hungry dog takes the bread even while beaten. The labour which a student puts in to attain a first division in the examination is never seen in his ordinary life. Thus it is often observed that some of the persons brought up in the poor families are very persevering and laborious. Some men perform such inhuman action due to the sex urge which they would never do in ordinary conditions.

2. Persistence. An animal cannot leave its work without achieving the goal of its motive. An animal wandering in search of food keeps on roaming so long as it does not get it. The fighting birds keep on fighting till either of them is wounded or runs away. Sometimes some motivated actions go on for years. A young man in search of a job goes on labouring for several years till he gets a suitable one. A lover determined to conquer his beloved, does not leave her even in the face of great difficulties. Even in the motivated behaviour of insects and animals much patience and persistence is observed.

3. Variability. Motive has a goal, hence it continuously changes with the veiw of attainment of goals. A hungry cat closed in a cage tries new devices to open it. Sometimes it tires this way, sometimes that and this change of behaviour goes on till it succeeds in coming out of the cage. A man with the goal of earning money tries hundreds of ways for it. Sometimes he purchases a lottery ticket while at other times he is busy in some business. In fact, the motivated person goes on changing his ways till he arives at the way successful for the achievement of the aim.

4. Restlessness for the Attainment of the Goal. the motivated behaviour is goal-directed. The restlessness observed in such a behaviour persists so long as the goal is not achieved. For example, the goal of hunger is food. Till the food is taken the restlessness disappears. The goal can be conscious or unconscious. Sometimes the man knows the goal of his motive, but at other times it is only after long efforts and trial and error that he knows the real object which will bring his restlessness to an end. The physical and the mental motives have physical and mental goals respectively.

5. Extinction of Restlessness After the Attainment of the Goal. The restlessness of the motivated behaviour exhibits itself in following ways of the fulfilment of some internal want or desire and extinguishes as soon as that want or desire is fulfilled. A thirsty animal roams in search of water. As it gets water it drinks it and the restlessness is gone. There are only two ways to get rid of the restlessness of the motive. Either the tension should be removed or it should be changed. The tension can be removed by the attainment of the object. Sometimes conflicts are observed due to tensions between more than one motives at the same time.

Types of Motivation

M.K. Thomson has classified motivation under two heads:

A. Natural Motivation

Natural Motivation is of the following five types:

1. Bodily Goals or Motivation. These motivations are nothing but bodily or physical needs, like hunger, thirst, sex, *etc.* Certain motivations are caused by physical activities such as respiration, throbbing of the heart, digestion, circulation of blood and working of the glands etc. These motivations are inborn and inspire a person to fulfil the needs of the body. By causing change in the glands of a person, it is possible to bring him to the normal situation. Such a situation will be helpful for the information of motivation.

Various experiments that have been done, put forward the conclusion, that in future, by physical and operational experiments and chemical activities, it shall be possible to bring about changes in the glands of the person. Such a change shall give rise to requisite of natural and required motivations.

2. Habit. Habit is a form of nature of a person. A good habit of a child shall be that which can bring about development in his character and help him in achievement of education.

3. Feelings and Emotions. Pain and pleasure, joy and distress are the natural feelings and experiences of human nature. This aspect of the nature and the personality is very helpful in that system of education. Where an atmosphere is aimed to be created, which can bring about the development of the character of the students and help them to educate themselves. This aspect of the personality should be very cautiously handled, otherwise, it can have adverse effect.

4. Emotional Motivations. Those motivations, that inspire us to bring about the fulfilment of certain emotional needs, are called "Emotional Motivations". Emotions are awakened by the outside stimuli. These stimuli are part of the environment. The teachers should try to create such a healthy environment that the sublimation or motivation of the emotions may be possible.

5. Instinct Motivation. Instincts, as already said, are inborn powers and they inspire the physical organs of the individual to take to certain jobs. Unless a person has satisfied his instincts, he remains restless. Teachers, in order to provide for their satisfaction, should present a normal atmosphere for the students.

Other than the above five main motivations, there are certain other motivations as well. These motivations are also part of natural motivations. It shall be wise to have an idea about them as well.

1. ***Social Motivations.*** Due to inspirations from social environment, a person takes to certain activities. These activities are guided by the emotions and the instincts. Normally certain motivations are awakened for the fulfilment of social needs. They express themselves in the following forms:

   (a) Gregariousness is a natural instinct of man. It is therefore natural for him to be guided by social motivations.

   (b) The man has a great social consciousness of getting a place of respect in the society or to get his Self-regarding sentiment fulfilled. Consequently he tries to do certain good things in the society.

   (c) Due to social motivations, a person takes up those jobs that are good from the point of view of the society or which are appreciated by the society.

2. ***Individual Motivations or Motivations of Self.*** Those motivations, that inspire a person to satisfy his personal needs are called individual motivations, beauty, knowledge, faithfulness, competition, ideal, hero worship etc., are personal needs. These needs inspire a person to fulfil his personal desires.

3. ***Desires.*** It is the duty of the teachers to create in the students, the desire to acquire knowledge and achieve success. Is the teacher succeed it is, he shall be achieving a great task.

4. ***Recreation and Play.*** Programmes of games and play are joyful for the students. In plays, elements of direct motivation are present. The elements can therefore, by very nicely utilized for imparting education to the students.

5. ***Direction and Imitation.*** Children have the tendency to imitate. If proper direction and examples are presented before them, they can improve the power of motivation. They can also lead them towards success.

6. ***Other Natural Motivations.*** Other than these things, man is also anxious to have knowledge, love, faith, office, ideal, rest, leadership, achievement of wealth etc. It is quite possible to utilize all these motivations of the child in the field of education. It is clear, that in human nature there is enough material for Natural Motivation.

7. ***Appreciation and Self-expression.*** It is natural for a man to be inclined towards such goods goals, that give him importance and greatness. Social appreciation is another form of this feeling. It is, therefore, necessary to provide students the opportunity to observe these things.

B. Artificial Motivations

Artificial motivations are of various types. These motivations are not present in the human personality. They are part of the environment or the society. It is useful for the teacher to know and use them. They are being given below:

1. Reward and Punishment. In the works of the school this serves as a very important and useful motivation. It has the following steps as well:

(a) Punishment is a negative motivation. Sometimes it is not very useful for children.

(b) Reward is a positive motivation. Reward may be physical, social, or normal. It is very dear to the students. Teacher should try to use this motivation in such a way that the students may grow into useful future citizens.

2. Cooperation. It is also a strong motivation. The teacher can use it as a medium of education. In the Project Method of Education attempt is made to develop a spirit of cooperation amongst the students. This motivation can be well utilized.

Functions of Motivations

In modern educational psychology every possible effort is made to base the education of the child on its motivations. Modern education aims at the excitation of one or the other motivation in a child in order to make any and every kind of education natural and normal. Various motivations in a child are useful in education in the following ways:

1. Escape. In a child one finds the motivation of escape conjoined to the emotion of fear. The intelligent teacher arouses fear and a disgust towards bad things in the child. He also tries to prevent fear and escape from action in many unnecessary cases. Meaningless fears are thus eliminated.

2. Pugnacity. The instinct of pugnacity of combat is a universal motive. The most important fact that accelerates or excites it is restraint. A child whose means of locomotion are stopped by the simple expedient of being placed under restraint will go red in the face and cry at the top of its voice. Conflict starts the moment one removes a chick from the hen, or makes fun of an irritable individual or prevents an animal from fulfilling and satisfying its motivations.

The object of animal in turning pugnacious is to remove the obstacle preventing its progress or to defeat the obstacle. As long as the individual fails to defeat the obstacle or to remove it from his path, his internal, physiological and psysiological disturbance continues. The pattern of pugnacity or combat is not the same in all animals or individuals nor are the implements common to all. Animals having long nails or teeth use them in warfare. In most animals it is the male who is pugnacious. He combats the animals of different species, and other males of his own species for supremacy over the females or for food. It is possible that the instinct of the pugnacity is somewhat depressed by the female hormones. Human beings and some other animals are known to threaten before actually attacking. Proverbially it is the monkey who is the best exponent of this behaviour pattern. Some animals threaten by showing their teeth, others by making offensive noises while others show their ungentlemanly instants by hanging on their chests. Forms of pugnacity are modified by age, intelligence, social and cultural influences and social behaviours. The pugnacious motivation of cultured individual finds expression is more indirect manner. His animosity continues over the years, and his vengeance is achieved in many devious and indirect ways. Litigation is only a form of conflict and it is very common in cultured societies. In fact, it is difficult to believe that pugnacity is only an instinct or an internal motive whose single object is conflict or fight. The motivation to competition may be innate but the pugnacious motivation is activated only when the fulfilment of a motive is obstructed. Anger results in conflict but sometimes anger finds expression in more devious and uncommon ways.

3. Repulsion. The intelligent teacher does his best to develop the motive of repulsion in the child for unsavoury and undesirable expendient.

4. Sex. Sex motivation of a person may be turned into more acceptable outlets such as dancing, music, art, etc., by the teacher. And, particularly in the adolescent stage, this motivation can be restricted and moulded to provide the desirable development in the adolescent.

5. Parental Motivation. To this motivation is conjoined the emotion of pity. This motivation finds its expression in the older child's love for his younger counterpart and for other living beings.

6. Curiosity. Curiosity is the most important motivation from the educational viewpoint. It is a fundamental motivation without any definite biological basis. When any living being is confronted with any new or unrecognised object, it is natural for it to desire a complete knowledge or understanding of it. Curiosity in human beings is accompanied by the sense of surprise. Almost all individuals are desirous of knowing new things and new places. When a child is handed something it has not seen before, it will immediately turn it over and explore it to the best of its ability. The child is always ready with an unending list of questions. He never tires of asking questions even if the parents tire of answering them till he is forced to rebuff the child.

7. Gregariousness. A child is gregarious by motivation and he naturally wants to remain with the group of friends. A child does not desire solitude. The teacher can make the best of this instinct and help in the social development of the child. The teacher should keep an eye on the various group tensions that develop within the school and also try to evolve healthy competition, cooperation and team spirit in the children. Blind faith in small groups may be turned to more productive channels when it is turned to love of country and philanthropy. In this way, the child becomes socially mature.

8. Self-assertion. The motivation of self-assertion occupies an importance place in the child's character. To it is conjoined the sentiment of self-respect which helps the child steer clear of all undersirable activity and to concentrate only on the desirable one. In order to develop self-respect, in the child, the teachers must put before him examples taken from the child's own environment. If instead of punishing a child for his mistake, the teacher tells him that such foolishness is not expected of him or from one of his upbringing, then the child will abstain from repeating it. He will also be remorseful. Once the motivation of self-assertion is fully developed, the individual makes his own efforts to progress in life, since he does not want to live the life of an insect but wants to hold his head high in society.

9. Self-submission. Of course, the motivation of self-submission may prove to be a hindrance in the child's development but the sensible teacher can turn it towards himself and arouse feelings of respect for the teacher and a healthy regard for discipline in the child. Students are prone to accept teacher's mandate without questioning so that success in education becomes possible.

Techniques of Motivating Students

1. Set Induction. It means the introduction of the lesson. It links previous knowledge with the present knowledge. It is known as the skill of introduction or set-induction skill.

2. Stimulus Variation. It means changing of gestures and positions by the teacher. If a teacher does not change his gestures and positions during the teachning process, it becomes bore and lacks in interest. Hence, it is necessary to provide the training to the teachers in the skill of changing the gestures.

3. Illustration. There are two teaching methods-continuous lecturing method and demonstration method. The pupil-teachers should explain the concepts through examples and by displaying pictures and charts. It is called the illustrating skills.

4. Lecture. It is concerned with the effective presentation of the content. The teacher leaves his impressions by using many techniques and tactics through this skill. It is also known as 'Communication skill'.

5. Probing Questions. it is concerned with the questions to be asked about the content in more depth. It stimulates the cognitive development of the pupils.

6. Closure. It means to finish some task, *i.e.,* in class the pupil-teacher exhibits various behaviours. If we divide these behaviours in smaller units, these are termed as 'skills'. When a pupil-teacher delivers lecture and sums up properly and in an attractive way, the skill is termed as 'Closure Skill'. The lesson remains ineffecitve in the absence of proper closure.

7. Skill of Explaining. It means—use of explaining or connecting links to link the statements or systematic information. When a teacher shows his behaviour while explaining the pupils about 'What', 'Why' and 'How' regarding some facts, principles and concepts, that behaviour constitutes the skill of explaining.

8. Skills for Class Management. Both—social as well as educational activities performed in order to create proper environment for learning in the classroom. The performance of these activities needs special skill. As these activities manage the class it is called 'Skill for Class Management'.

9. Use of Black Board. It is very essential in the class. Its use also needs special training. The necessary components of black-board work are clarity of handwriting, legibility and rationale of black-board work etc.

10. Increasing Pupil Participation. It is concerned with increasing pupil participation which means—'Pupils' direct behaviour which is observable. This includes both responses and reactions of the pupils along with their own new activities.

Motivation (Caused Behaviour)

Motivation is essential to the operation of organizations and class-room activities. No matter how much equipment and audio-visual aids a teacher has, these things cannot be made use of unless students are motivated. From psychology we learn that normal behaviour is caused by certain reasons. These reasons may relate to a person's needs and or the consequences that result from acts. Motives are expressions of a person's needs. Hence they are personal and internal, Incentives on the other hand, are external to the person.

There are various ways to classify needs. A simple but significant one is (1) Basic physiological or primary needs, and (2) Social and psychological needs, called secondary needs.

Conscious Action Arises from Needs

Diagrammed very simply, the relation of needs to action is shown in the figure below. Needs create tensions that are modified.

Steps 1	2	3	4	5
Individual Needs Motives Tension	Environment	Wants (Tension) ↑ Positive Negative Incentives	Perception	Action (Tension release)

1. ***Physiological Needs.*** Some of the physiological needs are food, water, sex, sleep, air to breathe and satisfactory temperature. These needs arise out of the basic physiology of life and are important to survival and preservation of the species.
2. ***Secondary Needs.*** Secondary needs represent needs of the mind and spirit, rather than of the physical body. They develop a variety of motives in each person. Many of these needs are developed as one matures. Examples are rivalry, self-esteem, sense of duty, self-assertion, giving, belonging and receiving affection. The secondary needs are the ones that complicate the motivational efforts of teachers.

Characteristics of Secondary Needs

1. They are strongly conditioned by experience.
2. They vary in type and intensity among people.

3. They change within an individual.
4. They influence behaviour. It is said, "We are logical only to the extent our feelings let us be."
5. They are often hidden from conscious recognition.
6. They work in groups rather than alone.
7. They are nebulous feelings instead of tangible physical needs.

Although human needs have been classified as primary and secondary, they are inseparable in a particular human being. The state of the physical body affects the mind, and the state of mind can affect the physical body. In fact, medical research shows that both chemistry (a physical condition) affects the emotions and feelings. According to the renowned psychiatrist, Dr. William C. Menninger, "The psychiatrist believes that the mind and body are inseperable—the holistic concept. The former tendency to regard the mind and body as separate has been discarded. Now we study the physical, the chemical, the psychological, and the social factors of every individual who comes to us for help."

The Expectancy Model of Motivation

Motivation in the expectancy model developed by Victor H. Vroom, Porter and Lawler and others, has been defined as the strength of drive toward action. The model shows that a person's motivation toward an action at a particular time is determined by the outcomes (valence) of the action, multiplied by the strength of a person's expectation that the action will lead to the outcomes. The expectancy model shows that motivation leads to increased effort. The increased effort will lead to outcomes that represent desired goals.

$$\text{Valence} \times \text{Expectancy} = \text{Motivation.}$$

Valence refers to the strength of a person's preference for one's outcome in relation to others.

Expectancy. It is the strength of belief that a particular act will be followed by particular outcomes.

A Diagram of the Expectancy Model

Valence × Expectancy
↓
Motivation
↓
Action
↓
Outcomes (Goal Attainment)
Satisfaction

Various Theories of Motivation

Following theories of motivation explain motivation with all its distinct varieties. We may find that these theories supplement one another and point towards the same truth.

1. ***Pawn Theory.*** This is based on the transcendental approach to the problems of life. According to this theory, we are a 'pawn', a puppet, an instrument in the hands of God. Both classical and Freudian Psychologists land Behaviouristic theories of learning derive their strength from this. This pawn theory passes on the responsibility to some 'mysterious power' which is something intengible.
2. ***Instinct Theory.*** McDougall is said to be the originator of this theory. According to him, "The "human mind has certain innate or inherited tendencies which are the essential springs or motive powers of all thought and action, whether individual or collective and are the bases from which the character and will of individuals and of nations are gradually developed under the guidance of the intellectual faculties." McDougall put forward a list of 41 instincts and attached 14 emotions with them. This theory was

very popular in Britain with Nunn, Burt, Ross, Hughes and Valentine etc. However, the American Psychologists do not find any weight in this theory.

3. ***Energy Theory.*** No energy, no motivation. According to Freud the source of physical energy is Eros and according to Jung, it is Libido. As a matter of the fact this theory offers no explanation.

4. ***Need Theory.*** There are two sets of needs: *(i)* Primary or biological, and *(ii)* Secondary or psychological. The more intense the need, the more the motivation.

5. ***Stimulation Theory.*** All inner and outer stimuli that bear upon a person at one time constitute his psychological field and determine his behaviour jointly through interaction.

6. ***Social Theory.*** According to this theory, causes of the social behaviour are to be found in the social environment, there are two streams of this theory:

   (i) *Cultural Pattern.* According to this view, an individual is cast in the mould of the culture to which he belongs. The different cultures would, therefore, produce different types of personalities.

   (ii) *The Field Theory.* According to this behaviour is caused by the interaction between a person and his environment.

7. ***Behaviour or Learning Theory.*** This is more elaborate than the need theory. Hull and his associates are the supporters of this theory. The theory has three main tenets:

   (a) All learning involves reward in the sense that only those responses that reduce need or drive are stamped in;

(*b*) All motivated behaviour is based on needs and desires; and

(*c*) Needs may be biological or psychological, primary or secondary.

Maslow, Tolman, Hebb and Mowrer do not share this view. They argue that all learning is not like that. Learning can be cognitive type also. It is not only the 'need reduction' but also 'avoidance of pain' that goads one to learn.

8. ***Depth Theory.*** Freud is the main protagonist of this theory. The spring of action is unconscious which is dark, ruthless, very powerful and illogical. Special exploratory techniques are needed to dig out the unconscious. Unconscious motives influence our conscious thought and conduct.

Adler's Theory

Alfred Adler was born of a middle class family in Vienna in 1870 and died in Scotland in 1937.

Alfred Adler was one of Freud's earliest pupils but gradually he began to develop ideas which were not in conformity with those of Freud and others in Vienna Society. When these differences became very sharp he was asked to present his views to Vienna Society. Adler resigned as President of Vienna Psycho-analytic Society and a few months later, he broke off his relations with Freudian psycho-analysis. He formed his own group which came to be known as *Individual Psychology*.

Main Concepts Put Forward by Adler

Adler's view-points can be stated under a few general headlines:

(1) Fictional finalism.

(2) Striving for superiority.

(3) Inferiority feelings and compensation.

(4) Social interest.

(5) Style of life.

(6) The Creative selt.

Fictional Finalism. Shortly after Adler terminated his relations with the circle that surrounded Freud, he came under the philosophical influence of Hans Vaihinger whose book *The Psychology* of as if had been published in 1911.

Vaihinger propounded the idea that man lives by many fictional ideas which do not have any counterpart in reality. "All men are created equal", "honesty is the best policy" and "the end satisfies the means", enable man to deal more effectively with reality.

Adler took note of this philosophical doctrine of idealistic positivism and propounded his own design. Adler found the idea that man is motivated more by his expectations of the future than by the experiences of the past. Neither Vaihinger nor Adler believed in predestination or fatality.

Adler like Jung identified Freud's theory with the principle of casualty and his *own* with the principle of finalism.

He states, "Individual psychology insists absolutely on the indispensability of finalism for the understanding of all psychological phenomenon. Causes, powers, instincts, impulses and the like cannot serve as explanatory principles. The final goal alone can explain man's behaviour. Experiences, traumata, sexual development mechanisms cannot yield an explanation but the perspective in which these are regarded, the individual way of seeing them, which subordinates all life to the final goal can do so."

The final goat may be a fiction, that is, an ideal which is nonetheless not attainable. This is a very real spur to man drivings and the ultimate explanation of his conduct.

Adler believed; that a normal person could free himself from the influence of these fictions and face reality when necessity demanded. This is something that the neurotic person is not capable of doing.

There were three stages in his thinking:

(i) to be aggressive;

(ii) to be powerful; and

(iii) to be superior.

Adler's concept of superiority is something very analogous to Jung's concept of the self or Goldstein's principle of self actualization. It is striving for perfect completion. It is "the great upward drive". Adler writes "I began to see clearly in every psychological phenomenon the striving for superiority. It runs parrallel to physical growth and is an intrinsic necessity of life itself. It lies at the root of all solutions of life's problems and is manifested in the way in which we meet these problems. All our functions follow its direction. They strive for conquest, security, increase, either in the right or wrong direction. The impetus from minus to plus never ends. The urge from below to above never ceases. Whatever permises all our philosophers and psychologists dream of self-preservation, pleasure-principle, equalization—all these are but vague representations, attempt to express the great upward drive."

Striving for superiority or perfection is innate, that it is part of life. In fact it is life itself. It is a prepotent dynamic principle. Alder admits that the striving for superiority may manifest itself in a thousand different ways, and that each person has his own concrete mode of achieving or trying to achieve perfection.

Inferiority Feelings and Compensations

Adler stated that inferiority feelings are not a sign of abnormality. They are the cause of all improvement in man's lot. Inferiority feelings may be exaggerated by special conditions such as *pampering* or rejecting the child which may result in abnormal manifestations, such as the development of an inferiority complex or a compensatory superiority complex. But under a normal situation the feeling of inferiority or a sense of incompleteness is the great driving force of mankind. In other words, man is pushed by the need to overcome his inferiority and pulled by the desire to be superior.

Social Interest. Adler was an advocate of social justice and a supporter of social democracy. He enlarged his conception of man to include the factor of *social interest*. In its ultimate sense, "Social interest is the true and inevitable compensation, for all the natural weaknesses of individual human beings."

According to Adler social interest is inborn. Man is a social creature by nature and not by habit. However, like any other aptitude, this innate predisposition does not appear spontaneously. It has to be brought to enjoyment by guidance and training. He believed in the *benefits of education*. Adler spent a great deal of his time in establishing child guidance clinics, in improving the schools, and in educating the public regarding proper methods of rearing children. Social interest replaced selfish interest.

Style of Life. It is the most distinctive feature of his psychology and is the recurrent theme in all of Adler's writings. Style of life is the principle by which the individual personality functions. It is the whole that commands the parts. It is the principle that explains the uniqueness of a person. Everyone has a style of life but no two people develop the same style. One person tries to become superior through developing his intellect, while another strives to achieve muscular perfection. The intellectual has one style of life, the athlete another. The intellectual reads, studies and thinks. He lives a more solitary life than the active man does. He arranges the details of his existence, his daily routine, his relations to his family, friends and acquaintances, in accordance with his goal of intellectual superiority. Everything he does, he does with an eye to his ultimate goal. All of a person's behaviour springs from his style of life.

Stage Forming Style of Life. The style of life is formed very early in childhood by the age of four or five. His attitudes, feelings, apperceptions become fixed and mechanized at an early age. It becomes extremely difficult to change style of life at a later stage.

What Determines the Individual's Style of Life?

The Creative Self. In essence the doctrine of a creative self asserts that man makes his own personality. He constructs it out of the raw material of heredity and experience. He states, "Heredity only endows him with certain impressions. These abilities and impressions, and the manner in which he experiences them—that is to say, the interpretations he makes of these experiences—are the bricks or in other words, his attitude in life which determines his relationship to the outside world." The creative self gives meaning to life. It creates the goal as well as the means to goal.

Concluding Observations. To conclude it may be stated that Adler gave a humanistic theory of personallty which was the antithesis of Freud's conception of man. By endowing man with altruism, humanitarianism, cooperation creativity, uniqueness and awareness, he restored to man a sense of dignity and worth that psycho-analysis had pretty largely destroyed. Adler offered a portrait of man which was more satisfying and more hopeful.

Psychological Self-psychoanalytical Class-room Motivation

Jung (1875–1961), a famous Western psychoanalyst who transcends both Freud and Adler and goes deep into the human psyche revealing some of its mysteries. He seems to be more of a philosopher and less of a psychologist. Starting as one of Freud's associates he started differing with him and by 1912 he developed serious ideological and personal differences and founded his own school named Analytical Psychology.

Jung considers Life itself as an 'ever living fire' and self-realization as the aim of life, which is far beyond satisfaction of sex and seeking of an easy-chair high prestigeous job. There are, of course, persons who are mad after these two things, but this does not minimise the importance of 'self-realization'. We may brush aside such differences as individual differences.

Jung does not question the importance of sex and status but he goes beyond these. He often appears to attack Freudian Concept of Sexuality. He stresses certain clear-cut aim of life before the individual. He states, "I have observed that a directed life is in general better, richer and healthier than an aimless one, and that it is better to go forward with the stream of life than backward against it."

We are living in an age of anxiety and tension and lawlessness in the outer world. Western man expects that psychology should be able to assist him in understanding the incomprehensible factors of life. Jung thinks that there cannot be law and order in this outer world so long as man does not feel at home in the inner world, in his own soul. Jung is very near the living process of the soul. He wants to lead people to responsible attitude towards life and a responsible way of living, suited to the peculiarities of each man. Jung is optimistic about human nature.

The Structure of Self

Jung does not deny the outer world but he gives importance to the inner world and the deep-seated unconscious. He gives a complete picture of the "Self" with its various aspects in the outer as well as the inner world. Jung thinks that the term 'self' stands for the integration of the various aspects of the personality, conscious and unconscious. Development of personality takes place when an individual chooses his way and separates himself from the crowd. His concepts about the different aspects to the self are woven into one integrated whole.

He accepts conscious as well as unconscious. But his concept of unconscious is entirely different from that of Freud.

He thinks that the unconscious is the matrix out of which the conscious has been evolved. Unconscious is not evolved out of the conscious but the reverse. Consciousness is the product of growth, whereas unconsciousness even existed before the intellectual self began to function. Our consciousness arises from unknown depths. Jung's concept of the unconscious is that of something vaster and more comprehensive. According to Jung unconscious was just not the dumping ground of the repressed desires from the conscious (as Freud thought).

Jung admitted Freud's explanation of the unconscious but felt that it was only a part of the vaster unconsciousness, which is shared by an individual with all other people in all places and at all times.

Jung has classified unconscious, in two types:

(1) Racial consciousness.

(2) Personal unconsciousness.

Racial unconscious consists of primitive beliefs and modes of response handed down over centuries. We call these ancient was of thinking as 'archetypes.'

The unnoticed, forgotten or repressed incidents of each person's life form personal unconscious. Here he agrees with Freud.

The unconscious of an individual is opposite to his conscious mind and is complementary to it. The unconscious tries to correct and moderate the conscious.

We can compare the picture of the mind given by Jung with compensatory aspect of a photograph of a range of mountains mirrored in a lake below. Just as each mountain has its equal and opposite reflection, in the same way each mental attribute has its equal and opposite complement. To Jung, therefore, a man is both better and worse than he knows. The coward is a brave man and the brave is a coward in his unconscious; the romantic is realist and *vice versa.* Different layers of unconscious according to Jung are as follows:

(i) Animal life;

(ii) Primitive ancestors;

(iii) Ethnological groups (races);

(iv) Nations;

(v) Clans; and

(vi) Family.

He further observes that conscious mind permit itself to be trained like a parrot, but the unconscious does not. Our uncanscious contains the experience of the whole race. Jung states, "Bady is a sort of museum of its phylogenetic history, so is the mind".

According to Jung the unconscious is more than just containing personal memories. The collective unconsciousness represents a sort of social memory. He also points out that certain identical customs are found in widely scattered parts of the earth. It has also been noted that Siblings' dreams are very similar even though they may be hundreds of miles apart in different milieus.

There is only racial unconsciousness at birth. It has got three things at that time:

(i) Individual instinctive reactions;

(ii) Ancestoral behaviaur; and

(iii) Ancestoral interpretations, *i.e.,* belief in ghosts, fairies etc. The unconscious forgets nothing. It is mnemic in nature.

Jung has archetypes, symbols:, Libido, Shadow, Persona and The Soul Images while explaining the concept of unconsciousness. These concepts are explained here:

Archetypes. Ancient ways of thinking and symbols or figures which explain life are called archtypes. Symbols are generally based upon experience of the individual but the experience of the individual is the experience of the human race, the collective unconsciousness. The collective unconsciousness is the "all controlling deposit of ancestral experience from untold millions of years" to which is added by each century small amount of variation and differentiation. These experiences are archetypes. Their sources are to be found in profound religious thought, in enduring literature and art which draw their universal inspiration from the depths of human psyche.

The archetypes are eternally inherited identical forms and ideas. The archetypes may appear as persons. They may appear as demons or as fabulous animals or natural forces or objects or geometrical forms and numbers, etc. Jung says, "Archetypes resemble the beds of river. An archetype is something like an old water-course along which the water of life flowed for a time, digging a deep channel for itself. The longer it flowed the deeper the channel, and the more likely it is that sooner or later the water will return."

Archetypes were and still are psychic forces which must be taken seriously. The archetype is a psychic organ present in all of us. They are complexes of experience that come upon us fatefully. They affect our personal life. We can never legitimately ignore our archetypal foundations.

Shadow. Shadow represents the unconscious and is closely related to us as the dark reflection of our conscious efforts. It may become monstrous and may actually overwhelm the ego-conscious. In one sense the shadow is a highly personal creation. In another sense it reflects the universals of human experience and is 'personal' only in a very limited manner.

Symbols. They are of greater psychological value as they are necessary openings to understand 'human experience'. They serve to reveal the depths of the soul. They are created by deep unconscious and are found all over the world. They appear in dreams, art productions, visions and fantasies. These symbols lead to the expression of archetypal, thinking.

Libido. Jung while retaining the Freudian term 'libido' gives it a different meaning. He means by the term a life energy underlying all natural phenomena, including the human psyche. He believes that sexuality is one manifestation of libido but not all. Libido is essentially creative and it takes many forms. For Jung libido is life itself. It may follow different channels, with the individual gaining maturity, Sexual is perhaps the most important among these but not the only one. He took it as the life urge. Jung suggests three stages of development. (1) Pre-sexual, upto three, four years the infant has epoch of sucking nutrition only, i.e., mouth zone. (2) Sharp changes take place when the child leaves the mouth zone and the individual develops and learns to turn from parents to the real world around him. (3) Libido gets direction in two ways—Introversion and Extroversion.

Jung's concept of the ego-conscious is similar to that of Freud's.

Persona. Persona is adaptively organized image of the self which all of us form in the course of living. It is forpted consciously as we develop our goals and ideals. Extroverts can hange persona as they change dress. It may differ at different times, places and persons, identification with persona is full of dangers, it represents the face show to the world. It is a necessity for social living.

The Soul Images. The soul image (Anima-Animus) lies deeper in racial unconscious. Every woman has her animus, the male component. The anima includes archetypal images of woman, the eternal mother, the virgin, the Harlot, the witch, the temptress, the spiritual guide like Dante's Beatrice.

Psychological Types. Jung believes that libido takes two directions—Extroversion and Introversion. Both are necessary for complete living. Freud's stress on sexual relations is extroversive and Adler's insistence on status seeking is introversive. Jung considers both these right but he goes beyond them and states that these attitudes complement each other. Even within himself the individual has the counterpart. The extrovert wants to a just himself to the reality of his environment and the introvert on the other hand seeks to adjust himself to the world which lies within himself. He thinks that the contents of the unconscious possess a greater reality than the things of the outer world.

Each type performs four functions—sensation, intuition, feeling and thinking. All the four are essential for ideal living, and should work in harmony. Sensation concerns the present intuition with the potential—what the living will be or has been, feeling gives us a sense of values and thinking tells us what the things is in an abstract manner.

Thinking coupled with intuition may take us away from reality and coupled with sensation, it may bring us down to reality.

***

Index

39. General Psychology	195/-
40. Distance Education in India	195/-
41. Teacher Education	195/-
42. Educational Philosophy	195/-
43. Science Teaching in Schools	195/-
44. Indian National Congress (New)	450/-
45. Indian Polity (Revised Edition)	395/-
46. New Comparative Government (Revised Edition)	350/-
Advanced Study in the History of Modern India	
47. (Volume-1: 1707-1813)	225/-
48. (Volume-2: 1813-1920)	325/-
49. (Volume-3: 1920-1947)	175/-
50. Handbook of Nutrition & Dietetics	250/-
51. Development of Education in India	195/-
52. A Text Book of Environmental Studies	195/-
53. Teaching of History	175/-
54. Administrative Thinkers	195/-
55. Research Methodology	195/-
56. Curriculum Development	195/-
57. Teaching of Science	175/-
58. Teaching of Mathematics	175/-
59. Principles of Educational & Vocational Guidance	195/-
60. Child Psychology	195/-
61. Abnormal Psychology	195/-
62. Indian Education in Emerging Society	195/-
63. Human Resource Management	175/-
64. Higher Education and Global Challenges	195/-
65. Teaching of Geography	175/-
66. Teaching of Social Studies	175/-
67. Teaching of English	175/-
68. Education for All The Indian Saga	175/-
69. Value Education in Global Perspective	195/-
70. Teacher Training	175/-
71. Public Administration	175/-
72. Public Relations & Integrated Communications	195/-
73. Educational Psychology	175/-
74. Introduction to Educational Technology	175/-
75. Textbook of Food and Nutrition	175/-

Lotus PRESS

Unit No. 220, Second Floor, 4735/22,
Prakash Deep Building, Ansari Road, Darya Ganj,
New Delhi - 110002, Ph.: 32903912, 23280047, 09811594448
E-mail: lotuspress1984@gmail.com, www.lotuspress.co.in